D1083153

METAPHYSICS OF
NATURAL
COMPLEXES

METAPHYSICS OF NATURAL COMPLEXES.

Justus Buchler

SECOND, EXPANDED EDITION

Edited by
Kathleen Wallace and Armen Marsoobian,
with Robert S. Corrington

Introduction by Kathleen Wallace

STATE UNIVERSITY OF NEW YORK PRESS

Published by
State University of New York Press, Albany

© 1990 State University of New York

For information, address State University of New York
Press, State University Plaza, Albany, N.Y., 12246

This volume is an expanded
edition of the work originally
published by Columbia University
Press in 1966 under the same title.

Library of Congress Cataloging-in-Publication Data

Buchler, Justus, 1914-
    Metaphysics of natural complexes/by Justus Buchler; edited by
  Kathleen Wallace and Armen Marsoobian with Robert S. Corrington;
  introduction by Kathleen Wallace. — 2nd., expanded ed.
        p.   cm.
    Includes bibliographical references and index.
    ISBN 0-7914-0182-0. — ISBN 0-7914-0183-9 (pbk.)
    1. Metaphysics.   I. Wallace, Kathleen.   II. Marsoobian, Armen.
  III. Corrington, Robert S., 1950-   .   IV. Title.
  BD111.B86   1989
  110—dc19   89-4416
                                                                      CIP

10 9 8 7 6 5 4 3 2 1

To

JOHN HERMAN RANDALL, Jʀ.

CONTENTS

PREFACE TO THE SECOND EDITION

AFTER THIS book (MNC[1]) was first published in 1966, Buchler wrote several more articles developing his general ontology and his view of metaphysics, as well as his *tour de force* on poetry, *The Main of Light: On the Concept of Poetry*, 1974 (ML). It was Buchler's intention to prepare a second edition of MNC to include the articles, "On the Concept of 'the World',"[2] and "Probing the Idea of Nature."[3] Unfortunately, an untimely stroke prevented him from doing so. With his permission we have undertaken this task for

1. Following Buchler's practice the following abbreviations are in use in the Editors' Notes and the Appendices:

TGT: *Toward A General Theory of Human Judgment*. New York: Columbia University Press, 1951; 2nd, revised edition, Dover Publications, 1979.

NJ: *Nature and Judgment*. New York: Columbia University Press, 1955; University Press of America, 1985.

CM: *The Concept of Method*. New York: Columbia University Press, 1961; University Press of America, 1985.

ML: *The Main of Light: On the Concept of Poetry*. New York: Oxford University Press, 1974.

2. Justus Buchler, "On the Concept of 'the World'," *The Review of Metaphysics*, 31:4, June 1978, pp. 555-579 (Hereafter, OCW).

3. Justus Buchler, "Probing the Idea of Nature," *Process Studies*, 8:3, Fall, 1978, pp. 157-168 (Hereafter, PIN).

him. This edition, therefore, includes these two major articles which develop and extend his ontological principles. These appendices are as per Buchler's express intention. The very slight emendations made to the 1978 publication of "On the Concept of 'the World'" are Buchler's own.

There are several points about categories, the "cognitive value" of philosophy and the systematic interrelation between his general ontology and the metaphysics of human process, which Buchler makes in his replies to critics at a symposium on the philosophy of Justus Buchler held at Fairfield University May 2-3, 1975.[4] The proceedings were published in a special issue of *The Southern Journal of Philosophy,* 14:1, 1976.[5] Additionally, in this second edition of **MNC** we are including selections from Buchler's "Reply to Reck: The Structure of the Whole, The Location of the Parts," and from his "Reply to Anton: Against 'Proper' Ontology," and the unabridged text of his "Reply to Greenlee: Philosophy and Exhibitive Judgment." We have abridged the replies to Reck and Anton for this volume in order to minimize the polemical context, while at the same time preserving Buchler's substantive points. In spite of the underlying polemic, the issues as articulated by Buchler are intelligible in

---

4. Sponsored by the Philosophy Department and Philosophy Honor Society of the University with the cooperation of the Society for the Advancement of American Philosophy.

5. Hereafter, all articles from this particular issue will be referred to with SJP and the page number. Such references appear primarily in the Editors' Notes to the text of MNC at the back of this book.

their own terms and, we hope, illuminating of issues which Buchler does not directly address elsewhere. The abridgments are entirely our own and we bear full responsibility for them. We encourage the interested reader to consult the full range of essays and most particularly Buchler's replies as they appear in the *Southern Journal*.

In 1977 Buchler prepared an extended commentary (heretofore unpublished) on the concept of contour. He entitled it "Notes on the Contour of a Natural Complex." We include it in its entirety in the Appendices, as it contains his last systematic formulation of these issues and was intended as supplemental to the original formulations in MNC. We have organized the material in the appendices according to chronology of composition as best as we can determine by publication dates and Buchler's own notes. Buchler made some slight editorial changes to "Notes on the Contour of a Natural Complex" after his stroke (i.e., post-1979), which we have observed here, but they do not in any way alter the substance of the text.

For this edition the original preface, text and notes have not been altered and page numbers of the text remain the same as the 1966 edition. In the Editors' Notes we have taken the liberty of adding cross-references for certain passages in the text. We have also quoted material which Buchler published elsewhere—most prominently in the 1976 *Southern Journal of Philosophy* issue—in which he develops or amplifies key concepts. These notes are marked with a dagger (†) in the margins of the text and are organized in the Editors' Notes according to page and line number. We have also updated the Index to include the appropriate references to the material in the Appendices.

KATHLEEN WALLACE
ARMEN MARSOOBIAN
ROBERT S. CORRINGTON

PREFACE TO THE ORIGINAL EDITION

THIS BOOK may be read as an independent essay. It may also be read as one of four books which form a larger theoretical undertaking. The other three are: *Toward a General Theory of Human Judgment* (1951), *Nature and Judgment* (1955), and *The Concept of Method* (1961).* In these three, the dominant concern is with a metaphysics of the human process, but the notion of natural complex has a major if informal role. My present purpose, in extending the structure, is to shape a position through concepts which are appropriately different in level of generality from the concepts I previously introduced but are discernibly continuous with them. For the justification of principles or ideas which are applied and not argued here, and for the reason why certain stances which others may consider problematical are not so considered by me, I can only refer the reader to the preceding works.

Over the years some minor shifts of emphasis and some variations of verbal usage have arisen within the larger undertaking. The basic approach and direction remain intact, and so does the underlying con-

* All are published by Columbia University Press.

viction of what it is important to do philosophically. Now as before, I rely on the reader's willingness to accept a highly sequential exposition in which the earlier and the later parts are mutually clarifying.

I have received a large number of remarkably apt criticisms and suggestions on the manuscript. To Gail Belaief, Lynne Belaief, Jerome Eckstein, Sidney Gelber, Douglas Greenlee, Joan McQuary, Milton K. Munitz, Robert G. Olson, John H. Randall, Jr., Stephen Ross, and Beth Singer, I wish to express warmest thanks. For the faults or imperfections of the book I alone, of course, am accountable.

I acknowledge with gratitude an award made to me by the Henry P. Kendall Foundation: it appreciably facilitated my work. And I welcome this opportunity to acknowledge the fellowship and stimulation of the Philosophical Group of New York.

J. B.

ACKNOWLEDGMENTS TO THE
SECOND EDITION

THE EDITORS would like to thank the following for granting permission to quote, either in whole or in part, articles that appeared in their journals: *The Southern Journal of Philosophy, The Review of Metaphysics,* and *Process Studies.*

We are grateful to Sidney Gelber for his critical yet sympathetic commentary. Our thanks to Dorothy McKenzie for her 1979 portrait study of Justus Buchler for this volume. We would also like to thank Southern Connecticut State University for providing a grant that defrayed the costs of typing this manuscript. Finally we thank Jean F. Alberino, who most genially and expertly typed the manuscript.

INTRODUCTION TO THE
SECOND EDITION

BUCHLER'S GENERAL metaphysical outlook is, by his own
original characterization, *ordinal*. The meaning of ordinality has been amplified and refined in the articles, "On
the Concept of 'the World'," (OCW) and "Probing the
Idea of Nature." (PIN) These articles are substantive
extensions of the system of categories developed in MNC.
They complete the system in so far as they round out
Buchler's original formulation of ordinal metaphysics.
But, there is also a sense in which no system is "complete,"
or as Buchler might say, has exhausted all its ramifications.
So the following commentary is offered as an articulation
of some ramifications of the concept of ordinality, without
purporting to be the final arbiter of meaning.

Ordinality means that every being or natural complex
is located in an order or orders. ("Natural complex" or
"complex" is the generic ontological term of identification. Whatever "is" is a complex, whether it be an entity,
an event, a possibility, a musical phrase, the speed of light,
a process, a child's wail, an individual's despair. See also
OCW 561-562.*) Ordinal location is not to be interpreted

---

* Here Appendix III, 233-234.

in merely spatial terms or in terms of set-like inclusiveness. Rather, it means "related to [some] other complexes in some [a given] respect." A complex finds itself in orders, so to speak, and is simultaneously an order for and locates other complexes. It may participate in generating new locations (relations) for itself and other complexes. To be a resident of London—to be located in that complex of geographical, political, social, economic, cultural, etc. orders—is to be related to, that is, determined by a variety of characteristic traits of that order, London. Thus, in this respect, London is the more inclusive order and the individual is located in London. On the other hand, the individual *qua* individual is also an order. Therefore, since being a resident of London is a trait, a subaltern complex, of the individual, the individual is a [weakly relevant] constituting relation of London. Thus, in another respect, London is located in the individual, the individual being the more inclusive order.[1] Of course, such "locatedness" in the individual does not constitute an integrity of London *qua* London. London, too, is a complex and has its integrity by virtue of being located in other more inclusive orders, e.g., the order of England, politically, geographically, economically, etc.; the order of English speaking metropolises; of cities with double-decker buses; of cities with underground trains; of cities with underground trains constructed by the deep-tunnelling rather than open-pit method; of Anglo-Saxon history;

---

1. Related to just this issue, Buchler points out that ordinal location exemplifies two of the various senses which Aristotle enumerates for "in": "the species, in one sense, is in the genus; the genus, in another sense, is in the species." (MNC 36) Also see MNC 16, and OCW 557 and 575, here Appendix III, 227 and 252-253.

of barrister/solicitor legal systems. While we can identify characteristic ones, the ordinal locations of any complex and
certainly of London are indefinite in scope. These locations and their unique inter-relation constitute the gross
integrity (contour) of London.

Since ordinal location is not merely spatial, let us
consider some nonspatial and nongeographical examples.
A family member dies. The grieving kin are in an order of
grief. The shared and distributively experienced emotion
is an ordinal location of each individual. The *family's*
grief is in each individual, just as, in another respect, each
individual is located in the wider emotional context or
order. The people of a society have a collective tempera-
ment or characteristic features. These are identifiable as
collective, as the wider personality structure, but they are
also present distributively in individuals. Individual
catholics embody values and attitudes of Catholicism.
Catholicism is in them, just as, in other respects, they are
in it. Lovers are in a love-relation, a relation largely of
their own making; the relation is a wider order than either
of them individually, yet it [the relation] is also, in
another sense, in each of them. Buchler himself gives
another apt example in his discussion of the assimilative
dimension of experience or proception: "What an individual assimilates is what he sustains, not what he feels;
though he may sustain an event primarily through the
medium of feeling, as when he is struck in the face or when
he is frightened by the prospect of death. But when, for
example, he is slandered by his neighbors, in the total
absence of awareness on his part, great changes may take
place in his possibilities and relationships, and the course
of his subsequent experience altered...." (NJ 138) The

individual in this case is located in an order of slander and the slander penetrates his self in determinate even if not conscious ways.

In addition to the feature of variable inclusiveness or reciprocal relatedness, there are two kinds of relation, strong and weak relevance. So, to return to our example of London, in one respect, London may be strongly relevant to the individual resident while the resident is weakly relevant to London. There may be another respect, however, in which London is weakly relevant to the individual (e.g., the individual *qua* lover) and there may even be a respect in which an individual resident is strongly relevant to London (e.g., a prominent and influential citizen of the city). Or, to take one of our other examples, Catholicism may be strongly relevant to an individual believer, while the believer as an individual may be weakly relevant to Catholicism. When a complex is strongly relevant to another complex, it is an integrity of that other complex. When a complex is weakly relevant to another complex, it is part of the scope of that complex.[2] But whatever the relevance, wherever two complexes are in relational position to one another, the relation always goes both ways, however apparently trivial some relation or determination may be. Therefore, there is no single or overall hierarchy of inclusive locatedness or relatedness since there can be no single dominant respect or order.

One implication then of ordinality is that the World cannot be a totality in the sense of the order of orders or the complex of complexes. There are many orders and com-

---

2. See MNC 22 ff., and Editors' Notes to p. 22 for further clarification of the concepts of integrity and scope.

plexes. They are not all related to one another, and neither can they all be located in some single, more inclusive order which itself has no ordinal location in another more inclusive order. In pursuing this line of argument in OCW, Buchler shows that such a conception of the World as the totality of everything (an order of orders) would violate the principle of ordinality. If the World were an order it would have to be limited, i.e., located in some other more inclusive order as the condition of its integrity, that is, of it having the character it has as world. But then it wouldn't be the totality of everything that is. In order to preserve the sense of exhaustiveness which the concept of the World connotes Buchler redefines it in such a way as to preserve the irreducibly plural character of the World. To do this requires giving up the idea of the World as the order of orders or complexes, the order in which everything else is located.

In "Probing the Idea of Nature" (PIN) Buchler argues against the view that nature is an order. It could not be an order of orders according to the same logic which governs the discussion of the concept of the World. Therefore, *if* it were an order it would have to be limited, *viz.*, located. If nature were an order, this would entail that some beings are not complexes of nature, that there are non- or supernatural complexes or beings. (There couldn't be beings with no ordinal location, because then they would not be complexes and therefore, on this view, couldn't be at all.) So would these be natural and non- or supernatural orders which would not locate or be relationally positioned to one another but which would locate their respective subaltern complexes? But, there would have to be more inclusive ordinal location[s] which would provide the basis for the distinctive traits, the integrities, of "natural" and "non-" or "supernatural" respectively. So since there would have to be such orders in order for the distinction to be possible at all, then for the sake of argument let us assume that it would be possible to specify the more inclusive orders for each. Even so, *if* each designation identified a kind of ordinal location and located other complexes in that respect, then each would still exemplify the principles and categories of ordinality. Therefore, the difference between the natural and the non or supernatural would not be an ontological one. The identification of kinds of complexes or orders is not illegitimate, of course, but merely as such it is not part of general ontology as Buchler conceives it. General ontology seeks to articulate the traits of being a complex at all and therefore, both the allegedly "natural" and "non-" or "supernatural" orders would be orders.

Evoking a distinction used by the medievals and Spinoza, Buchler notes the difference between nature natured (*natura naturata*) and nature naturing (*natura naturans*).[3] Nature is not just *natura naturata,* innumerable orders, that prevail or cease to prevail. The principle of ordinality also points to the dimension *natura naturans.* The meaning of this is intimated in Buchler's metaphor of "providingness."[4] Nature is not *a* provider or an order of providence. Rather, nature is the perennial availability and provision of orders (and complexes). "Providingness" signifies the fecundity, if you will, of nature.

So why does Buchler call complexes natural? In doing so is he obliterating an otherwise legitimate distinction,

---

3. See MNC 100 and PIN 165, here Appendix IV, 276.
4. See MNC 3.

albeit one which is not an ontological or metaphysical one? Or, is he making the stronger argument that the distinction between the natural and non- or supernatural is not a legitimate distinction? It is our view that Buchler would regard such a distinction as suspect for at least two reasons. One is because it tends to become elevated into an ontological distinction. The second is because it tends to carry with it an implicit, and sometimes explicit, commitment to a principle of ontological priority, namely, a commitment to the view that some kinds of being are more real than others. When the contrast is nature/non-nature, it is often nature which is regarded as more real. On the other hand, when the contrast is nature/supernature, nature often gets second billing. These not altogether consistent classificatory possibilities suggest that at best the distinctions are problematic, or worse, arbitrary.

On Buchler's view, ordinal metaphysics is based on an explicit rejection of a principle of ontological priority in favor of a commitment to a principle of ontological parity. Every complex is as real as every other. What a complex is depends on its specific ordinal locations. But that it is at all means that it is ordinally located and no less so than any other complex. To be, or to be real, is to be ordinally located and therefore does not admit of degrees.

So, why does Buchler retain the qualification "natural" in natural complex? He does not regard it as a designation which proposes a meaningful opposite:

> The term "natural complex" is not set up to be contrasted with "non-natural" or "supernatural" complex. The latter terms are made possible, as terms, by the procedures of logic and the properties of grammar; but they represent nothing discriminable that is not continuous with all other discrim-

inanda and all other processes of discrimination. When the term "complex of nature" is used instead of "natural complex," the impulse to ask whether there are complexes of an opposite kind is perhaps less likely to arise. Linguistic habits do not favor "Are there complexes of non-nature?" (MNC 6)

Buchler goes on in ML to say that "natural complex" is a pre-categorial term. By this he means that it is a generic term of identification for whatever is:

The expression "natural complex" (which we have been abbreviating as "complex") applies to whatever is, and therefore to whatever can be dealt with; to what is produced by men as well as to what is not. It is the expression we have been using for whatever we wish to include in our range of reference without having to specify a mode of being. (ML 103)

The word "natural" enriches the concept of complexity because it stands for the equal reality of any complex whatever. None can be consigned to lesser or elevated to greater ontological status. There are degrees and hierarchies of all kinds, but Buchler's point is that they are not degrees of reality. God is no more real and a fictional character no less real than any other complex or one another. Thus, "natural complex" adumbrates Buchler's principle of ontological parity.[5]

---

5. Ontological parity is the principle that no complex (no "being") is more "real," more "natural," or more "genuine" than any other. (MNC 31 ff.) It emphatically does *not* entail that there are no distinctions or priorities of importance, significance and the like. All it asserts is that none of these distinctions is a distinction of the greater or lesser being or "reality" of a complex.

The term "natural" is important, not as a qualification used in order to concede that some complexes can be "non-natural," but on the contrary as a reminder that *all* complexes are aspects of nature; that no complex can be dismissed or exorcised. Closely related to this usage is the conception of ontological parity.... In "natural complex" we are thus provided with a category (or more strictly, a pre-categorial device) by means of which a subject can be brought to a sphere of discussion in the most general terms possible. Such a category has advantages over others which have been relied upon traditionally to subserve a general encompassment prior to specification.... "Natural complex" enables us to talk of whatever it is that poetry may be concerned with and to include in the "whatever" not only public space-time particulars but any kind of actualities—actual parts of animals, actual traits of an illusion, actual revolutionary ideas, actual components of a dream; and any kind of possibilities—possible parts of animals and possible relations of men, possibilities of awareness, transformation, comparison, fulfillment and tragic defeat, life and death. To refer to what may become identified as a possibility of transformation by the term "an entity," or "a being," or "an object," at once assimilates it to the model of a "substance" or an individual. To refer to it as a natural complex involves no covert special model and no prior ontological classification. All that the term suggests at first blush is potential diversity and manyness within the unity of its reference. (ML 103-104)

In addition, the term natural complex anticipates Buchler's argument against ontological simples which begins on MNC 11 and of which he gives a succinct statement continuing in this same extended passage from ML (See also OCW 562-563, here Appendix III, 235-6):

The use of the term does indeed reflect a definite metaphysical orientation. It eliminates the idea that what we are concerned with can be regarded as "non-natural," as intrinsically and necessarily discontinuous with any of the possibilities or actualities of the world, as other than a nature of some kind, whether produced or not produced by man. It also eliminates the idea that there are or that we may be concerned with "simples." The simple, the seamless, the absolutely pure and non-complex, is in effect the traitless. To assume that any "what" or "that" is simple is to assume that it has no diversity of traits and therefore no trait in common with any "that"; it has only the trait which constitutes its difference from all others. Thus it is without relational traits, and is unlocated in the world. A simple could not be. (ML 104)

Finally, the term natural complex is suggestive of the accessibility of complexes to one another as well as to human probing and invention. The latter Buchler calls query, or the creative and methodic assimilation and manipulation of complexes. In other words, following Peirce's principle that nothing is intrinsically unknowable, Buchler refines and gives positive formulation to the ontological implications of this point:

One of the principal advantages of "natural complex" is an implication inherent in the uses of the term, namely, that every discriminandum whatever offers a prospect for query .... [I]n the most fundamental sense, complexity implies the likelihood of access, and this means continuing experience and query. A further implication of the idea of complexity will here be defended with concepts deemed best for this defense, the implication that the traits of any complex can never be regarded as fully and finally ascertained or completely circumscribed. A complex, if it is accessible at all, is analyzable and interpretable without end; or to speak in a more generic way, is manipulatable in an indefinite number of orders.[6] (MNC 5-6)

6. We point out that Buchler's doctoral dissertation was on Peirce and was published: *Charles Peirce's Empiricism*. London: Kegan Paul, Trench, Trubner and Co.; New York: Harcourt, Brace and Co., 1939. Reprinted by Octagon Books, Inc., 1966.

One of the key points which emerges from the above passages is the idea of continuity. Nature is not a totality, it is not an order, but every complex is a complex of nature. It is related to, continuous with and therefore accessible to an indefinite number of other complexes. "Natural" means that there is no such thing as that which is ultimately and *in principle* inexplicable. The natural, unlike the non- or supernatural, is available—potentially if not actually—to further discrimination and query. The non- or supernatural suggests remoteness or inaccessibility *in principle*. It's the *in principle* to which Buchler objects. There are many complexes to which we have no access other than the generalized awareness that there are complexes which exceed our grasp. But this is an empirical matter and not because complexes are *by definition* of a different stuff or mode than what is natural and accessible:

> [T]he way I use "natural" does not imply that the non-natural or supernatural is a lesser realm or a lesser reality; it implies that these notions are only confused ways of referring to nature. To call any complex non-natural would have to mean—using the formulation in ML (104)—that it is "intrinsically and necessarily discontinuous with any of the possibilities or actualities of the world." How can it be "other than a nature of some kind?"[7]

Art, poetry, God, as well as "trees and things" are all available for discrimination. They are all natural. By this Buchler does not mean that they are all the same kind of thing; Nature is not an order. Rather, their very complexity (their ordinality) establishes their continuity with,

---

7. Justus Buchler, "Reply to Reck: The Structure of 'the Whole,' The Location of the Parts," SJP 52, here Appendix I, 2.

and therefore their availability to other orders and complexes, including those of human query.

Buchler's system is starkly presented. The first chapter of MNC, "Rudimentary Considerations," sets the stage by framing certain fundamental questions and dialectically analyzing them prior to the introduction of the system's categories in the subsequent three chapters. The issues which Buchler formulates as being fundamental adumbrate the direction of his thought and the character of his philosophic commitments. They are not a catalogue of "traditional" problems, although Buchler does provide pithy analyses and reinterpretations of some recurrent issues in philosophy. Rather, the thrust of the first chapter is to orient one to the system's general character (its "demanding form of awareness") through analysis of selective "traditional" issues and through introduction of concepts and issues which are distinctive of this system.

Perhaps what Buchler says of Whitehead's system could also be said of his own:

A system like Whitehead's, and perhaps any major philosophic system, arises primarily not from the cultivation of diverse interests or from reasoned pronouncement on a large number and variety of problems, but from a new mode of discriminating complexes of nature, one which intrinsically aims to translate itself into a discipline of generalization. (It just isn't satisfactory to speak in terms of a "new way of seeing." Besides perpetuating the age-old bias toward sight as paradigm, this expression is not more applicable to systematic than to nonsystematic invention in philosophy.) The specific discriminations that exemplify the mode take the shape of a body of ideas dealing with complexes as such, though sometimes, as in Whitehead, also with the way the complexes have come to be discerned or framed. A system is

kindled, in other words, not by a desire to give answers to
standing problems, but by a demanding form of awareness
that requires conceptual ramification. Inevitably, specific
problems are coped with—both those which the new mode of
discrimination itself breeds and those which it construes as
traditional. The very source of a system's problems lies in its
gestation and application: there are discrepancies among its
assertions, there is darkness in the evolving portrayal; the
scope of its categories recurrently becomes uncertain; the
categories need clarification.[8]

In preparing this second edition of *Metaphysics of
Natural Complexes* it is our hope that it will stimulate
further clarification and ramification of the ideas of this
unique philosophic system.[9]

KATHLEEN WALLACE

---

8. Justus Buchler, "On a Strain of Arbitrariness in Whitehead's
System," *The Journal of Philosophy*, 66:19 (October 1969), p. 589.
Reprinted with small emendations in *Explorations in Whitehead's
Philosophy*, eds. Lewis S. Ford and George L. Kline, New York:
Fordham University Press 1983, pp. 280-294. The quotation is from the
1969 article.

9. In *The Main of Light* Buchler presents a concise summary of his
views geared to introduce the reader to the main concepts of his
metaphysics of human process as well as the general ontology as they
bear on the theory of poetry which he is developing. While it is no
substitute, the summary is useful in its own terms and as supplementary
to the original texts. See ML 87-101.

METAPHYSICS OF
NATURAL
COMPLEXES

I

THE RUDIMENTARY
CONSIDERATIONS

i

WHATEVER IS, in whatever way, is a natural complex. The entire sequel, in a sense, amplifies this statement. †
Relations, structures, processes, societies, human individuals, human products, physical bodies, words and bodies of discourse, ideas, qualities, contradictions, meanings, possibilities, myths, laws, duties, feelings, illusions, reasonings, dreams—all are natural complexes. All of these terms bespeak discriminations of some kind, and whatever is discriminated in any respect or in any degree is a natural complex (for short, "complex"). Precisely what kind of complex anything discriminated turns out to be; in what way its status, its location, its connections are to be interpreted; what traits it may or should be said to have after investigation or any other form of experience; is a distinct type of issue. Anything identified or discovered or imagined or discerned or inferred or sensed or posited or encountered or apprehended or made or acted upon— no matter whether deliberately or not—is here said to be "discriminated." There are initial and advanced phases of discrimination. The stress here is on the initial or minimal phase—on that which was not and now is present for us to take account of, to deal with.

In this basic meaning, whatever is for us, plays a role for us, is discriminated—grasped or marked out as having traits, and contrasted with what is other than it.

Although whatever is in any way discriminated is a natural complex, it does not follow that all natural complexes are discriminated. Whether all natural complexes are humanly discriminable, we do not know. In view of the fact that so much of what has surrounded men has been found out by them in distant retrospect or through the provocations of accident, it is fair to believe that there are complexes influencing them and influenced by them which are never found out. And in general, it is hard to avoid the conviction that, notwithstanding the power known as method, innumerable complexes of nature elude the range of finite creatures.

The concept of natural complex permits the identification of all discriminanda generically, without prejudicing the pursuit and the analysis of differences, of further similarities within the differences, of further differences within these similarities. Should we speak of nature as a "complex of complexes"? If this phrase can be justified at all, it cannot be justified all at once. Among other considerations, and in the light of the position to be developed, any complex is a complex of complexes. Although the phrase as applied to nature is not immediately felicitous, it is better than phrases like "infinite totality" and "system of systems." For it does not suggest a finished collectivity or an absolutely determinate whole, nor indeed a collectivity or whole of any kind; nor does it suggest immensity, as the terms "universe," "world," and "cosmos" do.

The idea of nature, in so far as it means not merely the common factor of all "natures" but the source of all that is, implies the perennial conceivability of complexes more inclusive than any that is dealt with. Nature in the barest sense is the presence and availability of complexes. It is the provision and determination of traits—providingness, if we must strengthen the emphasis, but not providence, not providentness. It provides man, for instance, with the possibilities, the circumstances, and the substance of judgment.

The concept of natural complex not only permits satisfactory generic identification; it permits various distinctions and categorizations. It encourages striving after the functions of generalizing precisely and portraying uniquely.[1] Precise generalization is twin to precise differentiation. Neither is possible alone for very long, even on the least philosophic and most highly restricted plane of investigation. But the essential philosophic direction, if not the immediate commitment of philosophic strategy, is from differentiation toward generalization; so that every triumph in the making of distinctions and the clarification of meanings becomes the greater philosophically in so far as it fortifies a conceptual structure which grounds and locates it.

So far as sheer generic breadth is concerned, "being" remains the inevitable term. So far as philosophic value is concerned, "being" and other traditional terms of generic identification, mainly "reality" and "existence," are required in certain types of context and are useful when treated with circumspection. But they suffer from many disadvantages and perplexities.

Their dubious status is indicated by the ways in which they have functioned. Thus philosophers for whom "being" is central have felt constrained to inquire into its relations with "non-being" or "nothing," or into "the being belonging to nothingness." Other philosophers have allowed the presence of discriminanda to which, not the term "reality" but actually the term "unreality" is applied. They have supported the notion that there are "degrees" of being and "degrees" of reality. Sometimes they have made "existence" synonymous with "being" or with "reality," and sometimes they have given it narrower scope, identifying it with that which is spatio-temporal or that which is temporal. For the most part, philosophers have not known how they should use "existence" *or* "being" *or* "reality" when confronted by problems concerning, for example, the relation between possibility and actuality. Many philosophers weaken the force of their ideas by this helplessness. A striking instance is G. H. Mead's allusion to "reality" as "existing": "reality exists in a present." The colloquial charity that is apparently expected or taken for granted does not condone the careless poverty of the usage. Nor is the usage without equally bad offspring. The present is said to be the "locus of reality," its "seat." [2]

The difficulties besetting the traditional terms of generic identification are the more evident when these terms are employed for instantial discriminations, singular or plural. No matter what it may be that is discriminated, we shall always find it expedient and desirable to call it "a" natural complex. But if we had to rely upon historical as well as twentieth-century ontological usage, we should surely hesitate to say that any one of the expressions "*a* being," "*an* entity," "*a* reality," "*an* existence" is applicable to every conceivable discriminandum. There is even a peculiar disparity in traditional habits of formulation, consisting on the one hand in a willingness to say that whatever is discriminable "has some kind of being," and on the other hand in an unwillingness to say that whatever is discriminable is "a being." There is also considerable awkwardness in the use of the plural terms "beings," "realities," "existences." The metaphysical applicability of all three is severely hindered by moral associations; that is, by associations which interfere with the desirable level of generality. Difficulties also beset the more colloquial terms that are widely used by philosophers for generic allusions—terms such as "things" and "objects." These are poor and clumsy when applied, say, to relations or laws.

One of the principal advantages of "natural complex" is an implication inherent in the uses of the term, namely, that every discriminandum whatever offers a prospect for query.[3] Some philosophers, whether enamored of ready-made standards or devoted to the ideal of calling a spade a spade, seem to distrust the very idea of complexity. But in the most fundamental sense, complexity implies the likelihood of access, and this means continuing experience and query. A further implication of the idea of complexity will here be defended with concepts deemed best for this defense, the implication that the traits of any complex can never be regarded as fully and finally ascertained or completely circumscribed. A complex, if it is accessible at all, is analyzable and interpretable without end; or to speak in a more generic way, is manipulatable in an indefinite number of orders.

ii

The term "natural complex" is not set up to be contrasted with "non-natural" or "supernatural" complex. The latter terms are made possible, as terms, by the procedures of logic and the properties of grammar; but they represent nothing discriminable that is not continuous with all other discriminanda and all other processes of discrimination. When the term "complex of nature" is used instead of "natural complex," the impulse to ask whether there are complexes of an opposite kind is perhaps less likely to arise. Linguistic habits do not favor "Are there complexes of nonnature?" If the concept of God is thought of as viable metaphysically, and not blankly endured as a stimulus to animism, it must signify a natural complex. Nothing jeopardizes the strong uniqueness of this complex. Historically and persistently, there attaches to it a customary formal scheme of traits. This scheme, adhered to in its essentials by widely differing philosophers, serves to maintain a level of gravity and primacy for the idea of God. It predetermines the complex to be interpreted, however different the interpretations otherwise may be. It provides the "rules" with which all versions are to accord. Thus men have recognized in effect that to God belongs great pervasiveness, inexhaustible value as a paradigm, symbolic richness, "supremacy." Such traits prescribe the sphere of relevance, the formula as it were, for ceaseless translation of the idea. Translation presupposes an "original"; so that when a philosopher wishes to use and adapt the concept of God, but fails to grasp the sense of the schematic requirement and fails to grasp the compulsion behind it, he achieves not the metaphysical or poetic perception he might have sought, but a somewhat hollow categorial freedom.

Even as echoed by men without the power of translation, the guiding scheme of traits is too constant, too substantial, to permit for the conception of God any specific or dominant role, its metaphysical character forever warring with the confusions of classic anthropomorphism. It threatens always to expose the insidiously comic aspects of that which is cast as father, judge, chief, even "creator." The persistence of the scheme mirrors a difficult, unresolved union of natural (though not universal) discriminations: of that which is always present yet always dark; of unaccountable imbalance, dissonance, and hunger; of perfection, remoteness, inevitability, mystery. That God should have been delineated, historically, in terms of vulgar finite analogies is in itself a kind of natural irony, though not an absurdity, seeing that analogies of one kind and another are native to the texture of speculation.

If God were understood in part as that complex of nature which preserves overwhelming contrast with the finite, then to God might be ascribed perpetual consummations of a related kind—delimiting all other complexes, opening human ways beyond prevailing limits, and constantly renewing in the experiential orders of the world (in the perspectives of man) that sensitivity to the similar and the different which lies at the base of query. The expression "God willing" is a recognition that the traits, the boundaries, that prevail or arise, govern the life of man. Limitation and situation give birth to the conative forces of overcoming, aspiring. The principle that there always are questions beyond the questions that have been asked, and complexes beyond and within the complexes that are known, besides being defensible as such, preserves the momentum of life and query. At least for man, absolute delimitation—perfect boundaries, incorrigible knowledge, total freedom from indecision (which is freedom from decision)—would be death.

The question whether God "exists" or does not is a symptom of deficiency in the categorial equipment of a metaphysics. The use of "exist" in such a context tacitly shapes a crude conception of the subject-matter under debate. In the metaphysics of natural complexes it could be said that God prevails, not for this reason or that, but because God is a complex discriminated, and every complex prevails, each in its own way, whether as myth, historical event, symbol, or force; whether as actuality or possibility. The critical question must be, not whether God exists, nor whether there is an "entity" which satisfies the scheme of traits by which the concept of God is perpetuated, but in what way a natural complex thus discriminated is to be understood, analyzed, and experientially encompassed; or, in what way it is to be further discriminated and found related.

By the same standard, to describe metaphysics as inquiry into "generic traits of existence" is unacceptable. "Existence" itself is too problematical, and not generic enough to be taken as the base.[4] Seldom is it realized or even observed that one function of an adequate category is to provide a just basis for distinctions, and not to blanket or transcend them. It is when deliberately wrought categories are eschewed, and terms like "exist" are applied indifferently, for instance to relations, concepts, possibilities, or physical bodies, that the distinctions among these complexes are ignored and suppressed. Nor will it do for a philosopher to say that he simply is not interested in a single concept applicable to all that is discerned. What happens in such a disavowal is that a term serving this function *is* actually used—say "entity," "existence," "thing"—but used informally, and without a rationale; and when several terms are used instead of one, there is the same lack of interest in their basic differentiae as there is in their possible subsumption under a term that is comprehensive.

Whatever the traits of God, then, God is a complex which various philosophers methodically discriminate and to which they variously assign a scope. To reject this way of approaching the issue is, of course, to render "natural complex" ineligible as the term for universal identification. The historic lack of a single and sufficiently versatile term has helped to encourage the suspicion of radical discontinuity in nature and has even seemed to vindicate periodic appeal to "the inexplicable." Far more commonly than the history of philosophic thought reveals or concedes, miracle implicitly functions as a basic category or as an extra-systemic bulwark. By many philosophers nature is regarded as the realm of the regular and even of the rightful, sometimes tarnished by the devilish and the "unnatural," too poor to contain deity and mystery, but pointing to these heights, and sporadically illuminated and mended in a way that passes understanding.

The "unnatural" that has been bequeathed by philosophic tradition to everyday discourse is not the non-natural, whatever that would be, but a natural complex which is (a) irregular in the sense that it does not obtain "for the most part," and (b) uncongenial to common standards of morality or taste. It is thus the irregular in both a statistical and a cultural sense.

"Natural complex" and "human complex," though they stand to each other as genus and species, are so immeasurably different in scope, that they oppose each other in a stubborn kind of way. Nothing is more customary philosophically than the phrases "nature and man" and "nature and art." These contrasts usually do not suggest a gulf that requires belief in absolute discontinuity and inexplicability. They aim to distinguish two orders, even if one is included in the other, and they suggest corollary distinctions bearing on the human process. Most doctrines of inexplicability betray theoretical fatigue. Man, like God, is interpretable through the most fundamental categories that philosophy can devise. Neither owns an ontological domicile. Of course, nobody feels obliged to prove "the existence of man." But both complexes are primal discriminations. They spread wonder, and not of the philosophic kind alone. When their ramifications are pursued they are found, as all complexes are, to harbor both actuality and possibility. Actuality and possibility alike feed wonder, which manifests itself variously, for instance in horror or elation.

iii

"Natural complex" is not a term set up to be contrasted with "natural simple." In common speech the "complex-simple" opposition is a practical way to distinguish between what men need or want to explore, and what they do not; between what they feel is divisible, and what they feel is not. But preanalytical feeling and practicality cannot settle or dictate to metaphysical investigation, nor can established philosophic habits. From the mere verbal availability of the term "simple," it does not follow that anything which is not a natural complex is ever actually designated or required to be assumed. Leibniz holds that since there are complexes there must be simples. This egregious *non sequitur* is partly an outcome of the tendency to think of natural complexes as clusters or bundles or containers or chains of traits: through disentanglement ("analysis") the units become increasingly clear. The tendency is also expressed by the idea that natural complexes are all "compounds" or "composites," divisible into components or elements, which are "without parts." But even when we confine ourselves to "composites," the Leibnizian inference is peculiar. For each composite can be divided into lesser composites, and so on indefinitely, without assuming any prior or actual presence of ultimate units; just as it is possible for a line to be divided endlessly without having to consist of minimal lines or [indivisible] points.* In the

---

* Words in brackets, unlike those in parentheses, will be used to qualify

elaboration of his metaphysics Leibniz manages to abandon, not the notion of simplicity, but the equation of simplicity with indivisibility, as Locke too had done in many contexts; and Locke and Leibniz likewise depart, even strikingly, both in principle and in practical argument, from the cluster conception. But the influence of the tendency in question has been tremendous.

The conception of natural complexes as clusters, besides reflecting a coarse conception of analysis, breeds confusion and triviality. It gives rise to the kinds of problems that are solved by repudiating the orientation which underlies them. One of these is that in a "cluster of traits" the traits seem to be more "real" than the cluster. For it is supposed that (a) a trait does not depend upon a given cluster for its being, whereas a cluster depends upon given traits. Or that (b) although a trait requires a cluster for its being, it is the same trait no matter what the cluster, whereas a cluster is not the same without the same traits.

The term "trait" probably is the most satisfactory of the terms that can serve to identify a constituent of a natural complex. It is more neutral and more general than, say, "quality" or "property" or "attribute," which alike may be designated as traits. At the same time, of course, the term is as good as the uses to which it is put. Not only (a) and (b) but another confusion needs to be disowned and remedied—it has been disowned more easily than it has been remedied —namely, the conviction (c) that there is something

what follows rather than what precedes them. Although they are not strictly required, they are introduced as possibly helpful.

of which a trait is a trait, something to which a group of traits "belongs." This is an understandable conviction, and it may be fundamentally sound in its core. The classic difficulty lies in the associated suggestion that the something to which a trait belongs is not itself a trait or analyzable in respect of traits; or the suggestion that what the traits belong to, as contrasted with the traits themselves, is "primary" in its being.

From this bog we begin to emerge when we conceive of every trait as a natural complex, and therefore of every natural complex as constituted by subaltern complexes. Every complex (complex of traits) is thus a constituent of some other complex and includes other complexes as constituents of it. Stated in what will prove to be an important equivalent way, every complex is an order of complexes and belongs to an order of complexes. Every complex may belong to more than one order, and conceivably to any number of orders.

We may now clarify and cut across (a), (b), and (c). Traits do require for their being a natural complex in which they are "located" (as subaltern complexes). There cannot be a complex without traits or subaltern complexes. A trait may be located in more than one order of complexes. A complex may be spoken of justifiably as the same even if not all of its traits remain the same. No complex *need* be spoken of as a "trait," and no trait *need* be spoken of as "belonging" to a complex. A complex need be seen as trait only when it is considered as subaltern in a [more inclusive] complex. And a trait need be seen as belonging to a complex only when this complex is considered in terms

of what is subaltern to it. Since any complex has subaltern complexes and is subaltern in some other, and
since "subaltern complex" means no more than "trait,"
the term "subaltern" has no moral or valuational significance.

These preliminary formulations represent a generalization and neutralization of the maxim of Anaxa-
goras, "Neither is there a least of what is small, but
there is always a less . . . But there is always a greater
than what is great."

When we consider a natural complex such as a common "thing," say a tree, we require no great wit to
discover that its "constituent traits" cannot be thought
of as all literally or geometrically enclosed within it,
or stuck to it. The container analogy, though actually
a dull relative of the cluster, has been even more
influential in the thought habits of both laymen and
philosophers. It is nurtured by an allied tendency to
think of complexes typically as objects of perception,
and of perception primarily as visual. Philosophers
do not like smell. If through the ages smell, or even
hearing, had been the exemplar of sense perception,
the approach to the constituent traits of things would
have been very different. At the other extreme from
the container model is the subtler relative of the cluster, a chain of traits spread out in time. Such a conception is not intolerable but only narrow, that is, not
representative of all complexes; for not all complexes
are happenings. But even where happenings are the
traits to be emphasized, the chain can never be regarded as exclusively temporal, perfectly linear, and

perfectly distinguishable; nor, when distinguishable, as perfectly single and separable.

The tree's relations to light and air, its typical visual effect on an average observer, are its traits even as are the color and texture of its bark. Its potentialities for a span of life are equally traits, and these are designated either by an account of diverse conditions that inhibit and promote its growth or, more abstractly, by the formulation of principles. No adequate analysis of such an object could limit itself to the enumeration of components within a container or cluster. It might even neglect gross details in favor of, let us say, implications drawn from a hierarchy of plant forms. Scientific procedures and the increased influence of pragmatic or operational techniques upon definition have surprisingly little effect upon metaphysical articulateness or the refinement of metaphysical categories. This is not at all to say that philosophers are blind to methodic developments in science, or resistant to what is implied by such developments. It is rather to say that scientists, whose actual experience is incongruous with a crude conception of traits, contribute little to a discursive recognition of the crudity. For one reason or another, philosophers and scientists alike find it more congenial to think of dispositions or powers as traits than to think of relations or of unfamiliar possibilities as traits. The stubborn influence of common sense suggests that traits are "possessed." Powers seem more precisely locatable than relations. To possess a power sounds better than to "possess" a relation.

Even when a tree is non-scientifically analyzed, even when it is regarded not with a view to description or explanation but with a view to depiction in a series of drawings, its visual "elements" may be less fundamental than its visual possibilities. The aggregate of its visual representations is an exhibitive analysis. We emerge with a tree that is made, re-presented. We "actualize" some of the traits, traits known as possibilities. These possibilities, like any other traits, are located "in" a complex. "In" and "within" are recognized by Locke as implying pertinence to an order rather than literal enclosure. This is true whether he speaks of ideas "in" a mind or qualities "in" a body or properties "in" the signification of a name. The principle that "things, however absolute and entire they seem in themselves, are but retainers to other parts of nature" is not simply an emphasis on remote or unsuspected causal dependencies, but an emphasis on what a "thing's" traits *are,* on how to ascertain the *thing's* traits.[5] It is not merely an emphasis on the explanation of the thing, but on the adequate identification of a complex. It helps to make clear why the cluster or container habit of approach to traits is unsatisfactory not only for complexes like an electron, a revolution, or a disenchanted man, but for the innocent and otherwise reassuring presences, a tree, a cloud, a stone.

Henceforth traits or subaltern complexes will be regarded as "constituents" of a complex. Constituents, it will be found, may or may not be "parts," and parts may or may not be "components." The assumption that all constituents are components is what encourages persistence of the view that every natural complex is reducible to simples.

iv

The idea of ontological simples, of irreducible components of nature, implies belief in absolute termini of analysis. Its appeal is not hard to detect. It seems to yield the assurance of a "foundation" for knowledge, and a stable or reliable foundation. It seems to provide "real" or "ultimate" elements. It seems to certify that familiar things, if they do dissolve, do not dissolve into nothing and are not lost.

Whatever can be discriminated (framed, grasped, identified) is related to that within which or from which it is discriminated. An element or simple would need to have traits of relatedness to the complex of which it is an element and to other phases or constituents of the complex, not to mention anything of a world beyond. It would stand in certain relations and not in others. For the relations in which it could stand, it would need to have aptitudes or tolerances. It could not have the same eligibility or the same aspect toward everything and nothing. Yet, as a perfectly simple, homogeneous trait it would also have to be single, unrelated, and unqualified. And this means that it would be unlocated and inaccessible. Its relationless freedom from all multiplicity would include freedom from relation to any knower or manipulator. To call it "indescribable," as we so often call that which we have had difficulty in describing, would be a far more serious matter than is ordinarily realized. A simple would not only lack the possibility of being described; it would lack all possibilities. Any possibility it had would be a trait, another trait, and would mean plurality. It would be indescribable for the truly good reason that it would be indiscriminable. The irony of the "simple" is that as a simple it must be perfectly "determinate"; yet as lacking all traits that would mark out its place in the world, it must be perfectly "indeterminate." Its "being" or "reality," its ontological status, as the case turns out, is exclusively verbal.

If the notion of a simple actuality is fictitious, can there not be a simple possibility? But the way in which a possibility obtains is analogous to the way in which an actuality obtains. A possibility is related both to other possibilities and to actualities. There are certain possibilities because certain actualities obtain, and there are certain actualities because certain possibilities obtain. A possibility is therefore doubly related: to the conditions which make it a possibility and to the conditions which actualize it. But a simple possibility would be one with a single, indivisible trait, and it could not be thus doubly related. The question is whether it could be related at all. If it is related to one other possibility, it would have to be unrelated to all other different possibilities. If it were related in any respect, it would have to be unrelated in any other respect. If it were related to another possibility, it would have to be unrelated to any actuality. If it were related to an actuality, it would have to be unrelated to any other possibility. Yet there seems no reason whatever why any possibility should not be related to, comparable with, and distinguishable from an indefinite number of others. The traits of a possibility consist minimally of a range of conditions which its exemplification admits and a range which its exemplification excludes. This is ordinarily formulated in terms of the "implications" of a possibility. When we say that it is possible for the earth to be inhabited only by plants, we imply the presence and absence of innumerable actualities and other possibilities. When we say that it is not possible for the sum of the angles of a Euclidean triangle to be either less or more than two right angles, we include and exclude innumerable other possibilities.

The most naive and yet by far the most obstinate attempt to evade natural complexes is found in the notion of "simple qualities." These qualities ("like red"), it is held, manifestly "have no parts" and are perfectly homogeneous. We are seldom told what is to be understood by "quality" in this context, being supplied instead with stock, common-sense illustrations of "qualities," which are alleged to be "indefinable" and "unanalyzable." Thus at the very outset confusion reigns. For when it is contended that a certain kind of quality or any particular quality is unanalyzable, or the term designating it is indefinable, this has nothing to do with the analysis or explanation of the general concept of quality; taking refuge in the contention does not confer exemption from the latter problem. In any case, so much in human history has been held to be indefinable, indescribable, and unanalyzable, that a few more intuitive pleas are drops in the bucket. Ontological simplicity, with its stubborn opaqueness, has been ascribed *both* to the so-called highest genera ("being," "the one") and to the supposedly most con-

crete and individual actualities ("basic facts," "qualities of sense"). The highest genus is "simple" because
it is the common denominator of everything else. The
most concrete fact or quality is "simple" because it is
the common denominator of nothing else. Neither,
we learn, has "parts."

How are we to test whether a quality does or does
not have parts? Is spatial expanse a "part" of red? Is
brightness? Or contrast with an environing ground?
Whether these are "parts" or not, they are certainly
constituent traits, and indeed the kind of constituent
traits without which red is not possible. When it is
protested that it is the "sense quality" which is simple,
does this expression somehow get rid of the quality in
any other respect? A "sensation of red" has the traits
that the "quality of red" necessarily has, such as expanse or spread-outness, and contrast of hue and background. These traits are what "red" minimally is and
means, and what the sensing of red is and entails. The
term "red" is the name for a natural complex. And so
is the term "spread-out." The metaphysics of natural
complexes denies the discriminability of anything without ramification and constitution—of anything unrelated and not located in an order, of anything free of
traits affecting and affected by other traits.

The underlying dissatisfaction with the view that
every quality is a natural complex, whether in its relation to other qualities or in its relation to sensing, rests
on two informal arguments that tend to linger.

The first is that if expanse, contrast, and other traits
are present in the case of a specific quality red, they
are also present in the case of qualities other than red,

for instance yellow, so that in each case there must be a unique and distinguishing residuum, and it is this which is the simple irreducible red or yellow. But the circumstance that two complexes have common or similar traits in no way interferes with their respective status as complexes. And this circumstance is even an indispensable condition of discrimination. Distinguishability is not an affair between perfectly simple or single qualities. On the contrary, *absolutely* unique qualities would be non-comparable. If any complex may belong to more than one order, then theoretically there is no limit to the number of similar traits that two given complexes may have while remaining different and distinguishable. The difference between complexes, in other words, may be revealed by their location. Where, for instance, in an order of classification two traits are considered abstractly and found to be the same, in an order of analysis the structure of the traits may be quite different.

The second lingering argument is that certain "whatchamacallits" (we mustn't beg the question by calling them "complexes") are "unities" first and foremost, and that if they are constituted of plural traits these traits are irrelevant in a peculiar way. The confusion in this argument will become evident; but by way of contrast it provides opportunity for the statement of a metaphysical truth, namely, that every complex has an integrity. Whatever the boundaries or limits of complexes may happen to be, whatever may be the conditions under which these limits obtain, wherever these limits may lie, any complex has just the status, just the relations, just the constitution that it has. This is its integrity, that in which its being "a" complex and "that" complex consists. Integrity entails both uniqueness and commonness. A complex has not only an integrity but also a "scope." The scope of a complex will be defined subsequently in a cumulative way: by consideration of its forms, by comparison with the idea of integrity, and by its role in the definition of relation.

The integrity of a complex is always conditional, in the sense that it is minimally determined by the location of the complex in this or that order of complexes. A complex has an *integrity* for each of its ordinal locations. The continuity and totality of its locations, the interrelation of its integrities, is the *contour* of the complex. The contour is itself an integrity, the gross integrity of that which is plurally located, whether successively or simultaneously. A contour is the integrity of a complex not in so far as the complex transcends all orders but in so far as it belongs to many orders. The *identity* of a complex is the continuous relation that obtains between the contour of a complex and † any of its integrities.

One way of looking at integrity is in terms of its implicit recognition within the human order—or, what in effect is the same, within the order of continuing interrelation between human and non-human complexes. The expression "*a* complex" is the most insistent verbal mode of setting apart whatever is discriminated and regarded as whole. It suggests an integrity in the formation of which man has had a part. Discriminations are, so to speak, framings of complexes from the welter of complexes. They may or may not be conscious. In so far as they serve needs, they make for long-term good or evil whether or not they express intentions. But they also arise in non-instrumental profusion, punctuating the life of man by virtue merely of his sentience or of his situation. Nature provides the human animal with dim alternatives, and he, destined as he is in one of his dimensions to accept, frames with a robust disrespect for actualities.

The process of discriminating, framing, selecting is the pulse of human utterance. Utterance ranges from the primordial maneuvers and responses—those which men cannot help making and which are humanly taken for granted, but which nevertheless vary individually —to the most intricate methodic products. Depending upon which essential aspect of the human process is emphasized, utterance may be seen as "production" or as "judgment." Man produces (a) by acting in relation to the integrities among which he finds himself, (b) by contriving new integrities, and (c) by propositionally structuring integrities in order to affirm or test his suspicions. He is the creature that judges the complexes of nature by producing in these three modes. In practice these modes are most often intermingled beyond recognition. But their analytical separation and preservation is imperative if a theory of the human process is to fit, with any adequacy at all, the animal that has stumbled fantastically among peaks and troughs.

The products of men are made possible by natural complexes that lend themselves to identification. Each product is a complex that has its own integrity, even if it is of momentary duration and small importance.

A product emerges in just the way it does, and has just the multifariousness that it has. Whatever the product, the fact that it is a product, that it is an integrity, means that it has a unitary aspect. And likewise, whatever the complex, the fact that it is a complex implies unity (or unitariness) in some respect. Every cross-section of nature, every combination, temporal stretch, accident, or flicker has an integrity in an order. Thus the view that certain complexes are unities "first and foremost" is without meaning. It makes sense only to say that given complexes are unities of such-and-such a kind, in such-and-such a respect. The integrity of a complex belongs to it not in spite of but because of its multiplicity and relatedness.

v

All natural complexes are relational, though not only relational. Any complex is related to others, though not to all others; and its traits are related to one another, though not necessarily each to every other. Whatever is, is in some relation: a given complex may be unrelated to another given complex, but not unrelated to any other. A complex related to another complex in one respect may not be related to it in another respect. There is no end to the relational "chain" of a complex; and there is no end to the explorability of a complex, whether in respect of its relational traits or any other. A relation as such is a complex, analyzable as all are. No complex is inherently "more of a complex" or "more complex" than any other, nor unqualifiedly "simpler" than any other. The whole is not simpler than a part, nor a part simpler than the whole.

The genus is not less analyzable than a species, nor a species less analyzable than the genus.

The principal qualification that must be made, partly because of dominant habits in human discourse, applies to complexes in an order of estimation; that is, in a certain sub-order of the human order. Here we may speak, with entire justification, of differences in "simplicity" or "complexity." Yet even here, since any one analysis can be pursued as indefinitely far as any other, the differences lie not in the relative number of traits belonging to a complex or its analysis, but (a) in the relative importance assigned to it, or in the relative interest aroused by it, and (b) in the relative adequacy, at a particular time, of the devices employed to manipulate it deliberatively. This is what is meant by the apparently commonplace opinion that some problems or some objectives are simpler than others. Importance and interest are themselves, of course, natural complexes, and they are related to the complex of purpose, which is the chief factor determining the boundaries of certain types of perspective. There are also, to be sure, compulsive conditions of nature that influence estimations of what is important. Two of these, described in the next section, are the relative comprehensiveness and the relative pervasiveness of natural complexes.

In sensation the diversifying aspects of a complex (the complex sensed) are submerged. They are neglected by the sensing organism. (Whether a sensation is "pure" or not is beside the point.) In sensation, no less than in all other processes and situations, man is both manipulating and assimilating complexes of the world available to him. Sensing is a way of functioning wherein the deliberative aspect possible to manipulation is all but irrelevant. Sheer sensory feeling is a relation between complexes. It is a relation which men seem always to have regarded as the most primitive form of encounter. By some, notably some philosophers, it is regarded as the only form of encounter.

If we distinguish between sensation, sensory perception, and sensory observation, we may regard these as levels of sensory encounter informed by respectively greater degrees of conjecture or probing. All three are discriminative, but differently discriminative. It is not merely what they discriminate but how they discriminate that defines the levels. Actually, while still in a sensory capacity, we may encounter quite different aspects of a given complex—for example, a complex in its status as a symptom or in its status as a problem. The difference in the levels lies in the relative accessibility—accessibility to *sensing*—of the order within which the sensed complex is located. Observation yields greater access, sensation lesser.

Not all complexes can be sensed. But those complexes that are available to sensation are encountered just as integrities, integrities-without-qualification. They neither are, nor are encountered as, ontological simples, perfect homogeneities. They neither are, nor are encountered as, indivisible. And they may, or may not, be encountered as undivided. In one respect, the "object" in the process of sensation engrosses it, and is thus an undivided whole. In another respect, constituent traits, together with their relative contrasts (divisions), are present together in the complex sensed.

In so far as the complex sensed is undivided, it may be called, not inappropriately, "individual." If what is individual in this meaning of the term is to be called "simple," then any natural complex that becomes sensed thereby *becomes* "simple." It is not by virtue of what happens to be sensed that this kind of simplicity enters the sensory relation; it is because of the nature of this relation that whatever is sensed acquires such simplicity.

Why should the three levels be called levels of "sensory" encounter? Because, it is sometimes assumed, an encounter of this kind is more "direct" than any other. But the definition of "direct" is very difficult. It is possible to think the other way round, of directness of encounter as that which is sensory in character. Is the perception of a "meaning," or of an emotional state, or of a mathematical similarity, or of a spatial relation, less "direct" than the perception of a color? And when we ask, further, whether the perception of a spatial relation should be regarded as "sensory" perception, the meaning of "direct" becomes still more indecisive.

In whatever way "direct" is to be defined, if we assume that sensation is the "most" direct of the three levels of sensory encounter, nothing implies that it must be instantaneous or devoid of gradations. Directness of encounter may continue indefinitely. As a phase within a wider sensory process, and beyond this, within an experiential process, sensation literally preserves certain kinds of integrities. The notion of sensation as an all-or-none occurrence of infinitesimal duration still carries extraordinary weight. It is probably perpetuated by the social need, or supposed need, for single trait-labels, names that are thought to facilitate communication. The fact, however, that children do not always sense in a way which harmonizes with the way their elders sense cannot be wholly attributed to their limited powers of expression and report—their relative lack of control over names. They appear to discriminate and to embrace what is not in accord with the standardized modes of sensory life. Thus the familiar view that children and poets have much in common is far from being precious or exaggerated.

Sensation is that kind of relation in which certain integrities as such become conspicuous, and hence expediently negotiable, utilizable. In sensation, we said, the many and different aspects of a complex are functionally annulled. But just as we may sense a complex-as-an-integrity, so we may methodically relate to that complex-as-an-integrity. *Methodically* we may submerge the contrasting traits within the complex. In our relation to a complex we may deliberately neglect or strategically disregard the relationality within the complex and the relations of the complex. But we cannot regard the integrity as somehow isolated in its being, or as intrinsically free of relation. We may speak of the integrity as "felt," but the assumption that there are integrities which can *only* be felt is without a shred of warrant. An integrity *need* not be inquired into. Not to inquire into it may be suitable to a purpose or circumstantially desirable. But to suppose that it *cannot* be inquired into, that it is not the "kind of thing" that can be "described or defined," is to suppose it the sole inhabitant of an order detached from every other order—in effect, to suppose it (in securely negative fashion) "non-natural." Dewey, who like innumerable others thinks there are "undefinable and indescribable qualities," qualities that are "ineffable," beclouds the natural status that he insists on assigning to these qualities.[6] A feeling is itself a complex that is analyzable, not a non-relational monadic ultimate. To analyze a feeling through an enumeration or description of its traits may be undesirable in certain types of situation. The description, like any other description, may be better or worse, more or less clarifying. To interpret and clarify the feeling through action, for instance, may well be the better course. And in certain types of situation it may also be true that to act is far less difficult (for some men) than to describe traits. But conditions of relative strategy and appropriateness aside, there is no good reason to believe that a description of traits is ever intrinsically less possible than an action.

Leibniz, who affirms the indubitable being of simples, at times equates simplicity with indivisibility, and at times equates simplicity with uniqueness. In terms of the latter inclination, he sees the "essence" of a so-called simple substance as actually a multiplicity of traits, but a unique multiplicity, a totality consisting of "all the predicates of which the substance is or may become the subject." [7] Here the simple is that which is *sui generis* but not necessarily unanalyzable. Whitehead, taking it for granted that "simplicity" means unanalyzability, distinguishes simplicity from atomicity, rejecting simplicity and accepting atomicity.

Atomicity he construes as genuinely individual being. And he regards his atoms as "final" or "ultimate" actualities, as the "really real" complexes.

vi

"For the meditating philosopher," says Husserl, "the world is only something that claims being." [8] Just what the world would amount to (for the meditating philosopher) if it lost its claim, is bewildering. Presumably it would still be tolerated, and allowed a role of some kind somehow, whether it were degraded, forgotten, or renamed. In any case, a metaphysics of natural complexes requires a quite different keynote. According to Randall,

"Reality" means either everything whatsoever—as we are here taking it—or else that a distinction of relative importance has been made. In any other than an evaluative sense, to say that only the Good is "real," only Matter is "real," only Mind is "real," only Energy is "real," is to express a prejudice refuted by a child's first thought or by every smallest grain of sand. No, everything encountered in any way is somehow real. The significant question is, not whether anything is "real" or not, but how and in what sense it is real, and how it is related to and functions among other reals. To take "the real" as in fundamental contrast to what appears to us, is to identify it with "the Good." . . . Such identification seems to have resulted invariably in confusions and insoluble contradictions.[9]

Now along with the notion of a complex as "unreal" we must discard the notion of some complexes as "less" and other complexes as "more" real. Let us contrast a principle of ontological priority—which has flourished

from Parmenides to Whitehead and Heidegger, and †
which continues to flourish in unsuspected ways—with
a principle of ontological parity. In terms of the latter,
whatever is discriminated in any way (whether it is
"encountered" or produced or otherwise related to) is
a natural complex, and no complex is more "real,"
more "natural," more "genuine," or more "ultimate"
than any other. There is no ground, except perhaps a
short-range rhetorical one, for a distinction between
the real and the "really real," between being and "true
being." Among the favorite perennial candidates for
the honor of "being" more truly or more completely
than anything else is "primary substance" or "primary
being." It has been the standing historical comfort of
"tough-minded" philosophers, preserving their confi-
dence in the solid concreteness of the spatio-temporal
individual.

No discriminanda can be consigned to "non-being,"
on pain of contradiction; for they have the being that
enables them to be discriminated. This being may consist in the being of a picture in a book; of an image or
a fantasy; of a plan private to one man or common to
many men; of a verbal expression; of a pain, a dream,
a habit, a fear, an error, a tradition, a bond among persons. Some discriminanda strike us as deserving no
further attention; others, as requiring clarification, action, or portrayal. Sometimes it is *said* that a discrimination has been made, even though people cannot ascertain that it has. Sometimes there is common agreement that a word or chain of words has not succeeded
in achieving a discrimination other than the pattern
of its own verbal being. Some philosophers think that

action, in contrast to thought, does not function to discriminate. But when there is a discriminandum, of whatever kind or status, *its* being has neither more nor less of being than the being of any other.[10]

The principle of ontological parity scarcely implies that there are no differences among natural complexes. On the contrary, it presupposes that no two complexes, in whatever order and however discriminated, are similar in all respects. Their discriminability forces us to preserve their integrity, or better, to acknowledge it. Natural complexes, moreover, differ in both kind and scope. Difference is so basic that every distinction good and bad, every opinion shallow or deep, every fiction, hallucination, or deception, every product social or individual, is recognized as a natural complex. Nor are distinctions of degree abolished; on the contrary, they are preserved. What is abolished is any inference, from *A*'s being less courageous than *B* or more skillful than *B*, that something is more or less real, of greater or lesser being, than something else. Little courage is not a lesser reality than great courage. The preservation of degree actually requires the principle of parity. Just as the principle does not warrant the attribution of higher reality to that which exemplifies a trait in higher degree, so it does not justify the attribution of lesser reality or unreality to that which exemplifies a trait in lower degree.

No distinction, then, is dismissed. It only awaits its analysis—the interpretation of "how and in what sense it is real." All complexes are equally "authentic" as complexes, distressing as this may be to certain points of view whose metaphysical orientation actually damages an ethical purpose which it is believed to support. The natural parity of all complexes, their ontological integrity, is what reveals all differences and makes it possible to ascertain them. The principle of parity obliges us to receive and accept all discriminanda. The conception of ontological priority, on the other hand, makes all ascertainable differences suspect, and instead of interpreting their relative character and ordinal location, always stands ready to efface them.

There are many possible ways of trying to justify the principle of ontological priority. It is a principle which seems to reflect a deep, standing need, and it lends itself to gratuitous affirmation and reaffirmation regardless of argument. We shall try to formulate a number of grounds for it, all different, and to show the untenable consequences which they entail. More important, perhaps, will be the concomitant opportunity to develop, by contrast, additional properties and distinctions in the theory of natural complexes.

1. Complex B, it might be held, is "more real" than complex A when A is dependent upon B but B is not dependent upon A. The forms of "dependency" are of course various. We may assume that causal dependency, in the strong sense of a complex having been produced by another which is its necessary and sufficient condition, is as persuasive as any other form. Causes, then, must be more real than their effects. Now since B, as cause of A, is itself the effect of a cause, and this in turn the effect of a prior cause . . . and since A, as effect of B, is also cause of a further effect . . . there seems to be only one major conclusion consistent with the initial supposition: that remoter causes are

more real than proximate causes. Each complex is more real than its posterity but less real than its ancestry. And from this it follows that the universe of actualities, to speak of no other, is becoming less and less real. The ensuing eschatology is grotesque. All the reality lost would have to be restored by an ontological resurrection if the Last Judgment were to be dramatically potent. Even an interpretation that would construe greater reality to mean greater goodness would fail dismally by this "dependency" criterion. Nothing is more obvious in the experience of men than the truth that an effect may be more admirable, more salutary, more encouraging morally than its cause; or the truth that human products are often much more important to mankind than their producers are.

2. Complex B, it might be held, is "more real" than complex A when A is [merely] a component of B, for B may contain not only A but other components. But as in the preceding position, an innocent-sounding assumption leads to stultifying results. If A is a component of B, and B a component of a still larger whole C, then B in turn is less real than C; and so on "upwards" (or "outwards"), so that only a universe or grand totality is truly real, while its most "minute" components or elements are least real. One ironic consequence is that what is putatively "indivisible" or "simple" emerges here as least real, instead of being an "ultimate." When the position is stated not in terms of wholes and components but in terms of wholes and parts, it is equally weak. All components would seem to be parts, but not all parts components. A man who is part of a religious movement is not a component of

the movement in the sense that a wall or a joist is a component of a house. In one respect, a man is part of a corporation; in another, the corporation is part of his life. In neither of these or various other senses of "part" is the part a component. If, without qualification, wholes are said to be more real than parts, the corporation must be more real than the man who is part of it; and at the same time the corporation must be less real than the life of the man who is part of that corporation. (It will be recalled that the generic term embracing "parts" and "components," as well as any other sub-complexes, is "constituents.")

3. Complex B, it might be held, is "more real" than complex A when the scope of B is greater or wider or more far-reaching than the scope of A. It is necessary to examine the idea of scope, with the purpose of showing that there are well-grounded distinctions in the scope of natural complexes, but that these distinctions actually render "degree of reality" an unsatisfactory and dispensable concept.

(a) B is greater in scope than A if it is more comprehensive or more generic than A. One complex is more comprehensive than another if it is not always a manifestation of the other but the other is always a manifestation of it. Juvenile crime is, let us say, a manifestation of the more comprehensive condition of social confusion and violence. Here the less comprehensive complex would also typically be called a "part" of the more comprehensive one. Being a sister is a manifestation of being a sibling: being a sibling is more comprehensive than being a sister. But in this case it is the more comprehensive complex that would most typically be called a "part" of the less comprehensive: being a sibling is part of what being a sister is or means. In each of the two examples it is possible, if less typical, to see the "part" in reverse. There is a sense in which social confusion is "part" of a juvenile crime; and there is a sense in which being a sister is "part" of what it can mean to be a sibling. The contrasting senses correspond to two of the senses which Aristotle enumerates for "in": the species, in one sense, is in the genus; the genus, in another sense, is in the species. If we consider once more the case of being a sibling as more comprehensive than and yet part of being a sister, we observe that the generic trait is part of a specific trait but not part of a "whole" in any obvious respect. To show it as part of a whole, we should have to frame and discriminate a natural complex that is somewhat different, and say that in another order the generic trait is part of the "whole structure of traits" which constitutes the specific trait.

(b) B is greater in scope than A if it is more pervasive than A. One complex is more pervasive than another if it is recurrent under more various conditions, or more widespread in its presence, or more extensive in its influence, or more diverse in its ramifications, than the other. A nation is a more pervasive complex than a stone in a cave, an ocean more pervasive than a swamp in a field. Being more comprehensive entails being more pervasive, at least in some respects. The class of physical bodies, which is more comprehensive than the class of sentient bodies, is also more pervasive in the spatial distribution of its members. (It is less pervasive, for instance, in the communicative powers of its members.) Being a sibling, which is more generic or comprehensive than being a sister, is also more pervasive because its occurrence is more frequent and widespread. But although greater comprehensiveness entails greater pervasiveness, the converse is not true. Nations are more pervasive than stones in caves, but neither more nor less comprehensive. To the extent that these are unrelated complexes, their comparative comprehensiveness might appear to be decidable not in terms of either as comprehended or embraced by the other but in terms of their respective divisibility, as kinds or types, into less comprehensive complexes. By this standard, however, there can be as many species of stones lying in caves as there are species of nations. The sense of overwhelmingly different magnitude that arises in a comparison of this kind, the sense that one of the two complexes "includes" far more than the other, boils down to a sense of relative pervasiveness. Although relative pervasiveness is often difficult to ascertain, this is a question of degree. In gross terms, if two complexes were selected at random, it probably would make sense to say that one was more pervasive than the other. In the matter of comprehensiveness, on the other hand, there is as likely as not to be an incommensurability of two randomly selected complexes, making the question of their relative comprehensiveness impossible to answer.

To vary the illustrations: in human affairs wastefulness may be more pervasive than planning, dullness more pervasive than imaginativeness. Even where two complexes, one of which is more pervasive than the other, are causally related, neither is necessarily more comprehensive than the other. Thus misunderstanding is a cause of divorce; it is a more pervasive human complex than divorce, but not necessarily more comprehensive, for divorce is not always a manifestation of misunderstanding.

Does the problem of incommensurability cast doubt upon the metaphysical goal of seeking to discriminate generic complexes that have the widest possible scope? No; the complexes sought by philosophy are deliberately selected for their commensurateness and applicability. Their comprehensiveness must be exhibited as a relation that they bear to numerous and diverse other complexes.

Thus comprehensiveness and pervasiveness are two forms of scope in natural complexes. There is no reason to believe that the kind of difference each represents gives any comfort to the doctrine of ontological priority. The scope of a complex is one of the factors in its contour or province. Lesser scope does not diminish the "naturalness" of a complex, nor does greater scope increase it. Nor is there any ethical significance in the idea of scope as such. Only when the ethical significance of a complex has already been established can greater or lesser scope be ethically relevant.

One impulse which motivates the doctrine of priority expresses itself in the concern that gradations in nature should be recognized. Herein lurks the deceptiveness of the doctrine. For to "recognize" gradation by seeing one extreme of a scale as the realm of the ultimately real, and the other extreme as the realm of the unreal or least real, is in effect to drive attention away from one of the extremes. For what is unreal is either impossible of query or unworthy of it. Consider the fatuity of a newly identified, newly located "unreality." Query, by its products, multiplies the complexes of nature. Can there be a more ludicrous idea than invention through the methodic discrimination of unrealities?

The scope of a complex, its pervasiveness and comprehensiveness, may also be regarded as its "inclusiveness." The latter notion has an unmistakable value, despite its somewhat indefinite character. There is much advantage to thinking of any natural complex as "including" traits or sub-complexes, or of an order of complexes as including complexes that are discriminable also in another order. Something like "inclusiveness" is pertinent to the understanding of what is meant by a natural complex. Every complex is inclusive, regardless of the way in which it is inclusive. Stated in the manner that has here been formalized, every complex has scope, no matter what the degree of its pervasiveness or the mode of its comprehensiveness.

4. Complex *B*, it might be held, is "more real" than complex *A* when *B* is more "determinate" than *A*. It is easy to see, at the very outset, that if the notion of determinateness varies, contrary conceptions can be made equally plausible. For example, where the "determinate" suggests the fixed and the eternal, forms are held to be more real than facts. Where the "determinate" suggests the concrete and the particular, forms are held to be less real than facts.

In a discussion of determinateness, the notions of actuality and possibility are inevitable. Most people

accept the twinship or correlation of the two in the
sense that if one talks of actuality one must talk of
possibility and vice versa. Nevertheless, philosophers
are less worried about actuality than about possibility.
After all, they feel, actuality is—well, actuality; but
just what is possibility? It does not occur to them that
the familiar presence of actual "things" does not clarify the concept of actuality. They are content with the
plain man's impression that the actual is near and
accessible, the possible remote and insubstantial. No
matter how primitive their metaphysics of actuality,
philosophers seldom hesitate to talk of possibility as if
it were illegitimately claiming to rival actuality in
rank. They warn against the danger of ascribing to
possibility the same status as actuality, but the typical
questions they themselves raise, about the "kind of
thing" possibilities are, and about where possibilities
could be, violate the warning in the most serious way.
Philosophers are wary of what some of them have
called "possible entities." It is worth observing that
we can hardly do without speaking of possibilities, but
can very easily do without speaking of "entities." This
term tends to obstruct, not only an adequate approach
to the conception of possibility, but an adequate approach to the conception of actuality. The relevant
considerations at the moment, then, are that the difficulties in the understanding of possibility do not justify
abstention from thought about the relation between
the possible and the actual; that the question, What
is the nature of possibility? does not interfere with the
recognition of possibilities and their significance; and

that the question, What is the nature of actuality? is not less difficult than the preceding question.

Let us state five conceptions of "the determinate":

I. That which is stable or constant.

II. That which is active and motive.

III. That which is not merely active but individual, or individually active.

IV. That which is "complete."

V. That upon which other complexes are more "dependent" than it is upon them.

And let us consider each of these separately.

I. This view of the determinate can serve as the basis of a contention—altogether opposed to the dominant one, according to which "determinate" at the very least means "actual"—that possibilities are more determinate than actualities. Thus: Some actualities are more stable or constant than others, but no actuality is as stable as a possibility can be. Actualities are subject to modification. Possibilities, on the contrary, are not; they remain intact, whether they are exemplified or not.

But in response to this contention: possibilities are mortal and modifiable, even as actualities are. The possibility of all Americans being literate by 1960 has ceased to obtain. Possibilities can be modified in their relation to actualities. In order to have a status that would remain perfectly intact, in order to be perfectly exempt from any kind of modification, a possibility would have to be totally unrelated, insulated from all actualities and all other possibilities. This means that it could not be located in any order whatever, and therefore could not have been discriminated as that possibility.

Are all actualities "subject to modification"? When the latter phrase is used and it is contended that they are, there is surely a certain model of actuality that is presupposed and that governs the answer. The question will have to be dealt with later in a number of contexts, along with the question whether any possibility is *not* "subject to modification." Answers will emerge, but not without the aid of additional categories.

II. This view can serve as the basis for a contention that actualities are more determinate than possibilities. For are not actualities agential and efficacious, and are not possibilities inert and non-efficacious?

But against this contention it can be argued that our ordinary notion of agency and efficacy is based on our disposition to think of one conspicuous type of efficacy associated with one conspicuous type of actuality. If a possibility merely as such cannot be said to yield a "result," neither can an actuality merely as such. Every actuality has limits. These represent "its" possibilities; in familiar cases they are sometimes called "powers" or "potentialities." Any "result" involves both an antecedent actuality and the possibilities resident in that actuality.

III. This view implies that, among actualities, individuals are "most fully" determinate. Since "societies," for instance, are constituted by individuals, and not the other way round, individuals are the "ultimate" agents.

But although societies cannot attain results that individuals can, they can attain results, and results that individuals cannot. Basically this is a commonplace of everyday belief, but it is also more than defensible metaphysically. For we cannot entertain the notion of a society, or even of a mere grouping, without taking seriously the relations that obtain among the individuals said to constitute the society or group. Nor can we recognize any complex as a society without recognizing the difference between an organization of individuals and an abstract number of individuals. A social complex is differently agential but not less truly agential than an individual.

And *are* societies constituted by individuals but not the other way round? If "constituted by" meant "composed of," the answer might be, yes. But to be a "constituent," as we have seen, does not necessarily mean to be a "component." What it means, more generally, is to be a trait that is relevant. The society of which an individual is member may enter into the complex that constitutes an individual, just as an individual may enter into the complex that constitutes a society. Indeed, so far as an individual at random is concerned, a society may be relevant to its integrity in a far more fundamental way than that individual is to the integrity of the society.

In the consideration of this point we have proceeded as if "actualities" comprised only individuals and societies (recurrently identifiable groups) of individuals. If relations and structures, for example, may be regarded as actual, then the question whether individuals are the "most" determinate actualities is even farther from resolution—or even more artificial and

ill-founded than we are thus far in a position to in-
dicate.

IV. This view can lend itself (a) to a claim that possibilities are more determinate than actualities, since
they are "complete" just as they are, without actualization, whereas actualities "become" complete and may
cease to be complete; (b) to a claim that actualities are
more determinate than possibilities, since they are the
"fulfillments" of possibilities, which as such are "un-
fulfilled" and hence incomplete; (c) to a claim that
societies are more determinate than individuals, having the completeness of a whole which transcends any
part; (d) to a claim that individuals are more determinate than societies, having the completeness that
consists in indivisibility, as contrasted with the divisibility of societies.

Each of these senses of "complete," (a)–(d), is a mix-
ture of plausibility and speciousness. Each is of very
limited significance. It seems far more significant to
note that whatever is discriminable as a complex is
fully as much a complex as any other; that any complex, whether possibility or actuality, is "complete" in
so far as it [inherently] has an integrity.

Nevertheless, it is desirable to continue the dialectic
of comment on each of the conflicting claims, the further to prepare for theoretical reorientation. (a) What
it means for an actuality to "become complete" or
cease to be complete is itself a nice question, and so is
the allied question, at just what point an actuality
may justifiably be deemed complete. (b) Every possibility is of course subject to actualization, but actualization does not complete it *as* a possibility. As a *pos-*

sibility, it is complete whether it is actualized or not. If, moreover, an actuality is the "fulfillment" of a possibility, this does not necessarily imply that an actuality is itself "fulfilled" or complete. (*c*) Why should a whole be more complete than a part? It is complete *as* a whole, and the part is complete *as* a part. There is undoubtedly an everyday sense in which, by a quantitative criterion, completeness is achieved when a vessel is filled or when pieces are assembled into a whole. But in these instances, the presence of a project waiting to be completed does not prove the point. For another project may be completed only when a vessel is emptied or when a whole is dismembered and separated into pieces. (*d*) There is no reason for that which is (allegedly) indivisible to be considered more complete than that which is divisible. The integrity of neither is a model for the integrity of the other. Neither relates to the other on a scale of degrees. And if a scale were constructed, it could be constructed to show the relative completeness and incompleteness of either.

V. This view can encourage a chaos of claims. (*a*) Possibilities are less dependent upon actualities than actualities upon them. For possibilities are what they are whether actualized or not, whereas actualities are what they are in virtue of the possibilities that there are. (*b*) Actualities are less dependent upon possibilities than possibilities upon them. For actualities are dependent upon other actualities: merely because they exemplify possibilities does not mean that they are products or effects of possibilities. (*c*) Societies are less dependent upon individuals than individuals upon them. For a society endures though each individual in it eventually perishes, whereas individuals never exist in isolation. A society is dependent only upon some present collectivity of individuals—but not on any given individual, not on any specific number of individuals, and not on the same collectivity. (d) Individuals are less dependent upon societies than societies upon them. For individuals are irreducible and societies are not. The same individual can be in either or both of two societies.

All the foregoing claims in V, (a)–(d), are invalid unless severely qualified. All the "dependencies" are co-dependencies. (a) It is true that specific possibilities do not require, for their being, actualization or eventual actualities: but in one or another sense they do presuppose correlative actualities, which precede them or are their contemporaries. Possibilities are "for" and "of" actualities. They are (to speak roughly until we come to Chapter IV) "conditions" for actualities and "natural definitions" of the boundaries or limits of actualities—however familiar or however bizarre these boundaries might appear to be. (b) Actualities are always actualizations of possibilities. If there were an exception to this, it would have to be an actuality which arose or prevailed regardless of any or all possibilities—whatever that might mean. An actuality is not the product merely of possibilities; but neither is it the product merely of actualities as such and unqualifiedly. It is a product of those actualities which provide the conditions or possibilities for it—that is, which make it possible, which (as we may say in some cases) have the power to produce it. (c) A society in which individuals simply "participate" is presumably like a box which continues in its identity though continually filled with new individual articles, or like a ship indifferent to the personnel of crew and passengers. But even a box cannot contain *any* number or *any* kind of articles, nor can a ship have *any* number or *any* kind of personnel if it *is* to be a ship. A society is more than a multiplicity of individuals, but not more than an order of individuals. The nature and continuation of the order is dependent at all times upon the traits of individuals and upon the relations among individuals which arise and which expire. (*d*) Individuals are inherently social or associational; no individual is without some mode of relation to other individuals. For as a natural complex it bears traits imposed by nature upon all complexes. It is related to those complexes which are conditions for its integrity, and in turn it has a sphere of domination or influence, which likewise presupposes association, or typical relatedness to other complexes. Finally, each individual, as a natural complex, is an order of traits. It is a society of subaltern complexes. It is no more and no less "irreducible" than any other complex.

Thus "dependence" is meaningful in various ways. But lesser dependence as a criterion of greater determinateness is reminiscent of the untenable versions of "substance" (if indeed the notion permits any tenable versions at all)—substance as less dependent than anything else: as the bearer of traits that is itself unanalyzable into traits, as the subject of predications that is itself not predicable of anything, as that which "is in itself" and is not in anything else.

The monstrous commitment facing such views is a notion of the fully determinate as that which is independent of traits. But philosophers never have been deterred from seeking a blend of the notion of determinateness with the notions of independence and completeness. Accordingly, that which is "in itself" is metamorphosed (for example, by Spinoza and Hegel) from that which is independent of traits to that which is the bearer of *all* traits and is therefore alone "truly" in itself.

But other philosophers have been unwilling to veer to this extreme and to identify the fully determinate with one basic order of traits, fearing that the notion of individuality is thereby eliminated. They have preferred to retain but to reinterpret the conception of a plurality of entities ("substances") each of which is complete. Completeness is thus held to belong not to the "ultimacy" of a universal order but to the "ultimacy" of its parts—to genuine "atoms" of reality. The completeness of each of these atoms or individuals lies, however, not in its "independence" but in its being uniquely "a system of all things" (for example, Leibniz and Whitehead). Traitlessness is banished. Completeness is reconciled with finitude. An individual or atom, though finite, is fully determinate, because unique relatedness to everything else is basic to its being.

According to Whitehead, these ultimate atoms ("actual entities") are "the final real things of which the world is made up. There is no going behind actual entities to find anything more real." These "final realities" are also described as "devoid of all indetermination," as "complete" (or "completely real"), and as "devoid of all indecision." They are not individual in a mere loose or rhetorical sense. Unlike what one might wish to identify, for instance, as an individual culture or nation, they have "absolute individuality." And as such, they have "an absolute reality." Actual entities are construed as "activities" and "processes." In so far as they are "grouped" into one or another kind of "nexus" or order, such as a "society," they compose a reality which alone has the property of "enduring." Societies, however, must not be confused with these "completely real things" of which they are composed. The actual entities or ultimate processes are themselves "composite" and "analyzable," and in "an indefinite number of ways." They have their own "component elements," of as many kinds as there are modes of analysis. Nevertheless, to *these* component elements "complete actuality" does not belong; they are "subordinate elements" only.[11]

It turns out, then, in Whitehead, that (1) the atomic actualities always have component elements; and that (2) the atomic actualities are always components in an order or nexus of actualities. Yet somehow the former kind of components, considered as realities, are less real, less "ultimate," than the latter kind of components. An atomic actuality is more real than its components, but an order of such actualities is less real than *its* components. Both that which goes to constitute an atom and that which an atom goes to constitute are less real than the atom. All this, curiously, in spite of the fact that the atoms are as inconceivable without their components as the components are without them; and in spite of the fact that these atoms are as inconceivable apart from an order as an order is apart from them.

It turns out, also, that (3) the atoms or "final realities" are actualities; so that actualities are more real than possibilities. This in spite of the fact that the atomic actualities do not endure but only become and perish, while "pure" possibilities ("eternal objects") neither become nor perish; and in spite of the fact that actualities are dependent, for their being, upon possibilities getting realized in them, while these pure possibilities are not dependent, for their being, upon any actualities—they are "the same for all actual entities."

It turns out, finally, that (4) possibility is "deficiently actual." Why this makes it less than "really real" is a puzzle; for by the same token, actuality should be "deficiently possible" or "deficiently eternal." Just what can be meant by a complex being deficient in that with which it is essentially contrasted, or to which it is essentially correlated, is problematical, to say the least. Is a male "deficiently female" and a female "deficiently male"? Is a society "deficiently individual"? If so, should an individual not be considered "deficiently social"?

An atomic theory of "ultimate actualities" is a type of metaphysical theory stressing the crucial role of "components." To be sure, Whitehead's components, as "processes," are a far cry from the tendency to think of building blocks as the model type of component. But not all natural complexes can be interpreted in terms of components, and especially not in terms of a single type. Whitehead conceives of his "ultimate actualities" as processes containing a phase in which they

achieve "full determinateness." The view of determinateness that is implied is an unnecessarily restricted
one. There is certainly a sense in which each phase of
a process is no less determinate than either the process
as a whole or its consummatory phase. Ontological
atoms, like their more familiar namesakes, can be relatively final in a functional capacity; that is, as explanatory or exhibitive devices accomplishing an envisaged
aim in a particular perspective. That atoms of actuality
should be unqualifiedly construed as the "really real
things" proves only that there is an aesthetic or meth-
odological bias, or an underlying predisposition of
common sense, the absolutist cravings of which are ap-
peased by the notion of actuality and not by the notion
of possibility.

No natural complex can be a metaphysical atom, unless we wish to hold that whatever is discriminable is
"atomic" in some respect, whether it is actual or possible, individual or social. Perhaps each is "atomic" in
the sense that there is an order to the nature of which
it contributes. Its own integrity is dependent on this
order, within which it is located. But at bottom, metaphysical atomism does not belong and cannot survive
in a theory of natural complexes. The required stretch-
ing of the notion of atom, to the point of abandoning
the analogical traits that lend it whatever value it
should have, serves no purpose. Since every complex
includes and is included in a complex, all atoms would
have to include and be included in atoms. All complexes would have equal claim; and if all complexes
are atoms, none is.

II

PREVALENCE AND ALESCENCE

i

EVERY NATURAL complex prevails. Does this appear to be a strangely incomplete statement? Explanations, of course, have to be made; implications have to be drawn. But the framework thus far provided should exclude certain interpretations at the outset; for example, that according to this statement, every complex must be recognized to "exist." The concept of natural complex, as a metaphysical category of unlimited applicability, cannot be significantly interpreted by a concept applicable only to some of its instances. It makes sense to say that whatever exists is an actuality. But there are actualities which, on the basis of considerations that will emerge, we might not wish to call "existences." And there are natural complexes which are not actualities—possibilities. Possibilities prevail as well as actualities. Are we saying, then, that to prevail is to "be"? We are not saying this, although we are assuming it perforce: a natural complex which has no being is a self-contradictory idea. In the present conceptual structure, a being which is not a natural complex is also a self-contradictory idea. To say that a natural complex has being is discursively unavoidable. But it is not very enlightening.

To begin with, a complex prevails in the sense that

it might not have been "provided" by nature, might not have been "constituted," but has been. The complex "obtains." This minimal sense could well justify calling every complex an "obtenance." The principle of ontological parity could be stated in positive terms, and without dependence upon the conceptual associates of "reality," to the effect that all discriminanda are obtenances, regardless of what else they are in comparison with one another. For certain purposes of emphasis and controversy, the principle commends itself in this [weaker] form. To say that every complex obtains underscores the idea that anything identified, whether as framed or as found, has an inviolability merely as such.

But beyond this, in saying (more strongly) that every complex prevails we are implying that it is ineluctable; that it has a sphere of primacy and domination; that it is restrictive and exclusive of other complexes.

Is there a sphere, then, in which each complex is *not* primary and dominant? And if a complex is exclusive of other complexes, does this mean that it may not also be receptive of other complexes or traits? It will soon be clear that although every complex must be said to prevail, prevalence is not the only basic dimension. Every complex is prevalent in a certain respect, in a certain way. This is true of the complex merely as a complex: it prevails as against some other complex that might have prevailed instead or in its stead. And this is true also of the complex considered as possessing traits or subaltern complexes: the complex prevails in one or another subaltern respect, any of its traits prevailing as against other traits which might have prevailed instead. The expression "might have," which is here required grammatically, should not lead back insensibly to the thought that only what is actual "prevails," as against what is possible. On the contrary, a possibility equally prevails, either as against any other possibility that might have prevailed instead, or as against the kind of world that would not have provided it or anything like it. The very concept of prevalence is introduced partly in order to permit recognition of possibility with categorial adequacy.

ii

Consider a complex commonly identified as a process; for example, the ebb and flow of the tides. The prevalence of this complex takes the form of a continuing occurrence, a recurrence. When we say that in a given order this process and not another prevails, we are identifying a specific *kind* of occurrence. But we can also say that, in a more inclusive order, a process prevails—not just this or that *kind* of process. It prevails, not as against another kind of process, but as against another kind of natural complex, as against the absence of process, the absence of traits such as continuation and recurrence.

Or consider a complex that is described as a structure, whether it be the structure of a bridge, of an inference, or of a poem. Here the prevalence lies in a kind of invariance. This is what prevails as against some other kind of invariance or some other kind of constancy. But again, the structure also prevails as against a complex in which the structural factor is of secondary moment. In the complex known as a history, the history of a man or of a people, the prevalence takes the form of an endurance amidst vicissitudes— of a limited span, a continuing identity, with spatial as well as temporal traits. In the complex known as a fact, the prevalence takes the form of a terminated and irreversible occurrence. A law prevails when complexes within a range of similarity always manifest themselves under certain conditions, however sporadic or regular these conditions may be.

A complex can be said *not* to prevail with respect to an order in which it is not located. For by the same token, what is located in that order prevails over what is not. Thus if every complex is prevalent in a certain respect, it is also not prevalent in a certain respect; and in terms of the innumerable orders to which it does not belong, it is not prevalent in innumerable respects.

But of basic importance is the consideration that even in an order to which a complex *does* belong it can be said not to be prevalent. Although as a complex it must always prevail in some order (in some "respect"), it may not prevail in every order to which it belongs.

A complex may cease to be prevalent in all respects ("cease to be"). Or it may cease to be prevalent in a particular respect in which it was prevalent—that is, by coming to prevail with a different integrity in its contour of integrities. It prevails in so far as it excludes other complexes, but what it may also exclude is a former integrity of its own. Now when a complex located in a given order is not prevalent in that order or ceases to be prevalent in that order, we shall say that it is *alescent,* or an *alescence.*

Alescent and *alescence* are derived (or subtracted)

from "coalescence," a coming together of complexes. The terms are suggested by the Latin *alescere,* to grow up, here converted to the sense of arising or (somewhat less generally) coming about or taking place. These approximations to "alescence," however, are rough, especially when separated from another group of ap-
† proximations. For alescence also signifies deviation or variation. It is that dimension of nature in which the specific integrities of complexes *initially* are what they are and how they are, whether in time, within an organization of traits, or within an order of encounter. It suggests origination or nascence or incipience, the incipience of growth, or of irrelevance, or of oddity, or of deterioration; the incipience of ordinal relocation or of difference within an order. Variation is difference in so far as it is initial.

We shall be as much concerned to show what alescence is not as to show what it is. Particularly unsuitable as an equivalent, for instance, is "becoming," which carries unacceptable implications both of a moral and a metaphysical kind; or "change," which (to mention only one difficulty) is not applicable to certain types of complex that can be alescent.

A complex is prevalent in so far as it excludes traits from its contour. A complex is alescent in so far as it admits traits into its contour. The same complex can be prevalent in one order, alescent in another. We shall say that *in so far* as it is alescent, it is not prevalent; *in so far* as it is prevalent, it is not alescent. An order implies relations among complexes. A given complex possesses its status in virtue of its sphere of relations, and it possesses a different status in virtue of a different sphere of relations, a different ordinal location.

A complex which ceases to prevail cannot, in one sense, be said to "admit traits into its contour." Its ceasing means that a contour of integrities ceases. But the ceasing, located as it is within a more inclusive complex or order, may mean that the latter complex is alescent—that it is admitting traits into *its* contour. A cloud is dissipated, a contract is broken, a threat disappears: traits are thereby introduced into the contour of an individual cloud mass, a social relation, a pattern of possibilities. But even the complex which ceases to be is admitting traits *as* it is *ceasing* to be—admitting traits of dissolution or destruction. Both this complex and the more inclusive complex, then, are alescent, each in its way.

Four forms of alescence may be distinguished, though they may be intermingled. In *augmentative* alescence a prevailing complex is extended, increased, or enhanced. In *spoliative* alescence there is loss or attenuation, expiration or extinction of a complex that has prevailed. In the third form, *coalescence,* a complex arises from a junction or intersection or novel configuration of complexes: there is variation in the world without deviation from any prevalent complex in particular, and without any particular complex having to be augmented or despoiled. The fourth form, *vagrant* alescence, involves that which has a "chance" or "dangling" character.

In the midst of a given prevalence, there may be alescence. (Conversely, where there is alescence, it is always in the midst of *some* prevalence.) Thus in the process of the tides, each wave that is idiosyncratic—that deviates from the typical pattern of all the waves—is an alescent complex. In the functioning of a machine, fluctuating quality of operation, from inefficiency and roughness to efficiency and smoothness, and back again, from uniformity to imperfection, is an alescent complex, or multitude of alescences within the more inclusive complex that prevails. In the ongoing history of a people or of an individual, the prevalence or continuing order seems to require numerous alescent stresses, from minor conflicts and ostensible discontinuities to crises and portents. Like all prevalences, a history embraces subaltern prevalences. It embraces subaltern alescences, of the kind just mentioned.

The language of a people is a prevalence within which there are phonetic and semantic alescences, complexes of differing scope. But the same language as present within another order, as a historical and geographical complex, is a gradual, prolonged alescence in the history of the people. A mountain range is a prevalence that once emerged as an alescence of the earth's surface and that now has its own subaltern alescences such as eroding areas, unexpected vegetation, agricultural improvement, and agricultural abuse.

Can we "step twice into the same river"? We can step into the same river any number of times, if we stay alive and the river remains accessible to us. The notion that movement and variation destroy or becloud the integrity of complexes, or that ceaseless flow somehow banishes sameness, comes from confusing the prevalence of a complex with some of its alescent traits.

The water of the river moves, and it isn't necessary to contest the idea that in a given area at two times the water is different. But the waters are the same waters, the prevailing waters. As an inclusive prevalence, the river is not just water. The spatial dimensions of the river bed comprise a constancy, a subaltern prevalence, in which the indubitable minute variations are negligible. So far as the act of stepping is concerned, even large variations would be negligible, or better, irrelevant. A step on dry land would not resemble a previous step in all respects any more than a step into flowing water would. Stepping, then, is also interpretable as a prevalence. The integrity of the complex is not affected by alescent occurrences within certain limits, though the integrity of some of its subaltern complexes must be.

In the midst of an alescence there is always a prev- † alence. Each of the constituents of an alescent complex prevails in some order to which it belongs. It has its own primacy: there is something which it excludes or precedes or supersedes. The alescence in which these constituents are subaltern is shaped, or continues to be shaped, just the same. For an alescent complex can be regarded as embracing but not as reducible to prevalent constituents. In so far as an alescence can be said to be "complete"—in so far as any complex can be said to be "complete"—it can be regarded as a prevalence in some order.

A spatio-temporal complex, say an "event" (an occurrence in so far as it is unique), may be concomitantly prevalent and alescent in its beginning. In so far as it is incipient, it is an alescence within a more inclusive complex. But in so far as it has already begun, to however minimal an extent, it is definitive occurrence—that which has the prevalent irreversibility of fact. Thenceforth, within the event, the concomitance may persist. The way is always open both for variation from a fund of occurrence and for the incipient within the more widely established. What is true of events, however, is not true of recurrences. The "beginning" of each instance of a recurrence, in the sense of the typical first stage or phase, is not an alescence but a subaltern prevalence.

May *every* prevalent complex have alescent constituents? (*a*) Some prevalences may have alescent constituents which do not affect the integrity of the complex. (*b*) Some may have alescent constituents which do affect the integrity of the complex. (*c*) Some seem not to have constituents which are in any sense alescent. To illustrate. (*a*) The physical laws of the solar system prevail, and the system prevails as a system, despite the occurrence of unprecedented events within the system. (*b*) In a vastly larger order of time, which includes the order within which the solar system and its laws prevail, this system may itself be an odd or eccentric event, a vagrant alescence. Or the larger order may be somewhat less pervasive, a historical or evolutionary order within which the solar system and its laws arise as a conjunction of circumstances, achieve a stable pattern and constitute a prevalence, and then cease to prevail. The sequence within the order would be: a coalescence, an augmentative alescence, a prevalence, a spoliative alescence. (*c*) In the order of reasoning, the law of non-contradiction is a prevalent principle with

no constituents that would seem to justify description
as alescent.

Besides the question just asked ("May every prevalent complex have alescent constituents?") two others
impose themselves. First: Is every complex that is prevalent in one order alescent in some other order? And
as part of the question we are prompted to ask
whether the principle of non-contradiction is an exception in this respect too. It seems justifiable to answer
that every prevalence *can* be an alescence in some
order; that even a law of logic *can* acquire quite another integrity, say in an order of speculation, or in
some other order of query such as literary or visual
art. In such an order it may assume all kinds of functions and relations, and be seen in various roles. Its
function as an inviolable governing principle of ratio-
cination may become irrelevant, even though the integrity of that function in a ratiocinative order is not
subject to spoliative alescence in the way that a physical
law is. But there seems to be no ground for saying that
every complex prevalent in one order *is* alescent in
some other order.

Second: Is every complex that is alescent in one
order prevalent in another? The answer to this question is easier and has already been given. For to the
extent that every complex is irrefragably a complex,
in its dimension of exclusion and identity and distinguishability, it prevails. In so far as a complex is
alescent, it cannot be prevalent, but there must always
be another respect in which it is prevalent. None of
these considerations affects the distinction or the
weight of the distinction between the two dimensions

of nature, nor does it make either of them more important than the other.

iii

Any concepts that are used to articulate the concept of alescence must be morally neutral as well as genuinely applicable to a great range of manifestations. What about birth and death, which are sharp, vivid categories? But if we are inclined to think of every alescence as either a birth or a death, we should be prepared to think of what follows a birth and precedes a death, namely a "life," and this, for a number of reasons, is metaphysically precarious. Despite all their descriptive and analogical advantages, the ideas of birth and death have implications which are hard to dispel and which would destroy their general applicability if not dispelled. (*a*) Birth and death suggest a "natural history," a typical history. But the beginning and ending of a natural history, in so far as they may be regarded as alescent at all, are scarcely the only kind of alescence. (*b*) Birth and death suggest "subjects" which are born and which die; and (*c*) they possibly suggest, in this connection, endurances. But vagrant alescence and coalescence do not typically involve "subjects" at all, while augmentative and spoliative alescence may characterize complexes which are not interpretable in terms of individual identity and which are best not interpreted as endurances. A clear type of alescence is variation of instances from the norm within a prevalence such as a physical law, which certainly cannot be said to endure in the sense that a man or a rock endures. Birth and death, then, are not adequate to explain alescence. They can only be regarded as themselves circumstantial manifestations of alescence. They can also be seen, in a more pervasive order, as prevalences, prevalences which take the form of awesome regularities.

Alescence is represented by variation, but it is neither solely nor necessarily the basis of variety. It is represented by deviation, but it is neither solely nor necessarily the basis of uniqueness. Among the prevalences of nature there is inexhaustible difference. The traits of any prevalence comprise a variety. Even if there were simples, since simples would differ, composites would manifest variety. The parts of an enduring "thing" are various, as are the stages, periods, phases, functions, or relations within other prevalences. Alescence is indeed the condition for the advent, and therefore the extension or increase, of variety. But complexes may be alescent without introducing variety at all. They may, for example, only terminate a prevalence. A dying may be like any other dying, but in its circumstantial introduction of a complex, in its arising as an event, it is an alescence which brings to an end the prevalent order consisting in an individual history.

Uniqueness, like variety, is not locatable in alescent complexes alone. It is part of the integrity of every complex. In the most fundamental sense, any complex is unique merely by virtue of its distinguishability from any other. But this sense is not trivial, because it cannot be by an absolutely "single" trait that any complex is distinguished from the complex most similar to it. The "single" trait is always an analyzable complex. Nor is it the different traits in a complex "outnumbering" the similar or common traits that determines "more" or "less" uniqueness. In any case, although it is significant to say that alescence is what increases the variety in the world, it does not seem significant to say that alescence is what increases uniqueness in the world. What does increase, but also decrease, by alescence is the prominence of this or that uniqueness in the perspectives of men. We should also guard against the tendency to think of alescence as necessarily "particular." A class of revolutionary ideas or of deviant happenings, a general trend of behavior, may be an alescence.

Augmentative alescence is not mere quantitative increase, nor is spoliative alescence mere separation or diminution. A cancer, a spoliative alescence, is a quantitative increase which conceals a pervasive decline of functions. In the complexes of ethical experience and in human distinctions of worth, the forms of alescence may be deceptive. An augmentative alescence may consist in the emergence of a value. And this may take the form not of an expansion or a literal growth but of a situation promoted, made viable—an evil relation disappearing, a cancer regressing, large bodies of incompetents reduced. On the other hand, a human corruption or decline, constituting a spoliative alescence, may take the form of an increase in burdensome detail, a growth of anxiety, a multiplication of codes and statutes.

A coalescence is an arising that is not traceable to any "single" complex. It is not reducible to augmentation or spoliation, though it may eventuate in either of these. It is an aspect of nature in which there is more "varying from" than "varying of." When numerous occurrences, each in itself perhaps inconsequential, are joined and patterned, a complex arises which is alescent primarily in so far as it adds to the configurations of the world without directly augmenting or despoiling anything in particular. If there is deviation of any kind in a coalescence, it is collective deviation from complexes which retain their general character. Historically, when individual traders found themselves tending to trade where others did and at the same time that others did, a center for an economic market arose. No distributive modification of economic practices directly took place, though inevitably, many augmentations and spoliations accrued.

Like coalescence, though without junctions or parallelisms, vagrant alescence is a varying "from." A meteorite falling in a certain path and landing in a certain place is a vagrant alescent complex. It is a variation from a diffused prevalence, but not a deviation from any prevalence in particular. Like coalescence, vagrant alescence may eventuate in other forms. When two opposing ice hockey players strike the puck simultaneously it becomes a "loose puck," veering erratically between the two goals or toward one of them. In this status, unmodified by anything else, it is a vagrant alescence. If shortly afterward the puck is hit for a score, there is an augmentation of one side's action and a spoliation of the other's. The loose puck may be seen as located in either or both of two orders (that is, as part of two complexes, one more inclusive than the other). It may be seen as part of an order which contains it as a vagrant alescence and which is succeeded by another order containing an augmentative alescence; or it may be seen as part of an inclusive continuing order which culminates, as it were, in an augmentation.

iv

Although every natural complex prevails in some respect, it is important to focus upon traits the comprehensiveness of which helps especially to clarify the concept of prevalence. We have indicated a number of these, such as continuation, recurrence, constancy, irreversibility, endurance. In a given prevalence there may be one or more. Whenever we think of a complex as a fact, or think of the factual aspect of a complex, the fundamental trait of the prevalence is irreversibility; endurance and constancy are not present or not relevant. In a process, for instance digestion, there are recurrences, constancies which are not recurrences, and endurances; there are also events, i.e., occurrences in their aspect of uniqueness. In digestion there are recurrent sequences: some of the sequences recur in wider spans, or less frequently, than others. There is a constancy that takes the form of a structure, the digestive "system." There are enduring organs, and these perform digestive functions.

Fact is occurrence in its aspect of finality: what is completed in the form, either of an event or a series of instances within a recurrence, is not modifiable except in its continuing effects. By contrast, process and structure are not unmodifiable. Whether we say, of a process or a structure, that it has ceased to be and has

been succeeded by another, that it has been transformed into another, or that it is the same with different traits, is in part a matter of discriminative emphasis
and in part a matter of linguistic or conceptual discre-
tion. Is "a complex with successive stages that are
similar" to be distinguished from "two successive complexes that are similar"? The distinction depends upon
what is discriminated as complex and what as subaltern
complex. The discriminations and the complexes discriminated are alike "realities." Selectiveness and
choice are among the realities of the world that play a
role in both the charting and the determination of
alescences.

A structure is a prevalence that may or may not involve recurrence but that always involves constancy of
some kind. Certain structures, for instance the structure of the fixed stars or the structure of an economy,
may be said to endure (whatever their duration may
be). We speak of them as endurances because we think
of them as having arisen. They are prevalences which
are founded upon an alescence in the past. We often
think of them as relatively distinguishable from that
of which they are the structure. The fixed stars might
have had a different structure, and so might the economy in question. The case seems otherwise with structures like the structure of a proof or the structure of a
poem. It is of dubious meaning to say that the same
proof or the same poem might have had another structure: they would then not be the same but another
proof and another poem. Accordingly, if in these cases
we say that the structure "endures," we must mean
that it is the proof or poem which "endures." But a

proof and a poem certainly do not endure in the same sense as a star or an economy. They do not have a "history" in the sense that a star and an economy do. They admit of spoliative alescence, but not in the same sense. And yet it can be said that all four of these complexes—the star, the economy, the proof, the poem—arose.

The contrast between the two pairs does not reduce to the difference between a complex which is a deliberate product and one which is not. For by this criterion, a star and an economy differ from one another at least as sharply as an economy and a proof do. Moreover, a garden or a bed spread, which are human products in the least complicated sense, are, in respect of their structure, actually more like the star and the economy than they are like the poem and the proof. For they are distinguishable from the structure that they "have," they exhibit a historical type of endurance, and they admit of spoliative alescence in the particular sense of internal decay.

Some prevalences have a temporal aspect, others do not. Consider the mode of prevalence we have called constancy. There are constancies, for instance, which consist of temporal sequences and cycles (the seasons). But there are non-temporal constancies which are also sequential (the series of integers) and in which there are periodic recurrences (odd numbers). The latter type of constancy, though non-temporal, is "applicable" to the discrimination and analysis of temporal complexes. This applicability is also true of non-temporal constancies which are not sequential (logical principles). There are temporal constancies, namely histories, in which sequences may be less important than endurances. A temporal constancy, and in general any temporal prevalence, may be of long or short duration. The history of an ephemeral insect is as much a prevalent complex as any other history. The season for fasting is not less of a prevalence than the winter season.

One reason why possibility has been considered so difficult to interpret by philosophers is its puzzling status in regard to the temporal aspect of actuality. A prevailing possibility may be either continuously present in a given order or recurrent in that order. Any possibility can be regarded as prior in time to its actualizations. This is true for what are sometimes called "remote" possibilities as well as "situational" possibilities. But possibilities also arise in the wake of [actual] occurrences. After the occurrences, we say that many other occurrences have "become possible" or "are now possible." Possibilities thus may be justly described as earlier and later. They may come into being or expire. And they may be brought into being or destroyed. Thus they can be either alescent or prevalent. Suppose, for example, that one author plagiarizes another. He thereby brings some possibilities into being and destroys others. One of the possibilities which arises is that he will be apprehended as a plagiarist. This possibility is an alescence, in the form of a deviation from an order of possibilities and actualities which constitutes a scrupulous life of authorship. In the subsequent order of complexes, this possibility prevails. Its prevalence helps to clarify, retrospectively, its previous character as (or within) an alescence—initially vagrant, then spoliative in an order of moral complexes.

Considerations of this kind make it difficult to accept, at least without further distinctions, the view that possibilities are "eternal." But they do not guarantee that all kinds of possibilities are temporal in the same sense. We shall postpone the question of the "effects" of possibility. Possibilities may be temporal in the sense of being prior to, coeval with, or posterior to given actualities and other possibilities. They may be said to endure in the sense of prevailing by continuous presence in a given order. This endurance may be brief, related to evanescent conditions; or it may be indefinite, related to stable conditions. For prevalent possibilities, like all complexes, are tied to other prevalences.

Does alescence always have a temporal aspect? Considered in its aspect as variation, it is a varying—that is, more than a mere difference. For difference, as we have observed, is present among all natural complexes, prevalent or alescent. In a human order like query the temporal aspect of alescence might appear to be all but universal. What arises for man in the process of wondering and probing arises in the cumulative sequences of experience. And yet, troublesome instances in a scientist's efforts to generalize, or resistant and elusive traits in a novelist's framing of a character, are varyings that cannot be regarded as primarily temporal, as arising in time. These obstacles, spoliations of texture, have their essential significance within a structure—a structure of ideas, of procedures, or of personality traits. And likewise, wholly apart from the human world, sheer interruptions of uniformity, among the flowers of a field or the diamonds of a mine, are deviations within a configuration of forms rather than within a succession of occurrences. These too are genuine varyings, not just differences. They arise in the sense in which a rock arises out of a plateau. The beginning or nascence is topographical rather than temporal. Over a large area the land is the same; at a certain place in this area, it deviates in character.

There may be no reason to believe that complexes typically deemed non-temporal, such as purely mathematical traits or abstract logical relations, admit of alescence *as* integral relations and possibilities. But neither does there seem to be any way of proving that they are exempt from alescence. A point in behalf of their inflexible prevalence is that without employing them inviolate no argument for conceiving them as alescent can be undertaken. This point affirms the inevitability of the prevalence in question, but does not establish its fixity in all possible orders. A counterpoint (of a type comparable to the original point) is that theoretical reflection cannot rule alescence out of the world. Suppose the prevalence of a possibility the formulation of which has the most abstract and intricate character. Actualizations are yet to come. In an order which contains *both* mathematical possibilities and the human manipulation of them, actualizations cannot be antecedently freed of all deviant and unexpected traits. These are the traits that are alescent in the order of query, where moral, mathematical, or aesthetic reflection accept no prior limits to discernment.

The contour of any complex, then, may exhibit the two natural dimensions, prevalence and alescence. In a given order, a complex must be either prevalent or alescent and cannot be both. It may be prevalent in one order and alescent in another. If it is alescent in an order, it must be concomitantly prevalent in some other. But not every complex must be alescent. Every complex can be *conceived* as being alescent in some order, such as an order of query. A complex may be prevalent in an indefinite number of orders, and alescent in an indefinite number of orders. With respect to any given complex, there are always orders in which it does not prevail and yet is not alescent either—orders to which it does not belong at all, i.e., orders in which it is not a trait or subaltern complex. The contour of a complex is the interrelation of its ordinal integrities. Alescence in a complex (the alescence of a complex) is the introduction of some different integrity within the contour of that complex.

v

The categories of prevalence and alescence must now be distinguished explicitly from various pairs of traditional categories.

"Permanence" and "Change." No major metaphysical concept has flourished with so dim a meaning as has the concept of permanence. It is futile to stake out the limits of this meaning by a survey of historical usages. In common discourse the term is applied as loosely as in metaphysics. The distinctions required by everyday practice carry no extreme claims. The "permanent" is what we cannot or need not encompass directly, and this is enough to distinguish it from the "temporary." When we produce a so-called permanent

abode or reform or agreement, we develop one set of expectations; when we produce something temporary, we develop another set. When that which is permanent or temporary is imposed upon us instead of being produced by us, we are not likely to develop our expectations in the same climate of feeling. Sometimes it is the temporary that is to be feared, sometimes the permanent. But in practical reflection on the distinction between the two we are rarely deceived. We do not seriously think of the permanent as everlasting but as matter for the long run, as negligibly variant, as fixed in the degree pertinent to human concern.

Metaphysically, permanence seems to imply something beyond "persistence," which presumably suggests the continuation of an integrity for an indefinite period. Persistence surely, and permanence equivocally, implies endurance. Permanence has been predicated also of that which is said to be perfect and immutable; of realities that are "unconditioned" or realities that are "simple," of traits that are "unconditional." When it relates to what endures, it seems literally to imply unending endurance. All these conceptions of permanence have an empty, fictitious ring. But they bespeak an ethical consciousness which is far from empty and which affects metaphysical discrimination in the form of a search, however ill-directed, for fundamental, illuminating traits.

Traditional metaphysics sees permanence as the twin, the necessary correlative, of "change." So does cracker-barrel wisdom: "what don't never change" is correlative to "what ain't never the same." "Change," of course, has played as important a social and moral role as "permanence." When interpreted as "more real" than permanence, it takes on the meaning of universal "flux." When interpreted as a condition making for the intelligibility of permanence, the two become polar and interdependent. Nevertheless, change is a more readily applicable concept than permanence, and much less dispensable. Unlike permanence, it is illustratable and discoverable. It allows for degrees, and for comparisons of scope. It suggests many kinds of measurements. At the same time, it is a less than satisfactory category for philosophic, as opposed to common, use. It is often contrasted, not with permanence but with constancy; and this, at least, replaces a dubious notion by a viable one. The constancy required for the occurrence of change need be neither a traitless "subject" underlying change nor an eternal "form" against which change is discerned; it need only be an order of complexes. But the polarity of change and constancy is imperfect. For regular or recurrent change is precisely one form of constancy.

Prevalence is not "permanence," and alescence is not "change."

1. Taking any of the aforementioned senses of "permanent," a prevalence may be impermanent. Nor, as we have seen, is prevalence to be identified with constancy or endurance or persistence. It is the genus of which these may be regarded as species.

2. Change may be present in a prevalence *or* in an alescence. In the prevalent constancy of the seasons there is "change." In the alescence of a hot day in winter there is "change." There is "change" in the prevalence known as a history, and there is "change" in an alescent trend within the history.

3. Change may be absent from or irrelevant to an alescent trait. Suppose that in a club the members of which are all classified by custom into a limited number of prepared categories the year after they are admitted, a given member is found to be unclassifiable. This state of affairs is an alescence within a complex. It is deviant, congruous in a way, yet passively incongruous. It does not change. If "changes" in membership or in the relation between individual members and the group can be said to be going on from time to time, or all the time, the essential problem is directly pointed up: relying on the category of change alone, how to distinguish between this and that moment of change in order to discriminate the trait in question.

4. To complexes which are not actualities, the idea of change is applicable only with circumlocution. Suppose that within a certain range of conditions there is a group of possibilities, and that in the group a new possibility arises. We might be able to say that the "complexion" of the group has "changed." But we cannot say that any given possibility has changed, or that the new possibility "is" a change. We can and should, on the other hand, say that both the group and the new possibility are alescent. A possibility has (for instance) augmented a group and a group has been augmented by a possibility. (Although the group as a group is quite distinguishable from the new possibility, this circumstance does not affect the relational variation, the relational "arising" in which the alescence consists.)

5. When the allegedly polar categories of "change and constancy" are applied to certain types of actuality, and even to what is sometimes regarded as the para-

digm condition of actuality, further difficulties present themselves. A spatio-temporal or temporal complex, an occurrence, an event, is located in more than one order of complexes. In the order where it is a brute finality, a fact, it is a prevalence. In the order where it is an idiosyncratic condition, or a variant, it is an alescence. Yet in each of these aspects, as brute and as idiosyncratic, the event is neither a "constancy" nor a "change." At best we should have to say that it "represents" or "reflects" a change. But just what change? Should we say that the order or environment in which the event arose has changed? But this would not have to be and would not ordinarily be the case. We could say, just as well, or preferably, that the order in which the event arose is still that order, the same order. Thus —and paradoxically in terms of the "constancy-change" polarity—neither the order nor the event may be said to have changed. We must patch up by saying either that the world has somehow changed now that there is such-and-such an event in it, or that there has been not a "change" but a "becoming."

"Being" and "Becoming." If being and becoming are to be regarded as opposite in the sense that neither is reducible to the other, the distinction is stultifying. It implies that becoming is "non-being," so that no matter what is discriminated as becoming, it somehow "is not." This particular kind of opposition emerges as an appearance-reality distinction. On the other hand, if the pair are not opposites in the sense described but are related rather as genus (being) to species (becoming), certain traditional problems crop up. Is "being" a genus which is describable in distinction from any of

its species? Is it "indescribable" in the sense that it is simple or pure? Is anything discriminable merely in its capacity as "being"?

Whatever the answers to these "problems" may be, prevalence is not to be equated with "being," nor alescence with "becoming."

1. If alescence were equated with becoming and prevalence with being, then, depending upon which version of the being-becoming contrast is stressed, alescence would be either "non-being" or a species of prevalence. The first of these alternatives is absurd, the second false. Alescence is no more a species of prevalence than the other way round. Both are dimensions of natural complexes, such that a complex which is not in the one dimension must be in the other and can be in both only by virtue of different integrities in its contour.

2. A complex prevails not merely because it is, but because it is in a certain natural dimension. To say that a complex is not prevalent but alescent is not to deny that it "is."

3. There are various special reasons why alescence cannot be identified with "becoming." (a) Even when becoming is dissociated from any categorial coupling with being, it has been invested by tradition with an emotional burden of meaning, so that it is regarded sometimes as the "most real" and sometimes as the "least real" aspect of nature. (b) "Becoming" often suggests a "subject" of becoming, even if such a subject is interpreted as the antithesis of a characterless substance. The dimensions of prevalence and alescence do not require the notion of a subject. An alescence

presupposes prevalences, but a prevalence may be preceded and formed by alescences. Grammatically we speak of a complex *as* alescent. But the complex is not the "subject" of alescence—it can only be the "subject" of our analysis. Alescence as such does not imply individuality, career, course, or aim in a complex. It implies an arising in an order; and as many traits or complexes as are relevant to the arising are "subjects." (*c*) "Becoming" suggests, not always but still too often, evolution, progress, or development, and even design. These concepts or conditions are of no special relevance to the concept of alescence. An alescence may be purposive or blind, felicitous or destructive. (*d*) Becoming is commonly regarded as characteristic of actualities, and is either made the basis of an argument that there are no other kinds of complex, or is contrasted with the "being" of complexes like possibility. In any case, whether or not we can say that a possibility "becomes," or that it "is a becoming," we certainly can say that a possibility is alescent, or that it is an alescence. (*e*) "Becoming" not only fails to coincide with the alescent, but it overlaps the prevalent. Thus it can be applied to the basic contour of a history—to that which makes the history a prevalence. Although the expression "coming about" is a less unsatisfactory approximation to one meaning of alescence than is "becoming," it is too bland, lacking in exhibitive force, and too awkward in import and use to qualify as a major category.

"The Static" and "the Dynamic." The meaning of these conceptions is at least as hard to find as the meaning of the two preceding pairs of conceptions. Any attempt to equate "static" with "prevalent" and "dy-

namic" with "alescent" would face the following obstacles, to mention no others.

1. Whether the alescent includes the "dynamic" or
not, it implies much more. For in the concept of an
"arising" there is included not just an origination but
the character of the complex involved. Alescence implies not just the arising of a difference, but the difference that has arisen.

2. We can speak of possibilities as alescent. Whether
we can speak of them as "dynamic" seems to raise a
different question altogether, the answer to which depends plainly upon antecedent clarification of the term.

3. The terms "static" and "dynamic" both seem
quite applicable to prevalences, the former not more
obviously than the latter. "Static" is applicable (if not
very wisely) to prevalent possibilities, facts, and certain
kinds of relations and structures. "Dynamic" is applicable to prevalent histories, processes, and certain
other kinds of relations and structures.

"Regularity" and "Irregularity." Although prevalent processes or recurrences might be counted as "regularities," it is not easy to see how such prevalences as
histories, possibilities, or facts could be. Regularity is
not even coextensive with constancy. Every regularity
might be called a constancy, but the converse is not
true. Regularity is commonly (and etymologically) associated with laws and rules. But laws and rules themselves may be either prevalent—in so far as they continue to be exemplified—or alescent—in so far as they
are complexes that arise originally as variations.

If we had to regard all alescences as "irregularities,"
we should have to regard all laws in so far as they

come to prevail, and all rules in so far as they are laid down, as irregularities. They are, however, not irregularities but new regularities. Considered even in relation to the order in which they arise, they are better regarded as deviant than as irregular. The need to distinguish their nascent character from their sphere of dominance is precisely what is to be met by the distinction between alescence and prevalence.

"Irregularity" is a manifestation of alescence, not its equivalent. The same may be said of "emergence," "chance," and "novelty." Chance and novelty, each considered by itself, also give the impression of being eligible as an equivalent of alescence. Considered in relation to each other, their eligibility collapses. An alescence may consist in a chance complex. Or an alescence may consist in a novelty. Yet there is no reason at all why a chance complex must be a novelty. And there is no reason at all why a novel complex must be a matter of chance.

"Stability" and "Instability." It is certainly possible, whether useful or not, to think of the complexes of nature in terms of stability and instability, although it is hard to escape the feeling that the difference between the members of this particular pair is a matter of degree, and that therefore the extremes are less strictly "opposed" than other kinds of "opposites." A continuum of relative stability also suggests the corollary that the extremes are limits of an "ideal" kind, that they are possibilities rather than actualities. Be this as it may, prevalence cannot be equated with stability, nor alescence with instability.

1. To think of alescence as instability is to neglect

such forms of alescence as cumulative accretion and novelty, and virtually to exclude coalescence. If every complex subject to variation were depicted as an instability, one would be justified in suspecting that the notion of "permanence" was the tacit basis for the depiction. And once again the emphasis would be on the originative factor in alescence to the exclusion of what is originated. What an origination amounts to, its character as a complex, might well signify "stability," whereas origination considered abstractly might signify lack of stability.

2. To identify stability with prevalence is to misunderstand the latter notion and to confuse different manifestations of it. Prevalence is not necessarily a matter of duration. Within a political revolution, a provisional government is a prevalence, despite the fact that by any historical standard it is a typical form of instability.

"Determinateness" and "Indeterminateness." What does it mean to say that a natural complex is or is not "determinate"? Philosophers have always been strongly inclined to think of actuality as the minimal condition of determinateness: what "is not yet," what is still "in the realm of possibility" is indeterminate. Even as an actuality, however, a complex is allowed to be partly indeterminate, when it lacks "definite" traits, when it has "unsettled" aspects. This view implies a "completeness" notion: if all the indefinite aspects of a complex were definite, all the unsettled aspects settled, the complex would be "complete" or completely determinate. To the extent that it makes actuality basic, a view of this kind tends also to lay emphasis on "concrete-

ness." The assumptions on which these emphases rest cry out for articulation.

There is no good way to dispense with the concept of determinateness. It plays a particularly useful role when we evaluate certain complexes in the human world. We wish to say, for example, that a meaning is relatively indeterminate, in the sense that it is open to expansion, to alternative constructions, to greater definiteness and precision. Or we wish to say that a man's obligations in his job are relatively indeterminate, that they have not yet been made determinate. The idea of something "fixed" or not yet fixed is an influential one in human affairs. To fix or make firm suggests, once again, completing. A decision or definition is presumably made determinate when it is "fixed" or "completed."

Is prevalence in some way connected with determinateness, and alescence with indeterminateness? The question is best answered after a number of other issues are clarified and dealt with.

1. In place of "fully," "completely," or "wholly," it is desirable to use the expression "in all respects." The phrase "fully determinate" would be replaced by "determinate in all respects." Then we would be clearly recognizing the principle that a given complex may be located in more than one order of complexes. And we would be forced to see that what is held to be true of a complex in all respects must be held to be true of it no matter to what orders it belongs.

2. No complex can be said to be indeterminate in all respects. It would not be a complex, and we would be contradicting ourselves by assuming that a dis-

crimination has taken place. The latter assumption implies that traits have been made to be or found to be located in an order. A complex indeterminate in all respects would have no traits. For each trait is a determination, implying the exclusion of some other trait and the imposition of limits—implying a prevalence.

3. Can a complex be determinate in all respects? Determinateness in all respects implies that all traits attributable to a complex are exhausted, and that the complex cannot belong to any more or fewer orders than it does. Now whether there are complexes of which this can ever be said is a moot question. That it should be said exclusively of actualities is hard to understand. If any natural complexes at all are subject to alteration or modification or environmental relocation, actualities are. The number of orders in which an actuality is located, and the number and kind of relations into which it may enter, are exhausted or closed only when the actuality ceases to be that actuality. And surely enough, this latter condition for determinateness not only has been taken seriously but has been made fundamental: an actuality is determinate in all respects at the point directly adjacent to its expiration. This is the point at which it is "complete"; or the point at which nothing else is possible for it.[12]

With at least as much plausibility, however, one could say that at the point of an actuality's expiration the various possibilities it has are also at the point of expiration, and that by not actualizing these possibilities it does not achieve "completeness." But suppose this point were ignored. The difficulties would not be ended. If it is at the point of expiration that an actuality is complete, then it is complete whenever it expires, early or late, and in whatever way, and no matter what kind of actuality it is. Whether in catastrophe or in gradual transmutation or in progression through a typical sequence, it can achieve determinateness in all respects only at an infinitesimal moment. However great may be the gap that we suppose between incompletion and completion, at that moment the gap is bridged perfectly and immediately. The paradox we are led to is that completeness is an empty and ghastly condition.

4. The kinds of actuality that are most often cited as determinate in all respects are fact and feeling. These, it is said, are just what they are and nothing more. They have a finality which makes them "fully actual." And indeed fact and feeling are sometimes identified as one, on the ground that the "immediacy" and the "complete" specificity of feeling constitute fact in the "ultimate" sense (Bradley, Whitehead).

(a) But every complex whatever can be said to be "just what it is." In any order to which a complex belongs it has an integrity. Its traits in that order can be ascertained and can be distinguished from the traits of other complexes. Whatever is said about the determinateness of "atomic actualities" can be said about the determinateness of all others. If there is an order in which an "atomic actuality" is a "subject," then there is an order in which a given actuality of any kind, and more generally, a given complex of any kind, is a "subject." If the atomic actuality is said to be determinate by virtue of its uniqueness, the same can be said for any other complex—a structure, relation, possibility, history, process, regularity. Each is unique, that is, just the complex that it is and not to be identified as any other. Any complex, no doubt, can be said also to be "like" some other. But an atomic actuality too is "like" other atomic actualities.

(b) "Just what it is and nothing more." If every complex whatever is just what it is, every complex also is "nothing more," and it takes no acumen to see that this is outwardly a tautologous emphasis. But there is a confusion that lurks here, and it is on this confusion that the case for "full actuality" rests. If we think of "what a complex is" as consisting in its integrity, we may be forgetting that an integrity, dependent on an ordinal location, is not necessarily coextensive with the contour of the complex. Since there is no way of proving that an integrity belonging to a complex, or any finite number of integrities, is all that there are— exhausts its contour—we are deceived in thinking of it at any *given time* as "nothing more." There is no way of establishing that a complex can have only a certain number, or no more than a certain number, of ordinal locations; or that it can have only a certain number, or no more than a certain number, of traits.

Any order to which an actuality belongs includes the effects, the influence, and the restricting limits imposed by that actuality. The order consisting of the effects of a feeling in temporal relation to the feeling as an original occurrence, provides the setting for another integrity of the feeling. The feeling as occurrent, the feeling as remembered, the feeling as important or unimportant in the enlarging temporal span, may all be regarded as different integrities of a natural complex. The occurrence, the remembrance, the importance, may each expire. The determinateness of each consists, not in the completion effected by its expiration, but in the distinguishability of its traits, in its discriminable integrity, in the difference it makes, in the way it is determined by other complexes, in the way it determines and limits other complexes.

5. Every actuality thus has a relative determinateness, a determinateness in given respects. Every actuality also has a relative indeterminateness in so far as it continues to have a contour of integrities, in so far as it may or may not belong to orders to which it does not now belong. Every actuality may be called "complete" in so far as it is an integral complex or integrity. Every actuality may be called "incomplete" in so far as any of its possibilities remain unactualized. If we consider the partly human complex known as a meaning, a complex which, like so many others, men seek both to shape and to explore, we can illustrate its determinateness and indeterminateness in conformity with the generic standard thus far provided. A meaning is determinate to the extent that we can identify it and can distinguish it within an order of complexes; to the extent that we can trace its relations to alternative meanings and other complexes. It is indeterminate to the extent that we are unable to ascertain the order or orders in which it belongs, or to the extent that it eludes control despite our resolutions and precautions.

Some philosophers believe that determinateness and indeterminateness are matters pertaining only to cognitive structuring and intellectual definition, and not to natural complexes in general. The common usage that corresponds to this viewpoint is the one in which we are said, for example, to "determine" who offended whom and why. Less compatible with the viewpoint is the equally common usage in which it is said that one thing causally "determines" another. Strictly, neither of these usages quite reaches the concept of determinateness. The possible opinion that this concept is more of a hindrance than a help to metaphysical inquiry may well be worth discussion. But if the concept is considered useful or essential in application to complexes which are thought about, which are subject-matter of knowing, it is arbitrary to assume and to leave unexplained a discontinuity between such complexes and complexes which have not become subject-matter—those from among which both thought and its subject-matter spring.

Any complex is determinate, whether it is related or unrelated to mind. Its gross integrity cannot be obliterated by decision, or deemed non-prevalent if it falls outside the range of finite intellectual machinery. It is determined by and determines other complexes.[13] And any complex also is indeterminate, not only because it has sets of alternative possibilities in which there has not yet been actualization, but because not all of its traits, including possibilities, may yet have arisen. Now among its present sets of alternative possibilities may be its emergence or non-emergence in [the order of] human experience. Its actual (actualized) emergence in human experience, say in an order of scientific awareness, may endow it with another integrity and make it determinate in a new respect. In this new respect, and at the very same time, it may constitute a "problem" to scientific minds. The solution of the problem by investigation would make the complex determinate in yet another respect. But not in *all* respects. For its relations within the order of investigation would not exhaust all of its possibilities, any more than its relations within another order would. And its traits within the human order may be far less pervasive than its other traits.

Thus (*a*) relative determinateness and indeterminateness belong to natural complexes, and not exclusively to the complexes known as minds or men, any more than actuality and possibility as such belong to minds or men. Nor (*b*) does relative indeterminateness belong solely to complexes-in-relation-to-men ("situations"), to existences which are "unsettled," "objectively" unsettled, supposedly because their relation to human or other organisms is unstable and disquieting, "unresolved." All complexes are relational, and accordingly it is necessary to speak of the *relative* determinateness of complexes. But organisms are not a necessary condition of this relationality.

6. It follows from what has been said that possibilities no less than actualities are both determinate and indeterminate. And it will become clear (in Chapter IV) that the present separate treatment of actualities and possibilities in the problem of determinateness is dictated only by the strategy required for argumentation. Consider the possibility that the next bomb exploded as a weapon will kill a million people. This possibility is determinate in its integrity of interrelated

traits. It is determined by actualities, such as the existence of bombs and the recurrence of explosions. It is determined by other possibilities, such as the possibility that bombs will continue to be used as weapons. It in turn determines actualities and possibilities—the actuality, among others, of men living in fear; the possibility, among others, that men will take remedial measures. At the same time, it is indeterminate with respect to its continuing location in orders of complexes, with respect to the occurrence or non-occurrence of an instance of actualization, and with respect to the place and time of such an instance.

7. The sense of "completeness" in which completeness coincides with integrity does not eliminate the familiar sense in which a part of that which is repeatedly exemplified, or a phase of a cycle, is "incomplete." (The seed, as a part or phase of a cycle leading to a mature organism, is incomplete.) On the other hand, the distinguishability and integrity of the parts or phases as such makes them as determinate as the more inclusive complex to which they typically belong. (The seed is a complete seed, complete as a seed.) Constituents are incomplete in comparison with the typical complexes which provide them with a typical function. The same cannot be said of the constituents of complexes which are atypical. Thus the constituents of an event or a history are best thought of not as incomplete but only as less pervasive. These constituents may have no more of a function as constituents than they have merely as complexes distinguished. Subaltern spans in a history may themselves be histories, different in scale but complete as such, like the order in which they

unfold. The sense in which they are incomplete is generically the sense in which the larger history itself is incomplete.

8. There is no essential connection between determinateness and prevalence or between indeterminateness and alescence. Every complex as such, we have seen, is determinate in some respects and indeterminate in others. A complex is determinate not in so far as it prevails but merely in so far as it has an integrity. An alescent complex also has an integrity. Any complex is indeterminate in so far as the contour of its integrities, its gross integrity, is not severed from the rest of the world; in so far as alescence is not foreclosed. A complex which is alescent is determinate in so far as traits have been admitted into its contour, and in so far as its traits are relevant to an order. Only when alescence is confusedly equated with some of its manifestations, such as chance, does its connection with indeterminateness seem to loom large. We cannot say, then, that for a complex to exclude traits from its contour (as a prevalence) is either less or more of a "determination" than for a complex to admit traits into its contour (as an alescence).

"The Intelligible" and "the Unintelligible." Should it be said that the prevalent is what is intelligible and the alescent what is not intelligible? In one of two dominant meanings, "intelligible" is contrasted with "sensible." In the other, it is contrasted with "unintelligible."

In the first meaning, the contrast is between that which is grasped by "intellect" and that which is grasped by "sense." But there are prevalences in relation to which intellectual activity (abstraction and the use of general notions) is commonly deemed most important, and there are other prevalences in relation to which sensory discrimination may not only be most important but may require a suspension of otherwise useful intellectual habits.

In the second sense of "intelligible," the contrast is between that which meets and that which does not meet the requirements of "knowability" (whatever these requirements may be). But that which is prevalent is not more or less knowable than that which is alescent. There are many different ways or avenues of knowing, whether the complexes known prevail or arise. In the Platonic tradition the intelligible is that which is fixed in its structure. By this standard, certain types of prevalence would obviously not be intelligible, histories in particular. Beneath both the "intelligible-sensible" and the "intelligible-unintelligible" distinctions there slinks the "unchanging-changing" distinction. But it has already been shown that "change" may or may not be located, or found relevant, either in a prevalence or an alescence.

There are individuals and communities of individuals who above all value the record and the effect of what happens to happen. Each addition to the record, even if sorrowful, is within the relative control of judgment, and the major type of gain is increase in the variety of things encountered. To be sure, the record cannot survive without dependence upon prevalent symbols, not to mention prevalent capacities, for without them the processes of recognition, communication, and comparison are impossible. But in terms of the

major *interest,* the symbols are combined and directed
in such a way as to dwell upon what has arisen and
what newly prevails, perhaps upon what is odd, as well
as upon its specific impact. The interest is not in the
illustrative or regular aspect of any complex: the importance of the predictive and the uniform is under-
played.

That there always have been, not only individuals
and groups of individuals, but periods and cultures in
which such an interest predominated, is beyond doubt.
To them the world and the complexes of the world are
not less "intelligible" but just differently assimilated
and manipulated (differently "experienced"), differently selected as materials for utterance. Where their
productive power takes on methodic form, the prospect for theory may sometimes be darkened; but at
other times it is actually strengthened by the vitality
of fresh perception. Knowledge does not vanish if we
can conceive of knowledge, of cognitive gain, as inherent in the molding or transmutation of complexes
† and in the effectiveness of action. So that even if the
standard called "knowability" is what is stressed in the
idea of "the intelligible," such a standard is hardly
lacking among men for whom the alescent dimension
of the world is uppermost.

III

ORDINALITY AND RELATION

i

EVERY COMPLEX is an order and belongs to an order of complexes. Thus orders are inclusive and belong to more inclusive orders. "Orders" and "an order" are to be distinguished from mere "order." When the question is asked, "In what order are these bricks to be arranged?" the tacit assumption may be that the bricks are not without order or pattern and that only a particular kind of order is at issue. Or the assumption may be that action is to confer upon the bricks order as such. The question, "When do these bricks begin to acquire order?" more plainly makes the latter assumption—that there may be complexes devoid of order. If the questions were made metaphysically self-conscious, they would take for granted order as such in any complex, and they would always refer only to some manifestation of order that falls within a range of recognizability or familiarity. Order, then, is inherent in whatever prevails. But this acceptance does not, by itself, introduce the notion of *an* order, of a complex as ordinal. Whereas the notion of order may be roughly equated with the notion of form or pattern, the notion of *an* order must be sharply distinguished from the notion of *a* pattern or *a* form.

Belonging to an order, being located in an order,

being in various orders, being an order, are conceptions indissociable from the conception of a natural complex. They are ways of representing its ordinality, and without these ways there would be no way of framing the conceptions of prevalence and alescence, or of possibility and actuality.

As sheer complex, an order exhibits limitation, multiplicity, and relationality. It is just in so far as the complex is limited that it possesses an integrity and a location. Multiplicity is crucial in the contrast between order and an order. Order by itself implies nothing about the distinguishability and integrity of complexes. It inheres in a complex without respect to the scope, and without respect to the constituents, of that complex. An order is a complex of traits in which multiplicity goes hand in hand with relationality. Strictly, if the relationality of a complex is taken, as it should be, to imply indefinite ramification and division, it already implies multiplicity actual and possible. But multiplicity then can be taken to *mean* at least the inevitability of distinguishable relations along with all else that constitutes a complex.

"An order" needs to be distinguished from "a pattern" or "a form." The two latter do not so clearly imply multiplicity, if indeed they ever suggest it at all. An order also needs to be distinguished from "a structure." Up to a point we can link the two, provided that "a structure" is understood, not in the sense of a form or configuration, but in the sense of an encompassing framework, as when we speak of a comprehensive structure or an adequate structure. But only up to a point. For "a structure," once again, may entail but abstracts from the idea of multiplicity. It suggests a constancy prevailing in an environment of both greater and lesser constancies, or in the midst of inconstancies. As itself a complex, of course, a structure is an order of a specific type; but it is too special to represent all orders.

An order is a sphere of (or for) relatedness. It is what "provides" extent, conditions, and kinds of relatedness. Despite the fact that in its multiplicity of traits an order is not "internally" limited, as an order among orders it is precisely what limits. Limitation must be thought of not on the analogy of a finite geometrical figure but in terms of integrity. A complex is an order, however, in so far as it not merely harbors or houses but locates its traits. It is when we think of a prevalence as harboring subaltern prevalences or alescences that we are thinking of a complex in its ordinality. Among other considerations, then, a complex is to be construed as an order because it necessarily has scope or inclusiveness.

The traits of a complex need not all be related to each other; yet all are, in a difficult but insistent sense, commensurate with each other. Unrelated traits may belong to the same order because "between" them there are traits of access, mediating routes. What this means, one may be tempted to say, is that if not every trait in an order is actually related to all others, every trait possibly is. But in the order of an individual history, does it make sense to say that the individual's first taste of ice cream at the age of three is even possibly related to the validity of the mathematical proof on which he is working at the age of forty? One need not go so far as to argue that although the activity of proving is part of the history, the validity of the proof is not. The latter does belong to other orders as well. But so do the other complexes of a history. The validity of the proof is related to the individual's process of inquiry, which is certainly part of his history. In any case, we are thrown back on the concept of commensurability by virtue of mediating traits. These are the traits that account for "an" order—for the joint presence, in a complex, of traits that are not related to one another. The validity of a proof may be related to a man's inquiries, and the early events of his experience may be related to his inquiries, even if the early events cannot be related to the validity of the proof. The man's inquiries mediate between the two; the two are commensurate by virtue of the mediating trait. What is commensurate with what else determines a complex, and determines for each complex the order that it is.

At least part of the answer has been given to a question which is companion to that about the nature of an order—namely, What does it mean for a complex to have limits or boundaries? This question might not seem troublesome if each complex had just so many ramifications and were cut off, somehow and somewhere, from the rest of the world. But the meaning of "cut off" would be just as troublesome, and in the primitive conception of a natural complex thus implied, the cluster or container conception of traits would be resurrected. The complexes of nature would turn out to be like a plurality of large and small figures with innumerable shapes, all in a random pattern of intersections and overlappings. The idea of intersec-

tion and overlapping is basic enough, but the neatly
bounded figures must be transformed back into less
neatly mappable orders.

If it is justifiable to say that wherever there is commensurateness or mediatability of traits, there is an
order or complex; then we are able to take the next step
and say, that in whatever way or at whatever "point"
there ceases to be such commensurateness, there is a
boundary or limit of the complex. Where traits incom-
mensurable at one point are mediated at another, they
belong to another and more inclusive order, the prevalence of which in no way erases the integrity of the
subaltern order. The limits of a complex, like any
other aspect of it, may be alescent.

Why are there the limits that there are? Why are
there the complexes that there are? The question why
that which prevails is what prevails and why that which
is alescent is what is alescent, *whatever* prevalences and
alescences they are, is a basic form for expression of
the sense of mystery, the primordial sense of mystery—
which is not alleviated by the resolution of those specific and recalcitrant issues commonly termed "mys-
teries" (the "mystery of Stonehenge," the "mystery of
living tissue"). The basic question may be rendered
in the form, "Why is all that ever prevails and is
alescent what does prevail and is alescent?" This is
quite different from the question, "Why is there a
world at all?" or the question, "Why is there something rather than nothing?" [14] The latter questions
(*B*-type) as distinct from the former (*A*-type) are concerned to ask, not why whatever prevails is what prevails, but rather why there are prevalences, why any-

thing prevails at all, why there are complexes. The formulation of these B-type questions entails a theoretical difficulty that the formulation of the A-type does not. One and perhaps both of the alternatives which it verbally posits seem hopelessly resistant to coherent interpretation. As an alternative to "There is a world" it posits "There is no world" or "There is nothing." Or if we would get rid of the circumstance that the actual statement of these propositions seems to make one of them tautologous and the other self-contradictory, the B-type questions posit as an alternative to there being something, there being nothing. Whether either of the alternatives thus posited and expressed represents a significant discrimination as such, and whether each of the alternatives is significantly discriminated from the other, is a considerable problem. Part of the problem is whether a question about "the world" should be treated analogously to a question about a finite whole, either with respect to how or whether it is a question, or with respect to how or whether it is to be answered. A-type questions posit alternatives which are comparable to each other. They find mystery in the actualities and possibilities that there are being *what* they are, *whatever* they are, other actualities and possibilities being either abstractly conceivable or hypothetically supposable without specification.

The primordial sense of mystery is not diminished either by general interpretations in theology or by specific explanations in science. In so far as theology aims to account for what prevails by tracing or attributing this to a grand Prevalence, it plainly begs the question. In so far as science "explains" specific prevalences by connecting them with others, progressively exposing traits of more inclusive prevalences, it leaves the primordial question intact. The specific answers do not affect the *"whatever* prevails as it does."* There remains the mystery why in all of the explanations that science gives *these* are the prevalences that are *there to be explained;* why these explanations, these connections, these orders, are what arise and what prevail.

ii

Historic phrases like "the natural order" and "the order of nature" suffer to some extent from the confused belief that order (as such) is arrangement, and that there is *a* basic arrangement which nature "has." Whether these phrases suggest that besides the natural order there is another, a non-natural order, depends upon the angle of philosophic emphasis. To say that nature "is" an order is more meaningful (or less perplexing) than to say that nature "has" an order. An order more inclusive than any other is certainly not easy to think of as a storehouse or receptacle of "all things." The "an" is disturbingly unsatisfactory. Although analogies are not inapplicable to the conception of nature, no single analogy is adequate; and the kind of conception we are dealing with seems to make mandatory the conclusion that no group or grouping of analogies is adequate except as a stimulus to metaphysical query. But if the idea of an order of nature does not emerge, orders of nature do. Among the subaltern orders that constitute and diversify nature are orders of possibility.

Nature is not an order of orders in the sense analogous to an outer circle admitting an infinite number of possible concentric circles. Nor is nature a hierarchy of orders all congruous with each other by virtue of their hierarchical location. For a version of *natura naturans* and *natura naturata* to be framed by a metaphysics of natural complexes, it is necessary to extinguish dormant assumptions: that whatever is, is determinate in all respects; or that all subaltern orders "ultimately" harmonize and blend; or that each subaltern order "ultimately" is a distorted symptom of the one basic order; or (similarly) that in the basic order everything is related in some way to everything else. The concept of nature should embrace the alescent and the prevalent. If *natura naturans* means prevailing and arising, *natura naturata* means what does prevail and what has arisen. But the engendered affects the engendering, as the engendering cumulatively modifies the engendered.

If *natura naturata* is "the world" or "the universe," then *natura naturans* is the order of provision and determination. It is reflected in the fertility of any complex whatever. Nature is not so much the order which contains or even includes all other orders as the order which permeates them all; not the order within which but by which new orders are discriminable and explorable, whether through assertion, action, or contrivance. Only such an order can make possible and justify the indefinite continuation of query.

The idea of "unlocking the secret" of nature is primitive and barbaric, despite its ostensible influence in the history of science and philosophy. It depends upon the assumption that nature is a unitary prevalence in which alescences are merely human expressions of probing. On such an assumption, there are no arisings but only duplications, no formations but only schedules, no determinations but only predeterminations. The fear underlying the outlook of many philosophies is that if nature were otherwise, the natural order would be inaccessible, and nature would be unintelligible. Those who have systematically rejected this approach—for instance, the evolutionary philosophers of the early twentieth century—appear to accept one form or manifestation of alescence, namely novelty, as the corrective category. Although they do not reduce alescence exclusively to human terms, it is mainly upon a certain type of alescence in human life, the surge of spontaneous feeling, that they build analogically their conception of a varied and "open" universe. When built, this conception of the centrality of feeling may well result, as it is sometimes said, in a human world writ large. If so, then nature and nature's God are once again writ small.

iii

By various means it has been iterated that when we think of a complex in terms of its traits or constituent complexes, we are obliged to think of both possibilities and actualities. A possibility, considered as such, as a discriminated complex, is related; it has relational traits; and its relations are to actualities as well as to other possibilities. Likewise, an actuality considered as such is relationally inseparable from possibilities; for, as we have seen, a complex which is actual and has no possibilities is a self-contradictory notion. Since every complex is indefinitely analyzable and relatable, it follows that no complex has more or fewer traits than any other. But if this is true, why is nothing quite so common as the discrimination of more and less, and of obviously different limits, among the traits that belong to specific complexes? A hummingbird has more bright colors than a starling, one man has more skills than another, one area has more sunshine and more foliage than another. And this is true of possibilities as well as actualities. If a building is to be erected in relation to one that is now standing, there is indeed an infinite number of possible, discriminable distances between them. But in another respect the possibilities are strictly limited in number: the new building can be either fifty feet away or less than fifty feet or more. A man has an indefinite number of traits, but only one skin color or only two eyes or only so much strength. A building has an indefinite number of traits, but only so many rooms or so much height.

Restrictedness and unrestrictedness, limitation and freedom from limitation, take the form of specific traits. They are traits of a complex in so far as it is an order and in so far as it inhabits an order. A complex occupies orders in which it is subject to specific restricting conditions, and orders in which it is not. In an order of gross color types or broad social groupings where gross color is recognized, men have a single skin color. In an order that includes personal, pathological, and various contingent conditions, men have many colors in their skin. In an order of conditions that currently determine American constitutional life, the possibilities for a president are to serve either one term or two. In an order embracing the entire ongoing and future history of American life, there are any number of possibilities for presidential tenure of office.

Every complex has both limited and unlimited aspects, and no "more" of one than of the other. Limitation and restriction are not to be equated with determinateness. There is no limit or restriction on the number of successors that an integer may have in the series of integers. Yet the series with its principle of succession is as determinate as any complex can be. To say that every determination implies a restriction is true if it does not mean that a determinate complex is limited in all respects.

A complex is alescent in so far as it "admits traits" into its contour. The "admission" is not to be construed as an absolute increase but as a variation of specific proportions or quantities, or a variation of status, in an order. This variation is what constitutes an increase in "variety." An alescent trait makes a difference, but it does not make any complex more or less of a complex, nor does it "add" a trait to a sum of traits, in an arithmetical sense. What an alescent complex "admits" is deviation from environing conditions or from a proximate past.

All complexes have scope, but not the same kind of scope. All are inclusive, but not in the same way. It certainly cannot be said that the scope or inclusiveness of any complex is the same as that of any other. But difference in scope has nothing to do with "number" of traits.

Consider now, not any conceivable traits of a complex, but only its relations, whether these be subaltern to the complex-as-an-order or obtain between the given complex and another. In either case, relations are complexes which obtain "between" or "among" other complexes. If we take at random any two complexes, they may or may not be related. If they are *related*, then each is *relevant* to the other. But each may be relevant to the other in either of two ways, presently to be defined.

What does it mean for two complexes to be related? It means that each is at least a condition of the scope of the other; that is, of the other's comprehensiveness or pervasiveness. Each is a determinant, a determining trait, of the other's scope. Every relational condition is necessarily one of an indefinitely large number. It may also be of major or minor status so far as the *integrity* of the related complexes is concerned. Relation is the measure of scope, as well as its peculiar determinant. The relations in the contour of a complex determine whether its scope is large or small.

Relations are the ramifications of a complex. Some branches turn inward and are more intertwined with themselves than with neighboring branches, some spread out and intertwine liberally and harmoniously, some crowd each other spoliatively. When two complexes are related, each diminishes, enlarges, or keeps constant the scope of the other. But related complexes may or may not affect each other's scope in the same way. And either may affect more than the other's scope. A master may enlarge the powers of his pupil while the pupil inhibits the growth of the master. A machine may promote the growth of an economic process while the process wears out the machine and renders it obsolete. The particles related to an evolving mass accrue to increase its size and are deprived of their independent motion. The relation of friendship may entail a mutual, progressive extension of scope; a symbiotic relation may entail a mutual, progressive narrowing of scope.

The influence of a complex, which constitutes it as pervasive, and the architectonic reach of a complex, which constitutes it as comprehensive, are themselves constituted by various subaltern relations. And scope, great or small, may be determined either by relations that arise or by relations that prevail.

iv

A relation (by definition) has bearing on the scope, but it may or may not have bearing on the integrity, of a complex. We cannot always draw a sharp line between the integrity and the scope of a complex. A variation in scope may, as such, constitute a variation in integrity, depending upon the kind of complex and upon the nature of its circumstances. The difference, however, is firm in principle, as the ensuing considerations should help to reveal. In order now to frame the distinction between relation and relevance, it is necessary both to recall and to introduce certain general observations about the integrity of a complex.

First, we recall the rather obvious but fundamental point that every natural complex has traits in common with others and traits peculiar to itself. Integrity cannot imply unique traits alone, for this means that a complex would be utterly unconnected with any other.

If its traits were all unique, it would be as undiscriminable and unlocatable as if its traits were all common.

Second, the integrity of a complex does not lie in the totality of its traits. The mere presence or absence of specific traits or constituents, without further qualification, would not result in a different integrity. And this would be true whether the traits in question were traits unique to it or traits that it had in common with other complexes. Whether the City of New York contained eight million thirty-three or eight million thirty-four residents would not matter to its integrity as a complex. Strictly, the difference in the number of residents would imply a difference in scope. But far more extensive differences in scope may leave the integrity of a complex unaffected.

Third, integrity is not to be equated with "individuality." The latter term in its most neutral sense serves to epitomize traits basic to complexes that are identified in a rather distinctive way. Just how this way is to be characterized, and just what the attributes are that constitute an individual is an extremely difficult question. But it is plain enough that not all natural complexes can be identified as individuals. There are relations, processes, possibilities, structures, laws, kinds, groups; and all such complexes, whether "general" or "particular," have an integrity. They all have a contour of integrities, and an identity (the continuing relation obtaining between their contour and any given integrity within it). But not all can or should be said to have "individuality." The integrity of a complex requires its having some traits that are unique. All individuals, as individuals, are unique. But not all unique complexes are individuals.

Fourth, what we have called the minimal condition of an integrity is the location of a complex in a given order. To every complex there are related certain others which affect its location (its presence) in a given order, and therefore its integrity. Any such complexes will be called *strongly relevant* to it. To say that one complex is strongly relevant to another, then, is to say that it is a condition of the other's integrity, that it either reinforces and sustains or modifies and perhaps destroys the integrity (a given integrity) of the other.

Consider the two complexes, rainy weather and the growth of wheat. They are related, and it makes no sense to say that rain is related to the growth of the wheat, but that the growth of the wheat is not related to rain. What we can say, given the typical agricultural order in which the complex known as the growth of wheat is located, is that the rain is strongly relevant to the growth of wheat, whereas the growth of wheat is weakly relevant to the rain. The wheat typically would not grow if there were no rain, but there would still be rain if the wheat did not grow or there were no wheat. In this order, the rain is strongly relevant to the wheat in the sense that it is a condition of the integrity of a complex other than itself. But although the growth of the wheat would not be relevant to the rain in the same way, it would affect the scope of this as of any complex to which it were related: the scope of rain increases according as it makes wheat grow in addition to making other forms of vegetation grow. A complex is thus *weakly relevant* to another in so far as it is related to that other in an elementary way, merely as a condition of that other's scope. The relation is a trait of each of the two complexes, but (in this order) a trait affecting the integrity of one and only the scope of the other; so that one complex is strongly relevant to a second, the second weakly relevant to the first.

Plainly, if a complex is a determinant of the integrity of another complex, it is also thereby a determinant of the latter's scope; for by the nature (definition) of relation, complexes that are related contribute at least to the determination of one another's scope, in the sense of keeping it constant, enlarging it, or diminishing it.

In a more inclusive order than the typical agricultural order, an order of which the latter is part, the growth of wheat might be strongly relevant to rain, even if intermediately, and with less "direct" efficacy than a naive conception of relevance would envisage. (The strong relevance of the rain to the wheat was not one of "direct" efficacy.) For example, if wheat did not grow, and the land were barren, and erosion occurred, and silt washed into lakes and streams, and streams began drying up, and evaporation were affected, rainfall would be affected. The state of the wheat then would be a complex affecting the integrity of weather in a geographic order.

The following generalizations may be made. (The third of these states what was given as a defining trait of relation, but the generalizations collectively augment the definition, as indeed the entire chapter does.)

If *A* is one complex and *B* is another, they may be related or unrelated.

If A is related to B, B is related to A.

If A is related to B, each is a determinant of the scope of the other.

If A is related to B, each is relevant to the other.

If A and B are relevant to each other, A is related to B.

If A is related to B, each may be either strongly or weakly relevant to the other.

If A is a determinant of the integrity of B, it thereby is a determinant of the scope of B.

If A is a determinant of the scope of B, it may or may not thereby be a determinant of the integrity of B.

If A is related to B in order O, it may not be related to B in order P.

If A is strongly (or weakly) relevant to B in order O, it may be weakly (or strongly) relevant to B in order P.

In one familiar order of complexes, the City of New York may be strongly relevant to an individual taken at random, while that individual would be weakly relevant to the city. But an extraordinary or historic individual might be strongly relevant to a city, as a source of major alescence in it. The class of all individuals in a city would have to be strongly relevant—indispensable to the prevalence of the city.

There is a relation between a law of property and an individual property owner. The law (again, in a familiar order) is strongly relevant to the individual, crucial to his integrity as a man of property, while the individual is weakly relevant to the law, which, though affected in scope by the mere relation, is indifferent, in its integrity, to his living or dying or ever having existed. Suppose, however, that the individual property owner *is* strongly relevant to the law. This may mean that his acts, his ideas, or his career as owner are the source of a major alescence of the law—that the law, owing to him, is widely disregarded, modified, or viewed in a novel way. Or consider the law in relation not to an individual but to the entire class of property owners, individual, corporate, and public. This class, merely as such, is strongly relevant to the law, in the form of a complex essential to its integrity. In the present instance the class is essential to the prevalence of the law: without property owners there would be no law of property.

We have just seen that a complex may be a determinant of another's integrity by being essential to its prevalence or by effecting a "major" alescence in it. Now alescence as such implies only the introduction of an integrity in the contour of a complex. And *A* may be relevant to alescence in *B* to the extent that not *B*'s integrity but only the integrity of a subaltern complex of *B* is affected. In such a case, *A* does not effect a "major" alescence in *B*. Thus within the given prevalence *B,* within *B* as inclusive complex, the alescence may be a negligible variation. The arrival of one more resident in New York is a new relation between one complex and another more pervasive one, a relation that increases the latter's scope; but the arrival is an alescence of negligible effect in the order under consideration. It would be comparable to the presence of a cork within one wave of the tide. In both cases, the alescence leaves intact the integrity of the more inclusive complex.

v

When two or more complexes are related, the character of the relation as a trait of the relata may or may not be the same for all of them, in the familiar sense that if brotherhood is the relation of A and B, their specific relational traits are the same, whereas if fatherhood is the relation of A and B, their specific relational traits are different. The usual way of putting this aspect of relatedness is that some relations are symmetrical and others are not. But in all cases, whether the relata be persons or other kinds of complex, there is neither more nor less relatedness on the part of any relatum. The law of property is as "much" related to the property owner as the property owner to it. There is an order of common experience within which it is held that A relates to B "more" than B to A, or that A relates "better" than B, or that B "fails" to relate. This conception has no metaphysical significance, although it certainly may be allowed its psychological and moral interpretation, as well as the right to be translated into less general terms. If A and B are related in any way at all, A may be more reliable and may confer greater benefits upon B than the other way round. What this means is, not that A is more "related" than B, but that there are subaltern aspects of the relation in which comparative estimation or comparative measurement is called for. The difference between A's performance and B's, or the difference between the way in which A regards B and the way in which B regards A, may be covered over by the more inclusive relation between them. No one would regard a biological relation of brotherhood or of fatherhood between A and B as admitting of more or less, although the subaltern constituents of A's relational complex may be radically different from those of B's.

Even in non-personal terms, when we speak of a "close" or "strong" relation, or of things "loosely" related, we are referring to kinds of relations, to different relations, not to amounts of relatedness. Among these kinds, some may be of indefinite duration, others ephemeral. Some may be stable, others easily subject to dissolution. Two employees of a firm, one with years of competent service, the other with a few months of poor service, differ not in the amount of the relation as such which each bears to the firm, but in the character of their inclusive relational complexes. Some relations may be much more important than others. Some may entail great widening or narrowing of scope among their relata or in one of their relata, others little widening or narrowing. The differences of degree found in the comparison of all these relations with one another are not themselves degrees of relation.

We have alluded to the sense in which certain subaltern complexes in a relation may admit of degree, even though relation as such does not. Speaking generally, certain traits admit of degree, even though "being," having traits, does not. Let us consider certain forms of relation involving readily measurable magnitudes. If A and B are sailors whose positional relation in a marching ceremony involves a consideration of height, then A is related to B as taller to shorter. And A may be not just taller than B but much taller, each thereby affecting the other's position. Or if A and B are runners, either in a particular race or in recurrent competition, then A may be not just faster than B but much faster, or faster by increasing margins, again with mutual influence. And a third runner, a third marcher, may be still faster or taller. All who are thus related are related in the sense of occupying a position in a series or hierarchy, and each is differentiated by degree from any other in the series.

We may formulate more exactly now the contrast between the degree of height or speed among those related and the absence of degree in their relation as relation. The relation of A and B consists not (i) in the magnitude of the difference between them, but (ii) in each being a constituent condition of the scope of the other. If relation admitted of degree, we should have to say that (i) is essential to (ii); that the degree of the difference between A and B is the degree of their relation to each other. But two complexes may be different in any number of ways, or similar in any number of ways; they may be more or less different, more or less similar—and yet not be related at all. *All* complexes differ in some respect. *Not* all are related to each other.

Some tree in a Siberian forest, we can assume, has a height that would measure more than the height of both A and B; yet, instead of being related to them in respectively greater degrees, it may not be actually related to them at all—it may be irrelevant to their scope. We could put together the words "some tree in Siberia is taller than A." But framing a sentence, which produces a relation among words, does not suffice to produce a relation among the complexes of which the words speak. It is a relation between A and B that brings with it or entails a difference in degrees of a given trait belonging to each. The trait-difference that admits of degree is a subaltern complex of the relation. This does not mean that the "relation itself" is traitless. What it means, rather, is that a subaltern complex is not to be identified with the complex in which it is subaltern; that the presence of a trait admitting of degree does not imply the presence of degree in the inclusive complex.

Can we say that relevance, if not relation, admits of degree? For if there is strong and weak relevance, is there not very strong and very weak relevance? But although the distinction between relatedness and relevance makes such a question understandable, and although relevance is directional in a way that relation as such is not, the supposed consequence does not follow. The contrast *here* made between strong and weak relevance is a contrast between that which affects integrity and that which affects only scope. Influence on integrity is "stronger" with respect to what it is in natural complexes that is determined. Since a determination of integrity is also a determination of scope but not vice versa, the terms "strong" and "weak" are justified, even though the suggestion of degree that is risked by the usage is neither intended nor accepted.

Now relevance is relation either with respect to integrity or with respect to scope; yet it is, after all, relation. From this point of view it might be thought plausible simply to reiterate that, whatever the differentiae, relation does not admit of degree. But such a disposition of the issue would be cavalier and unconvincing. If it is necessary to conclude that relevance, like relation in general, does not vary in degree but admits, instead, of innumerable modes, forms, and circumstances, it is also necessary to provide an explanation of persisting usages according to which some things are "more relevant" and others "less relevant"—say to the solution of a problem, to a situation which prevails, to a trend which arises.

Reverting to an earlier example, the law of property may be strongly relevant to an individual property owner, and the property owner weakly relevant to the law. Why can it not be said that there are complexes other than the law which are *more* relevant to the integrity of the individual, and that there are complexes other than the property owner which are *less* relevant to the scope of the law? Might not religious commitments be more relevant to the integrity of a property owner than the law is? Might not a property owner, weakly relevant to the law, yet be more relevant to the law than another individual who is also weakly relevant but not a property owner? And might not the latter be more relevant than still another individual who is weakly relevant but not a citizen?

So far as the problem of more and less is concerned, both relation and relevance are notions comparable, not to warmth, skill, or density, but to structure, being, or prevalence. It is not a matter of "how much" but of "in what way" or "of what kind." Among human individuals that *are* relevant to the scope of a law of property, property owners are not "more" relevant but relevant in a different way. Each of the individuals is located, but differently located, in the inclusive order of relevant complexes. This means that each is related to an aspect (or sub-order) of the law as a complex— for instance, to the law only as law, to the law as a social force, to the law as a symbol of authority, to the law as one law among many, to the law as one force among many, to the law as oppressive or beneficial. And again: religious commitments may be more influential than the law is in determining certain traits of a property owner's integrity. But if the integrity of a complex is what it is by virtue of *all* the factors that are relevant, none is *more* relevant than any of the others.

If *A* and *B* are players on the same team in a competitive game, we can say that *A* was more skilled than *B,* and that *A*'s play was the most pervasive of the forces in the game, but not that *A*'s play was more relevant to the outcome than *B*'s. Even if *A*'s play promoted the winning of the game and *B*'s jeopardized the winning, *B*'s play was not less relevant. For that which is spoliative affects the integrity of a complex along with that which is augmentative. The force making for augmentation may be greater than that making for spoliation. And the traits that *are* relevant can differ or be similar in any number of ways. Each way can be graded or scaled in terms of comparative importance. These comparative traits help to constitute the way in which each trait is relevant. All the actors in the play are relevant to the play, those with "small" parts and those with "large." If small parts are eliminated from the play, it is not because of their so-called lesser relevance but because their kind of relevance has been found to be either (*a*) a relevance to the play's scope and not to its integrity, making alteration of the play's scope desirable; or (*b*) a relevance to the play's integrity, making alteration of the play's integrity desirable. But the small parts and the large parts are all parts, the many relations are all relations, the little and the big realities are all realities. The principle of ontological priority, opening the way to the confusion of what prevails with what we want or do not want to have prevail, must be kept in exile forever.

Sometimes degree of relevance is thought of in connection with the development of a complex rather than in connection with the differences among complexes. It is said, for example, that the early writings of a poet have become "more" relevant to the basic character of his work, or that his current direction is increasingly relevant to the importance of his early work. That relevance can be said not just to prevail but also to arise in time is indisputable. Moreover, there is no fixed limit to the length of time that may belong to the alescence of a complex. But the arising of a relevance cannot be equated with an increase in magnitude of a trait already present. It is the formation of traits. The traits constitute a relation.

It seems likely that when philosophers, critics, or scientists think of "degrees of relevance" they are identifying these "degrees" with the comparative evidential weights that they assign in the *ascertainment* of relevance. The "more relevant" turns out to be the discriminandum that tends to improve an interpretation. Thus when it is stated that economic factors are more relevant to the course of a historical movement than psychological factors, the statement defines the tendencies that prevail in a search for links and connections. Once it is shown that economic factors are pervasive, and that psychological factors are not, the objective of the search is achieved. Then the purely nominal, rhetorical function of the expressions "more relevant" and "less relevant" becomes clear. No scientist, in any case, need concern himself over what the essential difference might conceivably be between a low and a high degree of relevance, or between a low degree of relevance and irrelevance.

In widespread practice there is an implicit distinction between relation and relevance, such that relevance is present *only* in human orders of complexes, or more strictly, in complexes subject to human manipulation. Thus what is said to *be* "relevant" is always a reflection, a trait only as reflected upon, a "consideration," something applicable to an argument, to a theory, to an interpretation. What is relevant is relevant only as evidence. On this view, relevance applies to the completion of a case, the examination of a belief claim, the resolution of a problem. (Narrow as the view may be, it is a step or two removed from the preposterous yet historically persistent view that relations as such are not complexes prevailing and arising in the world at large but are only modes of comparison made by men.) Relevance is conceived as that which matters, and the guiding assumption, plausible enough on the surface, is that something can matter only to man. The plausibility hinges on whether or not we rest content with the popular moral import, the limited import of the key phrase "that which matters." If that which matters were discerned in its continuity with that which makes a difference, a difference of any kind and not only a human difference; if it were discerned as a specific instance of that which prevails in place of something else, or that which prevails where it did not before, or that which arises and has effect; then the arbitrariness of confining relevance to orders of inquiry would be visible.

vi

The doctrine that each complex is related to every other (or, that no two complexes are unrelated to each other) has a singular appeal, even for those who are unable to defend it. A metaphysics of natural complexes reveals this doctrine as easily confused with the entirely defensible principle that every complex has an indefinite number of relations. The general problem and its many angles will not be reviewed here. Nevertheless, the following observations are pertinent at this point, and theoretical underpinning for some of them will come from the next chapter.

1. Possible relations are not actual relations. The thesis that all complexes are related to all others may mean either that they actually are so related or that there always is the possibility that they should be so related. The latter seems, on the surface at least, to be less sweeping than the former. But its acceptance, far from being a first step in the argument for the more sweeping position, breeds trouble for that argument. If it is possible for any two complexes to be related when actually they are not, is it also possible for any two complexes not to be related when actually they

are? If the answer is yes, then may not any complex be related or unrelated to all others? If the answer (to the original question) is no, then what distinguishes becoming related from becoming unrelated? These questions expose the force and intent of the original position. What the position amounts to is that every complex not only may but actually is, and not only actually is but "must" be, related to every other; that it is impossible for each not to be related to every other.

2. The view that it is possible for every complex to be related to every other is not at all more readily acceptable than the view that every complex actually is related to every other. Some think that the former view is a truism. They think that some relation or other between complexes is always "logically possible." Whether the addition of the word "logically" adds to the strength of the contention, or adds anything to the contention at all, is doubtful. But does the contention show that "a possibility" of universal interrelatedness *prevails?* It is arguable whether any such *possibility* is discriminated; whether what is discriminated as a complex is not rather the statement alleging the possibility —the word-structure making up a contention. The contention itself stems from a philosophic habit of believing that "to know what is possible" is fairly gratuitous—that this is much easier than "to know what is actual." But to establish a possibility, to show that there is a possibility of a certain kind in the complex under consideration, is on the same plane as showing that there is a certain actuality. Just as in a given order we may know what is possible without knowing all the actualities involved, so (with no less frequency)

we may know what is actual without knowing all the possibilities involved.

3. What of the contention that any two complexes are relatable in so far as they can be jointly considered or compared; that is, related to each other by joint relation to a comparer? For example, two complexes A and B may each be thought of by C. To generalize this, however, is no comfort: If X is related to Y and Z is related to Y, it does not follow that X is related to Z; nor is it guaranteed that X *will* be related to Z. But again, there is a formidable difficulty aside from this one. The "can be" begs the same question as before: does there *prevail* a possibility that any two complexes should be jointly considered? *Can* any two complexes be compared?

4. If all complexes are actually interrelated, is each strongly relevant to every other, or do instances of both strong and weak relevance prevail? (*a*) If weak relevance is accepted together with strong, the thesis breaks down. For if any complex X is weakly relevant to another, Y, it affects the scope but not the integrity of that other. That is, there are traits (subaltern complexes) of Y wholly independent of X. Some complexes, then, remain unrelated. (*b*) If only strong relevance is accepted, the very notion of weak relevance in effect becomes meaningless so far as the thesis is concerned. But this consequence, aside from its artificiality with regard to the evidence of human experience, is equally destructive of the thesis.

5. The destructiveness is shown by the reflection that if weak relevance is not adequate to the requirements of the thesis, neither is strong relevance. Some-

thing more is required, such as "total relevance in all respects." We are compelled to hold that when any two complexes are related, each of their subaltern and superaltern complexes is related to every other. But if each is related to every other, to all the complexes they include and all the complexes that include them, we must ask whether all these relations are one and the same or admit of differences among them. If they are all the same relation, we cannot say they are relevant to each other in all respects, for there are no respects. No relations can be distinguished, indeed no complexes at all can be distinguished, and the very notion of relation is not discriminable. If the relations do admit differences, then the traits by which a complex relates to a second or third complex will differ from the traits by which it relates to a tenth or eleventh. There will be something in the way it relates to the second which is irrelevant to the way it relates to the tenth. There will be, in other words, an order in which it does not relate to the second, and an order in which it does not relate to the tenth. Irrelevance is required if discrimination is to be possible and if the multifariousness of nature is not to be arbitrarily disregarded.

vii

When a complex B is relevant to another complex A, whether weakly or strongly, the relevance may be to A as typical (as representative of other complexes) or to A as unique, as different from other complexes. For example, a government's relevance to a citizen A may be nothing other than its relevance to any or all citizens. On the other hand, the relevance may be to

A not in so far as *A* is a citizen but in so far as *A* is *A* and no one else. In so far as it provides a legal structure, the government relates indifferently to all. In so far as it enforces this structure, it may relate to *A* in particular, say as a suspected criminal. Conversely, *A*'s relevance, weak or strong, may be to his government as government, or to his government as that government in particular. A complex may be relevant to another in either or both capacities, in either or both orders of relatedness.

If some complexes are relevant to a human individual as a citizen, others, in respectively more inclusive orders, are relevant to him as a man, as an organism, as a complex. The inclusive order consisting of all complexes which are relevant to an individual as a complex is what constitutes that individual's prevalence in the broadest sense—for he prevails in narrower senses too. The subaltern order consisting only of those complexes which are relevant to an individual as an individual is precisely what constitutes the order or course known as his experience, his prevalence as a historical creature.[15]

The inclusive order contains the contour of the individual. The experiential order, which is an order of historicity, provides him with the integrity that is characteristically and crucially human. It is within the latter order that still another basic order is made intelligible, that in which the individual has a moral integrity. Locke distinguishes between identity of a man and identity of a person. The identity of a man is to be found in the kind of prevalence or prevalent sameness whereby, under one "organization of life," he exists constantly both "forwards and backwards." The identity of a person is to be found in the kind of prevalence whereby he is self "to himself." As a man, the individual's being thus lies in his historicity or experience; as a person, his being lies in his consciousness and self-consciousness. With the details of this distinction and with its problems we need not be concerned: it conveys perfectly the idea of greater and lesser inclusiveness in the human order, and it provides the appropriate level of query for the metaphysics of the human process. It forces reflection on the question whether the moral integrity of an individual is best delineated or illuminated by the basic patterns of his life as a man or by the kinds of conscious choice that he makes as a person. The "moral integrity" of an individual should, of course, not be confused with the same phrase of eulogistic import used to designate a trait which is not universal. In the present sense, a moral integrity, like a historical integrity, belongs to each human individual. By virtue of this integrity, which belongs to him as a moral complex, he has a moral identity. The individual who is admirable and the individual who is repulsive are alike located in an order which makes these very traits relevant.

Within the prevalence of a history, what meaning can there be for the concept of alescence? Assuming that the origin of a history and its termination are alescences in a more pervasive complex, what could be the alescent traits in the course of a history? Is not every trait of a history constitutive of that history? Can any trait be at variance with what prevails *as* perpetual arising?

Now a history is truly a perpetual arising, full of augmentations and spoliations, and not simply a span of time, of what Locke called "perpetually perishing parts of succession." Nor is it like (another Lockean formulation) a "continued train" of successive "actions," "each perishing the moment it begins." [16] And although a history belongs to an individual as such or a society as such, it is never the history of a pure individual but of one that is both unique and typical. Each history as a history is unique and typical, and in this respect each is a "natural history" as well as a contingent and idiosyncratic order. Each history, in so far as it is the history of an individual or society that is human, represents (signifies) the human process. Now in a process, plainly, there are alescences which it is not hard to discriminate from the fundamental prevalence. And in a history so regarded, the "perpetual alescence" is like the [inevitable] variation of each stalk in a growing crop of grain.[17]

But besides the alescences thus inevitable in a history there are historical alescences whereby the human pattern itself is reinforced or is extended, and whereby each individual version of this pattern gets reinforced or extended as individual. Here the analogy, though imperfect and incomplete, is with that which accelerates and decelerates, which stays in one path or diverges from it, which moves through stages or is arrested in one stage, which is engendered, launched, propelled, and is as likely as not to career or collide. Whatever moves and endures has a direction, which is the net result of the relations among its constituent traits and the relations it bears to the complexes of the world. The dominant direction of any human individual, simply as a direction, admits of a distinction between repetition and innovation, and between rhythms of various kinds. Being the direction of a creature with the traits of its genus, it admits also of human appraisals that define it. The dominant direction of an individual is a complex with subaltern directions. It may be reinforced or modified by the possibilities and actualities relevant to the individual as an individual. *All* of these relevant complexes go to constitute the individual's "experience." Complexes "experienced" are complexes related, not "presented," to an individual. That a direction should be modified or reinforced is inherent in a historical prevalence. But each circumstance of reinforcement or modification, each incipient instance of efficacy, is an alescence.

Among the complexes to which an individual is related are his own products. A producer may be strongly or weakly relevant to his product, and a product may be strongly or weakly relevant to its producer. Each may bear either kind of relevance to the other at one and the same time. If this appears paradoxical, it is only because "product" is construed narrowly to imply something that emanates from a producer on occasion or at special times; something that necessarily has special significance for one who has chosen to produce. The paradox dissolves if whatever a man does, says, or makes, whether deliberatively or unknowingly, is regarded as his product, and if all products are regarded as utterances. Whether they are important or unimportant, all of a man's products are equally his and they "emanate" from him—in distinction from someone else—allowing, to be sure, for the frequent practical problem of distinguishing between the produced and the unproduced, or between one producer and another.

A producer is strongly relevant to his products in so far as they arise, but not necessarily in so far as they prevail. Not necessarily, for instance, to their status as social symptoms or to their value for other men. He may be forced to diverge from them, both from the products he has unwittingly spawned and from those he has lovingly bred. Products not only may prevail beyond the prevalence of a producer's life but may acquire an autonomy beyond the continuing prevalence of his intent, his method, and his vision. As common experience testifies, the actual function of a product in human affairs often is indifferent to, if not altogether remote from, the circumstances in which it was cradled. Thus over and above the origination of a product, the producer and the constituents of his utterance (such as intent or method) may be weakly relevant to it.

The kind of relevance will differ also according as the producer is related not merely to his product as a whole but to this or that subaltern complex of it. To some aspects of a product the producer may not be related at all. And this possibility applies not only to the product in its own prevalence beyond that of the producer, but to traits that were part of it in its origin. For these traits, though concomitant with other traits of the product, may have been outside the power and the activity of the producer, and may have remained uninfluenced before, during, and after the process of utterance. No utterance of an individual is ever subject to total control or "possession" by him. He is never complete "creator," that is, sole condition of its determination. This follows, first, from the impossibility of producing without the utilization of that which to some extent is already determinate; and second, from the nature of production as continuous and ubiquitous in the history of the individual.

What is true of the producer's relevance to the product is true of the product's to the producer. Some products are relevant only to the scope, others also to the integrity of an individual or a community from which they have sprung. An everyday type of implication latent in this point is that not everything a man says or does is representative of what he "really is." The specific, definite understanding of what constitutes a human individual's integrity is supremely difficult, and the line between scope and integrity is harder to trace in affairs human than in any other kind of complex. The source of the problem is plain enough: the expiration of a man's history is ordinarily not the expiration of his role in the history of other men or of the community in which he produced. His products may continue not only to vary their relations but to wax and wane in their force, and the effect of his prevalence may be what it is not because of the labor that was his but because of some vagrant alescence, some small phase of his drift. So too the force of a man's history may owe what it does to the sheer facts of his natural location, more than to the utterances of his productive experience.

IV

POSSIBILITY AND ACTUALITY

i

THERE IS NO "realm" of the possible. But neither is there a "realm" of the actual. There are no "pure" possibilities which never are related to actuality, or which are actualized out of the blue—arising in no particular order and relating to no particular order. But neither are there "pure" actualities, exemplifying no possibility and having no possibilities. There are no "possible entities" which wear the character of actuality without being actual. And neither are there "actual entities" which monopolize or specialize in determinateness and are void of anything but actuality. Pure possibility and actuality is as much of a confusion as pure relation, pure individuality, pure fact, pure structure. Purity as such is as fictitious as simplicity. The very notion of "entities," which is the most mischievous catch-all in metaphysics, is covertly modeled after the notion of "primary substances," the alleged ultimate subjects of occurrence and of predication.[18]

It should be clear by this time that the kind of question which may profitably be asked about possibility is not, Are there "possible entities"? or, Where are possibilities to be found? or, Are possibilities real (are they "really real")? or, Is the real an expression of the possible or the possible an expression of the real?—but rather, What is entailed in saying that a possibility is located in an order of natural complexes, and in what way is a possibility, as one kind of natural complex, related to other kinds? [19] This question is not an easy one, but it can be answered. It bypasses the sheepish attitude to which philosophers submit and which they even enjoy in speaking of possibility. It assumes that with the help of other concepts something can be said about what possibility is, and not merely about what it is not. These concepts help to expose the inadequate common-sensism underlying questions like "Is there such a thing?" (it is nonsense to ask "Is there such a complex?") and "What being can belong to possibilities when, after all, it is on actualities that we stub our toes?"

Possibilities, we said earlier, are always possibilities *of* and *for;* a natural complex has certain possibilities —not any whatever. They are possibilities for it—or "the" possibilities for it. There are possibilities that such-and-such will occur, or will get done. These are, in some specific sense, traits of a complex, subaltern complexes in an order. And this is the chief consideration, no matter what may be the colloquial devices or mannerisms by which possibility is identified. Not only is a possibility a natural complex belonging to and traceable within a given order; it is always related to other complexes, however abstractly we are in the habit of considering it. Put in another way: a possibility is to be regarded basically in the same way as an actuality. Neither is "prior" to the other—"logically," "metaphysically," "epistemically." All actualities are interpretable in terms of specific relations, constituents, or ordinal traits. "An" actuality, like "a" possibility, prevails or arises in an order. Each is related to other complexes in the order—each to other actualities *and* other possibilities. Neither can be "by itself." When actualities are conceived of as being "by themselves," they are sometimes regarded as "substances." When possibilities are conceived of as being "by themselves," they are sometimes regarded as "essences." But for actualities and possibilities alike, the only tenable sense of "being by themselves" is as discriminable integrities.

Philosophers have wondered whether there are unactualized possibilities. The first impulse, of course, is to answer that one never can wait long enough to find out. But in a metaphysics which makes ordinal location fundamental for all complexes, the question is tractable, even if the validation process involved has its own kind of indirectness. First of all, a corresponding type of question can be asked about actuality. Are there actualities which fail to acquire possibilities that other actualities do acquire? If we say that some do acquire possibilities, we should be able to say that some do not. Failure and curtailment are identified commonly enough. It is necessary only to perceive that such conditions apply to complexes beyond the range of everyday identification. Whenever specific traits can be meaningfully affirmed of a complex, specific traits can also be meaningfully denied. But on a level where more general predicates are required, we become afraid of being trapped by grammar, and not without good reason.

The recognition of actualities curbed in their pos-

sibilities and of possibilities prevailing without actualization comes through the normal processes of pre-
sumptive and analogical inference. Nothing is more
familiar than contemplating or informally considering
a group of possibilities, or a number of actualities
classed together. When we say that illness prevented
a man from acquiring the potentialities belonging to
an individual with his training, or prevented him from
actualizing the potentialities that he did develop, we
are presupposing a group of comparable instances and
connected situations. If we can think of a complex as
ceasing to prevail, we can think of a complex as a possibility never actualized. The difficulty comes, less from
trying to think of a possibility in its *status* as unactualized, than from trying vainly to envisage, to all eternity, a possibility that would ordinarily be accepted as
such without evidence of its being actualized, but that
cannot be tolerated in its procrastination. In a metaphysics of natural complexes, it is not the possibility
that is to be blamed for the delay but the conditions
that preserve it intact.

Consider possibility p, which gets to be actualized.
The actualization brings about a new possibility r.
Possibility r never gets actualized; it expires as a possibility because of various other conditions which arise.
The conditions which bring about the expiration of
r bring about the prevalence of possibility s. Possibility s later is actualized. Thus possibilities that are not
actualized (and actualities that are curbed or restricted
in their possibilities) not only have their natural place;
it is something of a feat consistently to deny them. At

bottom, the denial would be a denial of possibility as such.

A possibility cannot be said to prevail or to arise if it is unrelated to any actualities, nor can an actuality be said to prevail or arise if it is unrelated to any possibility. Every complex that prevails as an actuality either arose under or is presently contingent upon limited, finite conditions. That is to say, it is an actualization. It derives from and reflects the possibilities of other actualities. It has its own finite boundaries, its own restricted connections. Its own possibilities are distinguishable from one another and from the possibilities resident in another complex. We are often told that the "realm of possibility" is far vaster than the "realm of actuality." For to each actualized possibility there corresponds an inestimable number of possibilities not actualized or as yet unactualized. But if every possibility reflects the presence of actuality in an order—even if many possibilities reflect one and the same actuality—the "proportion" between possibilities and actualities turns out to sound less queer, whatever it may mean to think of it in numerical terms. Traits are what count, not "realms." A given trait (of actuality) is inevitably connected with various and numerous other traits (of possibility). Conversely, a given [trait of] possibility reflects (belongs to an order of traits containing) an innumerable train of actualities.

Each possibility is conditioned by what else prevails and arises, whether actualities or other possibilities. When a possibility is actualized, this means that a complex has been modified; in the sense, for example, that an actuality with certain possibilities has been succeeded or augmented or permeated by another actuality. The complex may be modified either in scope or in integrity. It is modified in scope if, e.g., the actualization is one more instance of a recurrence. It is modified in integrity as well as in scope if, e.g., the actualization is a deviation from a recurrence.

With a recognition of the parallelism between possibility and actuality, the way is open for an interpretation of the difference. We will be asking, in various forms, and attempting to answer, what it means, respectively, for a natural complex to have possibilities and to be actual. Since clarification of the two concepts is reciprocal, it is necessary to shift back and forth in the main focus; and although the discussion has dwelt initially upon possibility, an adequately explicit conception of possibility is reached only late in the chapter.

ii

At the present point the problem that seems most threatening to this ordinal and dimensional conception of possibility lies in the status of what have been called "pure," "free," "abstract," or "logical" possibilities. Precisely how, in the first instance, to recognize the possibilities said to fall into these categories (or this category) is by no means clear. The issue, however, does not depend upon terminological considerations, and the principle that possibilities, like actualities, are always complexes that are subaltern in an order, will be shown to be illustrated by any "kind" of possibility. It will be shown in due course that "purely logical" possibilities are not different from any other.

Consider the possibility of a home run being hit in a game of baseball. In order that this possibility should prevail, and in order that it should be subject to actualization, there must be an actual game of ball and an actual situation of batting. The possibility is one in a typical group of possibilities, dependent upon previous decisions and continuing rules, to mention no other conditions. Consider, now, the possibility that for the next two years anyone in a game of baseball who tries to hit a home run will succeed in doing so. This outlandish possibility, no whit less than the preceding familiar possibility, can prevail or arise only in games of baseball, only in the actual course of playing; that is, in a well-defined order of complexes. Consider next the possibility that the rules of the game might have been radically different. This too is located in an order of actualities and possibilities, the more inclusive world of games and sport. And consider the possibility that there might not have been a game known as "baseball." This was a possibility prevailing in a human society with a history and with prevailing inclinations, a society marked by alescent events of varying importance. And no matter what possibility we discriminate or allege—the possibility that there will be no more games, that the human race will expire—we are speaking about a world in which the possibility prevails as a complex, about an order of complexes in which it is located as constituent.

What about the possibility that from a point outside

a given straight line an indefinite number of lines can be drawn which intersect this line? Here is not what would commonly be called a "contingent" possibility but an "inherent" or "permanent" possibility. The difference presumably lies in the trait that under appropriate conditions any attempt to actualize the latter kind of possibility will succeed. But *any* possibility will be actualized under conditions "appropriate" to *it*. The more important consideration applicable to the possibility about lines and points is that it is a possibility of or for complexes in an order—a spatial order, or a mathematical order, of a certain kind. The possibility that every even number is (will be found to be) the sum of two prime numbers, is a trait belonging to the number system. It presupposes other mathematical possibilities, and it presupposes actual relations among numbers.

Some possibilities are stable and continuous, others recurrent, others irregular or sporadic. Some are seemingly impervious to alescence, others are short-lived or unexpected by men. Some are regularly actualized, others seldom actualized, still others never actualized, though no possibility can be discriminated unless actualization is envisaged, posited, or conceived. Some possibilities are inferable in extremely abstract terms. Some, after being actualized, arise again or continue to prevail when the complex originally actualized ceases to prevail. Some relate to a definite or unique future. Others relate to an ongoing present or a *kind* of future, a typical eventuality. But each is located in an order, each is a trait of a complex.

The ordinal factor in the nature of possibility helps

to explain why major possibilities or groups of possibilities may or may not be indefinitely numerous.
Thus in the order (or world) of practices conforming
to rules—games, rites, legal conduct—possibilities
are classifiable. In baseball, a subaltern order of this
order, there is only one possible direction in which
a conforming batter can run when he hits the ball
fairly. In Roman Catholic practice, another subaltern
order, it is not possible for a believer to recognize
either more or less than seven sacraments. In a criminal
trial, the possibilities available to a jury seeking to
arrive at a verdict are few, though the number may
vary from case to case.

Why should not any complex taken at random have
the same possibilities as any other taken at random?
Is it not in their "potentialities" rather than in their
possibilities that complexes genuinely differ? For is
not a possibility, in the last analysis, whatever does
not entail logical contradiction? Does not "logical possibility" generically include all other kinds, and are
not purely logical possibilities present indifferently,
regardless of specific orders of complexes? And is it not,
then, true that it is "logically possible" to reject all
the sacraments and still accept Catholicism? And is it
not logically possible for a batter to hit a baseball so
hard that it flies into orbit as a satellite of the earth?
Neither of these suppositions "entails a contradiction."
Consequently, must not these and infinite other possibilities be acknowledged to belong to any of the
complexes heretofore mentioned?

1. The trait of "not entailing contradiction" is a
trait that belongs to all possibilities in so far as they

are prospectively actualized. It is a trait that accompanies any recognition that "such and such is possible." But it makes no difference whether we say that what is possible is possible "because" it does not entail contradiction, or that what does not entail contradiction does not entail contradiction "because" it is possible. If we ask how we decide what is and is not possible, the answer is that we discover or calculate as best we can what are the limits and boundaries of an order of complexes. If we ask how we decide what does or does not entail contradiction, the answer is precisely the same. Nor does the answer vary when we set about deliberately to construct a consistent body of statements or symbol complexes. Such a body of statements cannot be constructed otherwise than in (or in the form of) a system or order of rules and specifications. The latter constitute the limits or boundaries of the order within which the statements are and are determined to be "possible" ("free of contradiction"). When, instead of deliberately constructing an order, we try to decide what does and does not entail contradiction in our reflections about complexes that are antecedently determinate in some respect, the only way to do this is to ascertain the order (or orders) in which they are related or mutually relevant. It may well be that we never can finally ascertain what are the possibilities in any order—just where the boundaries of the order precisely do lie. Even in a formal order deliberately framed, there are no final guarantees of the guarantees —guarantees that the guarantees introduced to avoid contradiction do so. But this issue does not affect the conception of all possibilities as ordinal.

To hold that it is "logical principles" such as the principle of non-contradiction which ultimately determine "what is possible" is like holding that one side of a coin is more truly a side than the other. It could equally well be said that it is because of what is and is not possible that logical principles obtain. The usual formulation of the principle of non-contradiction is that it is "impossible" for the same trait to belong (or, that the same trait "cannot" belong) and not belong to the same subject at the same time and in the same respect; or, that a formula in a given system "cannot" be asserted and not asserted in the system.[20] The principle of non-contradiction itself might be regarded as a possibility characteristic of an order more pervasive than any other, or of an order overlapping all other orders.

2. If Catholicism without sacraments and the batting of a ball into astronomic orbit were genuinely possibilities and did not involve contradiction, they would be possibilities within orders quite different from the orders known as Catholicism and baseball. Such different orders would be much wider than the two familiar orders. In the latter, what is alleged to be "possible" is not possible at all and does entail contradiction. The reason the alleged "possibilities" seem not to entail contradiction is that the orders in which they are thought to be located (in which they are being posited) are tacitly stripped of various traits which would exclude them. In other words, the orders are covertly abandoned, although their social names ("Catholicism," "baseball") are retained, along with a number of superficially identifying traits. It is cer-

tainly not non-contradictory to accept a religion the essential traits of which one has rejected. As that religion is defined and structured, in so far as that religion with its limits ("rules") does prevail as the order under consideration, a contradiction has been introduced. Likewise, it is not non-contradictory to speak of a *baseball* as flying around the earth, if we continue to accept what is used and understood as such, and to accept the physical laws that prevail for such bodies, or even the order of grounded conjecture on the frontiers of physics. What yields the impression of consistency and possibility in each case is an order tacitly adapted to fit the novel instance of supposition, rather than the continuity of the novel instance with the original order of traits.

3. The novel instances may be possibilities in the worlds of Alice in Wonderland, Mother Goose, or Hollywood cinema. They may also be recognized as possibilities when they are suitably reidentified and reinterpreted, without deceptive location in an order which is itself dubiously identified. A religion, we say, might have been a "different" religion. A game might have been a "different" game. It is sometimes said that a distinction should be made between "real" and "unreal" possibilities. Strictly, all possibilities are "real." But if a function is to be attached to such a distinction, it may serve the purpose of exposing "possibilities" the integrity of which is arrived at by ambiguous or arbitrary means. These "possibilities" are "unreal" in the sense that they are misleading semblances of a complex with very different traits. In other words, although they are themselves natural complexes, such as actual word-

configurations, they are not possibilities in the sphere supposed.

It is desirable to qualify the statement that the questionable novel "possibilities" may become less questionable in their status if suitably reidentified and reinterpreted. Reidentification is a very difficult affair. It is a search for a different order. A search is not a linguistic exercise. An order is not always specifiable at one fell swoop. As long as the complexes in question are identified as the original complexes, as long as the terms used in the search for a suitable order remain the same despite variation, there is a commitment to traits. Even a decision to be arbitrary and "merely consistent" is not in advance assured of successful execution.

4. Complexes may surely be said to differ in their "potentialities." But potentialities (and powers) are kinds of possibilities, to be described in good time. Complexes therefore differ genuinely in their possibilities, whatever other qualifications or classifications are found to be pertinent.

There is a widely held view of possibility similar and related to the one just considered. Sometimes it is set forth with the deepest conviction, but sometimes also it is designed ironically, to show that the very notion of possibility is untenable. According to this view, the possibilities attributed to a given complex must have belonged to any causal ancestor of that complex, say a million years ago. Another way of stating the view is to say that whatever is now possible was always possible. This kind of error is effectively attacked by Bergson.[21] But the error does not lie, as he thinks it does, in the assumption that possibilities precede their actualization. The error lies rather in the assumption that a "logical possibility" for a given complex always was and always will be a "logical possibility" apart from that complex and regardless of what conditions prevail. If we wished to reject this assumption, and yet to contend something like this, "A million years ago there was the possibility that President Kennedy would be assassinated"—we should have to assume, instead, the prior presence of the complex to which the possibility was relevant. Since this kind of assumption is as bad as the other, any contention like the one just stated is seen to be unwarranted.

What can be said is rather something like the following. A million years ago there were certain possibilities resident in the orders of complexes that prevailed. Some of these possibilities were actualized, and accordingly another set of possibilities arose while some of the original possibilities prevailed. Then other actualizations . . . then other possibilities . . . until there *arose*, along with the alescence of a given *order*, the possibility that a person, a given complex in that order, the president, would be assassinated. To hold the opposing view is to assume a single indivisible order in nature within which all "possibilities" prevail eternally, that is, in total independence of what is alescent or specifically prevalent. Strictly speaking, in this one order nothing could be distinguished as alescent or prevalent. Everything would be inherently part of everything else, and there would be no discrimination at all. One possibility, then, could not be discriminated from another. There could be no possibility, but only one "seamless" actuality.

iii

There is a sense in which we should scarcely wish to dispute the old saw that it is on actualities, not on possibilities, that we stub a toe. But consider that stubbing a toe may be a possibility as well as an occurrence. When the occurrence comes, there is an actuality of stubbing. Before (and perhaps after) the occurrence, there is a possibility of stubbing. Nor do we actually stub a toe unless it is possible for an actual object to resist. At this point we need, first, to ponder the kinds of actualities on which one could *not* stub a toe, either literally or figuratively; and, second, to suggest that human experience is as much shaped and influenced by possibilities as by actualities.

What is the purview of the term "actuality"? To what sorts of complex should "actual" be applied, and from what withheld?

1. Is the actual (as contrasted with what some philosophers pejoratively call the "merely real") the physical? But there are complexes like aims, thoughts, or poems which are either non-physical as such or not exclusively physical, and which are produced or discovered as actualities.

2. Is the actual "that which has come to pass"? Formulation in the present tense, "that which comes to pass," seems to miss the intent. It suggests a regularity and a prospect but no assurance of consummation. Even "that which has come to pass" is less than safe in its suggestion of actuality. "Come to pass" and "happen" must be distinguished from "arise." For there are possibilities which arise. These have a temporal aspect. They can be dated approximately. The

expression "come to pass" and "happen" must therefore be taken as applying not to that which is merely temporal but to that which is terminal, with [temporal] antecedents. But even when these slight refinements are made, it seems clear enough that tonal relations, physical ratios, and space, which have not come to pass, at least in anything like the preceding sense, are as actual as physical bodies and wars are. There is even a more elementary difficulty. "That which has come to pass" is not a philosophically adequate way of identifying certain familiar types of actuality. It applies to wars, but does not without equivocation apply to physical bodies. Physical bodies have come to pass in the sense that there are configurations of matter which are continuous with but different from previous configurations of matter. But physical bodies scarcely have come to pass in the sense of being happenings. Events happen, but not bodies, even when bodies are analyzed in terms of constituent events.

3. Is the actual that which is subject to sensory encounter? Among philosophers, statements like "The actual world is the sensible world" are so frequent that we may well wonder what is the conceivable justification. It seems too obvious to note that one may encounter another's way of thinking, a meaningful pattern of action, or an aggressive person, in all of which the sensory element, if present, may be accidental or irrelevant. But what if we eliminated the qualification "sensory"?

4. Is the actual that which we can be said to encounter? But we can encounter possibilities as well as

actualities. When our friend lies gravely ill, we encounter the possibility of death. We encounter familiar and unfamiliar possibilities. Possibilities may have an impact, even as actualities may, and it may be a dull or vivid impact. A stock objection is that it is our "thinking" about the possibility which we confuse with the "impact." But this objection applies equally to the actuality—isn't it our "thinking" about the actuality which we confuse with the "impact"? We think, willy-nilly, and we think about our dying friend in his absence as well as his presence. Whatever we think and in whatever way, it is the actual state and the imminent prospect we encounter that provides the complex thought *about*. If "encounter" is to be restricted to a narrow common-sense signification, in order to eliminate possibilities as encounterable, then a vast number of formidable actualities must also be regarded as not encounterable—distant stars and public opinion and biological evolution and the processes of memory. There is certainly *a* sense in which such actualities are not encountered and certain kinds of possibilities are.

5. Is the actual that which has "effects," that which is "efficacious"? Suppose "effects" to be construed in the broadest sense, which would include any kind of "result" and any kind of "consequence." Then we would recognize that the inclusion of a certain postulate in a deductive system results in the actual presence of certain theorems. And we might therefore decide to call the postulate, however abstract, an actuality. But this would not be the problem. The problem would be rather that, on so broad an "effects"-criterion

of actuality, possibility becomes actuality. A consequence of the arising of some possibilities is the arising of other possibilities. The possibility of extending foreign trade introduces the possibility of learning more about foreign economies.

Every natural complex, whether actuality or possibility, is efficacious. Whatever prevails or arises makes a difference. The traits of a natural complex provide and remove conditions for other traits. Concern as to whether the only complexes with efficacy are "material" belongs in a rather naive metaphysics. Efficacy is solemnly denied, for instance, to "ideas" and "thoughts," when behind the scenes and indeed long in advance, the criterion of efficacy has been tailored to fit that which alone is said to possess it. Perhaps the historic circumstances of philosophic speculation precluded a more useful way of expressing this bias—selecting and stressing material efficacy as one meaning of "efficacy," recognizing it as restricted, and interpreting the traits that belong to it.

If the "effects"-criterion of *actuality* is to be defended, then, "effects" must be limited to a certain kind. But what is to be the principle of limitation? Some philosophers believe that "fact" and "existence" (fortified by good vague doses of intuitive common sense) help to explicate the meaning of "actuality." But these terms, even when philosophic legislation tries to free them of their histrionic functions, usually produce more trouble than they remove. "Fact" is the lesser offender. But it is a manifestation, and not the differentiating condition, of actuality. It is not a manifestation of all actualities. It is not what characterizes actualities such as bodies and musical tones. They are not "facts." It is rather what characterizes events or specific occurrences and completed chains or patterns of occurrence, namely, their finality or ineradicability. The human appeal to fact as decisive ("These are the facts . . ." "In fact . . ." "It's a simple matter of fact . . .") is at bottom the appeal to what is finished, incontrovertibly recorded in nature; to [the supposed paradigm of] the determinate, or better, the terminate. When men urge one another to "examine the facts," they are surely alluding to the accurate ascertainment of traits; but beyond this, they are implying the completedness, the definitive status, of the traits that are to be ascertained.

The notion of "existence" is less readily tied down to an extractable core of meaning. The term has been used implicitly as an equivalent of "actuality," as an equivalent of "spatio-temporal actuality," and as an equivalent of both "reality" and "being." As an equivalent of the two latter terms it sometimes bears both an ontological sense and an honorific moral sense. To try to clarify "actuality" by appealing to "existence" is to jump from frying pan into fire. Whatever the scope of "existence" is taken to be, the rhetorical value of the term derives largely from the forms "exists" and "existed." The knowledge that something in question exists suggests, as it were, nature strong and active. Something imposes itself and commands response. In common practice, no other metaphysical term so directly suggests compulsion and challenge. What "exists" seems to require of men not merely discernment, not merely the sense of similarity and difference, but an energetic preparedness.

If one asks a philosopher to explain what he means by "actual," and he answers by pounding the table, or says in accompaniment to the pounding, "This—this is what I mean," he is not quite so eloquent as he intends to be. Such an answer can be given by anyone; any butcher or pipe-bender can designate some actuality. The philosopher is being asked, as philosopher, to interpret, not just to illustrate. He is being asked to use his philosophic resources, not to demonstrate that he has given up in advance. Unfortunately, in response to the question the pounding does not qualify even as a designation. There are too many actualities that cannot be pounded.

The encounter of men with possibilities is at least as important and extensive as their encounter with actualities. Actuality is neither more nor less fundamental morally than possibility. Men are reliant on, motivated by, surprised to discover, and frightened by possibilities. Their concern about gross ranges of possibility may even precede their knowledge of what is specifically possible. Possibility is the reach of actuality, actuality the ballast of possibility. When men rise to query, close regard for either the distinction or the relation between the two may become secondary. The philosopher and the mathematician, for instance, often investigate specific possibilities as discriminanda. They look upon the possible less as a complex accountable to or emanating from actuality, and more as a prevalence. The distinction between prevalence and alescence is in a sense more fundamental than the relation between possibility and actuality. But not more important. And awareness of the urgency and impact that can belong to possibility forces us to sharpen the account of the relation. The continual presence of possibility to men explains the great scope and diversity of human judgment. A possibility present to men may or may not be consciously recognized. It may be discriminated by the accumulation of learning and feeling, by the trial and fate of methods, by the momentum which carries judgment or production beyond orders that are immediately available.

iv

For the purpose of framing a conception of actuality, it is reasonable to cite not only instances of complexes which are commonly regarded as actualities, but instances which are not commonly so regarded and yet might justly be, and instances which have lain outside the pale of adequate categorization altogether.

When men encounter possibilities, the encounter itself is an *actuality*. Men actually encounter possibilities when they visualize future occurrences. They encounter possibilities in the course of reflecting, acting, and contriving, where they are constantly faced by alternative directions. They expect such alternatives before actually encountering them. This implies that it is also *possible* for men to encounter possibilities. Men who expect changes to occur in their world encounter possibility not primarily by calculating what may or may not specifically occur but by assuming a generalized prospect with certain limits. But whatever form the encounter with possibility may take, it always involves an actual tolerance of differing complexes none of which is regarded as a present actuality.

Encounter is a relation. We may recognize the possibility of a relation, or we may recognize that there is actually a relation. It is possible for A to be the husband of B, and A may actually be the husband of B. The relation of marriage entered into by A and B is an actuality, an actualization of the possibility. What may be questionable to philosophers is not whether this relation is "real" but whether it should be said to prevail as an actuality. To deny that specifiable relations as such are "real" is to countenance the absurdity of saying that complexes which have been discriminated are not discriminable. To deny, on the other hand, that relations can be regarded as "actual," is only to raise problems in the analysis of what it means to be actual. If a relation is never to be regarded as an actuality, it cannot be regarded as a possibility either. For as a possibility it admits of actualization. It must instead be interpreted "in terms" of possibility. But if individuals are related, what does it mean to say that the individuals are actual and the relation not actual? If the relation is not actual, how do we describe the difference between "A-and-B" on the one hand and "A-and-B married" on the other?

There is no guarantee in nature that all conceivable relations will be actualized, and no one expects that they will be. Yet there are certain fundamental types of relation the instances of which need to be recognized as actual but which philosophers are reluctant to recognize as such, partly out of bondage to the traditional equivalence vaguely assumed between "actuality" and "existence."

Take the relations between numbers. The definition of "number" is of course difficult and controversial. We may or may not want to say that numbers "exist" or that the relations between numbers "exist." But there is no reason to deny that the relations between numbers are actual; 5 is a successor of 4 and a predecessor of 6: these are actual relations. The divisibility by 2 of an even number as yet unspecified is a possible relation. Like all possibilities, it presupposes and reflects traits of actuality, in this instance the actual traits of numbers, in an order. The divisibility of any odd number by 2 is not a possible relation in the order of whole numbers.

Take the relation between a proposition which is asserted in a deductive system and another proposition which is logically implied by it in the system. There is a relation that prevails here, and it prevails as an actuality. The two propositions are actually related in a specific way. And whatever the natural status of "propositions" may be, it does not affect the actuality of their relation. If, on the other hand, in a given logical system two new and as yet unspecified propositions are to be formulated, logical implication is a possible relation between them.

Consider two possibilities, one of which is more comprehensive than the other. The possibility of a man building a house in less than a month is more comprehensive than (for it includes as one among many instances) the possibility of a man building a house in twenty-three days and nineteen hours. The relation between these two possibilities is itself actual—the former actually comprehends the latter. To philosophers who are inclined to ask "Where is it?" this must be doubly offensive. For in the present instance of relatedness, neither the possibilities nor the actuality are anywhere. Not anywhere, that is, except in the most fundamental location that there can be—an order of natural complexes. The possibility of a man building a house in less than a month is located in the order of architectural activity, in the subaltern orders of house building, of masonry and carpentry, of transactions in buying and selling, and in orders which parallel and intersect these, such as an order of social appraisal.

Along with the recognition that one possibility may stand in an actual relation to another—the alternative would be for the two possibilities not now to be related—comes the recognition that possibilities are actually similar to and different from other possibilities. The truth here is perhaps more easily seen for the kinds of possibility known as potentiality and power. A potentiality is not an actuality; but the "possession" of a potentiality, say by a living creature, is an actuality. One creature's powers exceeding another's, or differing from another's, is an actuality. Sometimes a power is itself loosely spoken of as an actuality. What is being tacitly identified in such cases is the repetitive pattern in which the power is actualized ("exercised," "exemplified"): the actuality referred to is not "a power to do so-and-so" but "the possession of a power." [22]

Thus actualities prevail among possibilities, even as possibilities prevail among actualities. And this indicates anew the peculiarity of the idea that there must be infinitely more possibilities than there are actualities. Corresponding to every one of an indefinitely large number of actualizations, but not to every actualization unqualifiedly, there was more than one possibility. But for each possibility there is always more than one actual relation in which it stands, an actual relation either to other possibilities or to actualities.

It is awkward to say that a possibility is actually related to an actuality—as awkward as to say that an actuality is actually related to another actuality. Strictly, it is complexes that are related to one another, possibly or actually. And it is in orders of complexes that traits of actuality or possibility are located. But when, for example, a new possibility arises some time after a certain actualization takes place, there is an actual relation of posteriority. A possibility may therefore actually precede or succeed either another possibility or an actuality in a train of related complexes. The complex containing the possibility of educational expansion in the nineteen-fifties arose coevally with economic expansion. The possibility was subsequently actualized in educational expansion, and it also preceded another complex of government policy, a complex with a new group of actualities and possibilities. Retrospectively, each of these is traceable to previous actualities and possibilities; that is, each can be shown to stand in actual historical relation to complexes with the possibilities and actualities prevailing at an earlier time.

Many philosophers will never be persuaded that in the "actual world" there are significantly different orders of actuality. Their intuitive conviction favors a rough, tough, brute core that marks "true" actuality; it favors a privileged order ("the" actual world) that is pre-eminent even if other orders of actuality have to be conceded. Accordingly, a traditional source of puzzlement is the status of creatures like Apollo or unicorns or Hamlet. Surely unicorns are not actual in the "true" sense of the term? Not, of course, in the way that horses on my neighbor's farm are actual—just as horses on that farm are not actual in the way that contracts or inferences or sorrows are, and just as these are not actual in the way that intellectual trends or numerical relations or economic traditions are. Apollo, Hamlet, and unicorns are human products. Specifically, they are contrivances, or products of art. Products of any kind, like complexes that are not products, have traits of both actuality and possibility. Once the order which contains unicorns is produced, it has its distinctive possibilities and actualities: unicorns are actually white; it is not possible for unicorns to talk. Literature is more perplexing to philosophers, even to the aestheticians among them, than any other of the socially established arts. Its products, after being conceded a spatiotemporal term in the form of paper, ink, and furrowed brows, are supposed to vanish into the "imagination," with no metaphysical nonsense permitted. Sculpture and painting somehow fare better. No one refers to their products in the way that literary products are referred to—as works of "fiction." Strangely, a sculptured Apollo is more acceptably actual than the creature of literature that bears the same name.

Complexes about which philosophers have felt helpless and unclear they sometimes describe as "subsisting." This term has been applied both to possibilities and to the actualities which cannot be regarded as spatially or temporally located. "Subsistences" traditionally have no home but heaven (or limbo), and they have been said, either reluctantly or jubilantly, to be in some sense "non-natural"—which is also, it will be remembered, an appellation occasionally used for so-called indefinable or indescribable "qualities." Some "realm" or other is always systematically reserved for subsistences. The understandable reaction to them is to move away from them, usually very far. And so an opposite extreme interprets what it calls "non-existing entities" as verbal confusions which designate nothing, as verbal disguises for much more familiar "entities," as aberrancies of one sort or another.

The two extremes are equally desperate, and they have always worn the visage of *ad hoc* fabrications. When interest is shifted from the classification of entities to the natural location of complexes, the better way is at hand. According to an influential type of current procedure, never mind the troublesome complex and pay attention to the linguistic expression at issue; pay attention to rules and usages. There can be no doubt about the frequent appositeness of this advice. But in more far-reaching metaphysical investigation we shall often do better to turn the maxim around: never mind the linguistic expression, either its formal grammar or its habitual usage; pay attention precisely to the troublesome complex, and trace its relations to complexes whose natural location seems more accessible. It is better to seek and try to define

a broader conception of actuality than to relegate difficult and compelling complexes to the doubtful dignity
of a classification apart. All levels, all modes of actuality, have their own natural environment. The least
familiar of them, like all the others, are more than
verbal and less than magical.

v

Consider two contradictory traits. They are sometimes
both found to prevail as possibilities in one and the
same order of complexes. They are never both found
to prevail as actualities in one and the same order. A
given tree will possibly grow to 100 feet and possibly
not grow to 100 feet. It never will actually grow to
100 feet and actually not grow to 100 feet. The principal consideration with respect to actuality is that if
mutually contradictory complexes are actual, they
never prevail in the same order; if mutually contradictory complexes prevail in the same order, they are
not actualities.

The conception of actuality is thus framed by a contrast between actuality and possibility on a crucial
point. All prevalences restrict and exclude, but not all
in the same way. Actualities are exclusive and restrictive in a way that possibilities are not. In this "way,"
enunciated by the preceding paragraph, actualities always are exclusive, no matter what the order; whereas
possibilities sometimes are and sometimes are not, depending on the order. The same point may be stated
with a different focus: So far as its traits of actuality are
concerned, any order is always exclusive of traits in a
certain way; but so far as its traits of possibility are

concerned, the order is not always exclusive of traits in that way.

The pitfalls of terminology here are treacherous, and there is an ever-present threat of misleading formulation. To speak of a possibility prevailing means that it is actualizable. Contradictory traits may both prevail as possibilities in the sense that both are actualiz*able*, both are eligible for actualization, given certain conditions that obtain. Now, although we can say that contradictory traits are sometimes both *found to prevail as possibilities* in an order, it is tricky to say that contradictory traits are sometimes both *found to be possible* in an order. For the usual (and often quite acceptable) suggestion of the phrase "found to be possible" is "found to be actualized." Contradictory traits may both be actualizable (eligible for actualization) but never are both actualized in the same order.

The danger of confusion can be further illustrated by asking why, if contradictory traits may both prevail as possibilities in an order, it does not follow that "round squares" are possible. But again, the words "are possible" here carry over from another context the import "found to be actualized." At any given time roundness and squareness are both possibilities (both actualizable) in a lump of dough. But at no time are both together actualized as the shape of that lump. Further, though roundness and squareness both prevail as possibilities in an order, "round squareness" never prevails as a possibility; it is not actualizable.

Another pitfall of usage threatens to confound the original distinction. We said: (1) Contradictory traits are sometimes both found to prevail as possibilities in an order. We did not say: (2) Contradictory possibilities are sometimes found in an order. We did not say (2) because it is ambiguous. It *can* be taken to mean the same as (1), and then there is no problem. But by analogy with certain customary locutions, statement (2) might be taken to mean "It is possible for contradictory traits to coexist in an order," and this is false, because to coexist is to be actual.

It is accurate to say: (1a) A given tree will possibly grow to 100 feet and possibly not grow to 100 feet. It is not accurate to say: (2a) It is possible for a given tree to grow to 100 feet and it also is not possible for that tree to grow to 100 feet. Statement (2a) is false because it consists of two component statements which contradict each other. It asserts that there are some conditions under which a tree will grow to 100 feet, and that there are no conditions under which a tree will grow to 100 feet. It is a statement not about contradictory traits which prevail as possibilities but about contradictory traits which prevail as actualities. The locution "it is possible . . ." "it is not possible . . ." means "there are actual conditions which *allow* . . ." "there are actual conditions which do *not* allow . . ."

The conception of actuality in terms of the ways in which a prevalence is restrictive is designed to contrast it with possibility. (a) It is not designed to lead to the *discovery* of what is actual, to tell where to find actualities. (b) It is not designed to provide a "sufficient" condition for actualities to arise. (c) It presupposes complexes with traits, such that there are traits of possibility and traits of actuality. (d) It is designed to allow the inclusion, as actualities, of all the less

familiar and allegedly "problematical" instances posed
in section iv.

These instances exhibit the kind of restrictiveness
that any other actualities exhibit. A possibility never
both actually precedes and does not precede another
possibility in the same order. In the serial relations
of integers, 5 is never both actually greater than and
not greater than 4. In a given deductive order, a proposition q is never both actually implied by another
proposition p and actually not implied by it. In the
[literary] order of mythic creatures, unicorns are never
actually both all white and not all white, any more
than horses are, whether they are horses in a literary
order or an order of farm life in Vermont. Apollo is
not actually both graceful and ungainly, whether in
sculpture or epic. Hamlet cannot be said both actually
to have loved and actually never to have loved Ophelia.

"Which are the non-actualities?" will be an inevitable objection. "Isn't any figment, any wild fancy, an
actuality if it is merely shown to meet the conditions
stated? When we think of pink elephants, are they
actual just because we can't think of them as also not
pink?"

Neither righteous indignation nor the appeal to
laughingstock examples will dissolve the analysis. The
pink elephants *thought,* the *images entertained,* the
discriminanda, are complexes, and they prevail in the
way that they prevail. It is not the funniness of the
prevalence that is pertinent here but the type of restrictiveness that belongs to it. The integrity of an
image is not less or more of an integrity than that of
an animal spatio-temporally located in Africa. The

fact that the complex is *produced* does not render it "non-actual" but, on the contrary, exposes its actuality together with the kind of determinateness that such an actuality has. The fact that it is produced in an order of thought or imagery, the fact that it does not "correspond" to some *other* actuality, has no bearing on its ordinality and its ordinal location. A produced actuality does not need a previous actuality as model. We think of things that resemble other things and of things that do not, just as we paint pictures that resemble spatial models and pictures that do not. The "pink elephants" example is traditionally selected to support an association of actuality with "efficacy," confusing one manifestation of "making a difference" with all manifestations. It is also traditionally selected because of the assumption, latent or otherwise, that the trivial is less "real" than the businesslike or the serious. The principle of ontological priority can denigrate the trivial actualities, but it cannot "de-actualize" them.

vi

Is it "possible" for 5 to be greater than 4? In a typical mode of philosophic expression, it is not possible because it is "necessary." And by the same token, it is not "possible" for 4 to be greater than 5; although in this case the reason it is not possible is not that it is necessary, but that, instead, it is "impossible."

According to the metaphysical determination we have made, that which specifically makes it impossible for 4 to be greater than 5 makes it possible for 5 to be greater than 4. And the conditions within this order

which make the latter possible also make it the sole
possibility, that is, "necessary." The prejudice that
stands in the way of recognizing this more general
approach and the more general usage that it entails,
stems, first, from the feeling of superfluity in the usage,
and second, from what is more than merely an in-
grained feeling, the mistaken assumption that what is
possible means only what is not yet actual or actualized.
But a complex which is actual may yet continue to be
possible. It is possible for a man to be sick; if he is
actually sick, it still is possible for him to be sick or
to be well. Analogously, it remains possible for 5 to
be greater than 4, albeit this is an actuality. The
conditions which make it possible, since they continue
to prevail, continue to make it possible. Expanding
the rationale of the matter: The possibility of 5 being
greater than 4, and the correlative impossibility of 4
being greater than 5, is a trait belonging to the complex known as the system of arithmetic. The fundamental traits that determine arithmetic and the number system are what make possible, and what preserve
the possibility of, a certain asymmetrical relation prevailing between the numbers 4 and 5. Where there
are "necessities" in an order, these are either actualities none of whose contraries is possible, or possibilities in relation to which there are no contrary possibilities that prevail.

vii

The contour of a natural complex was described in
Chapter I as "the continuity and totality of its locations, the interrelation of its integrities." The possibil-

ities of a natural complex are those traits which define its contour (or any of its integrities) in so far as this contour is to continue or be extended. This *defining* is "by" the complex. It is inherent in the complex. It is constitutionally basic. It is the kind of trait partly illustrated by the way in which an animal's sense organs define the immediate environmental prospect before it, or by the way in which a surveyor's instruments define the boundaries of a plot of land. In generalized terms, the traits of a complex define its contour (or, delineate a contour), and those [subaltern] traits which define or chart the "prospect before it" are its possibilities. On this conception of what may be called natural definition, every trait defines, and a possibility is one kind of defining.

Both etymologically and historically, definition has been construed as the setting of bounds or limits. Definition as the marking out, explicitly or implicitly, of the meanings of words—of complexes whose basic location is in an order of grammar or an order of behavior—is one type of limiting and of setting bounds. The dominant emphasis on this type in certain trends of thought seems to rest on the assumption that any other conception of definition is a threat to philosophic clarity. This in turn rests on other assumptions and issues: about the role which attention to clarity should play in philosophy; about whether clarity itself is best achieved by initial restrictions on procedure or by critical procedures that follow the free activity of philosophic reflection; about the nature of clarity, and whether it is achieved in one fundamental form or in many forms.

Beyond the issue concerning *what* is *subject* to definition—words only or other natural complexes as well, and perhaps complexes without restriction—lies the equally important issue concerning *how* definition is *accomplished.* Is definition, the marking out of bounds and limits, something accomplished by men alone, or is it a more pervasive process which should be recognized as natural definition? Understood as a human product, definition has been thought to fall mainly within the area of assertive judgment; to consist of resolutions or procedures or conventions or stipulations or stated hypotheses or bodies of statements designed to abet the validation of propositions. Little room has been left for the conception of definition as effected humanly in the process of contriving or of acting and doing. For it is first necessary to recognize exhibitive judgment and active judgment as modes of human utterance no less fundamental than assertive judgment. Once the nature of man is conceded to embrace ways of marking out, determining, and charting the world that are not confined to the production of formulae, the transition to a still broader category is accomplished. Natural definition is the definition of natural complexes that is accepted in practice when, for instance, it is recognized that an image is defined upon the retina, or when it is recognized that a course of events has defined the options available for action. If we are to take linguistic usage seriously as opening the way to metaphysical insight, to the discernment of unsuspected yet fundamental traits in nature, we cannot ignore the full testimony of such usage. It is in the framework of natural definition that the nature of possibility is here considered.

A motor car in operating condition includes a certain range of possibilities among its traits. When the car lacks fuel, when its generator is disconnected, or when its steering arm is rusted; when, in short, the mechanism's conditions are significantly different and certain of its actualities cease to prevail, certain of its possibilities cease to prevail, though others arise. With its traits of actuality the mechanism defines its current situation—its position, its dimensions and proportions, its relations to the environment and to persons. With its possibilities the mechanism inherently defines a prospect for itself. With different possibilities, it would define or mark out a different prospect. It lies ready in one way or another. Some circumstances it will tolerate, others not. For some eventualities it is eligible, for others not. And this is true of every complex, whether or not any part of its prospect has ever been actualized.

The prospect peculiar to a complex includes trivial repetition and routine conditional actualizations as well as minor and major alescences. It is not to be identified with a specific or unique future, but includes whatever, in the complex, allows continuation or extension. If, in Euclidean geometry, from a point outside a straight line, only one line can be drawn that is parallel to the given line, this is a possibility relating not to a contingent or specific future but to a conditional and patterned future, including future methodic operations or whatever exemplifies the conditions whenever they do. Under certain types of spatial conditions, this possibility concerning a parallel line is part of the "prospect" for a complex with spatial traits. Likewise, as long as the conditions prevail which make it possible for 5 to be greater than 4, this possibility continues intact as part of the prospect for arithmetical relations and arithmetical operations.

There is another, equivalent, way of interpreting the nature of possibility, one which serves better to sharpen the distinction between natural definition through actuality and natural definition through possibility. A possibility is a *prefinition* of the relevant traits in the contour of a natural complex. Prefinition embraces both extension or continuation and rooted conditions of that which is to constitute the extension. The specification "relevant traits" underscores the truth that not all complexes have the same possibilities, that not all possibilities "always were." But this specification also allows complexes to have a possibility or various possibilities in common. They may all prefine the same relevant traits; or more precisely, they may prefine a body of relevant traits in common, whatever other possibilities distinguish them from one another. †

A possibility *is* an extension of a complex—an extension prefined. A possibility is that prevalent extension or continuation of the contour of a natural complex, whereby certain traits that are related (or, not related) to certain other traits will be related (or, not related) to the other traits. By contrast, an actuality is that prevalence of a natural complex whereby certain traits are related (or, not related) to certain other traits.

What is prefined in a complex is not its future as such, whether it be a future of novel or of recurrent and typical traits, but certain relative *limits*, the limits immanent in its prevalence. The extension of a complex as prefined is an extension whereby not merely *A* may arise (or continue to prevail), but also *A*-or-*B*, or *A*-or-*B*-or-*C*-or-*D*. The possibilities, the various extensions prefined, encompass all that is relevant to the complex.

A prefinition may include, but should not be confounded with, a suggestion or signification. Prefinition is a matter of traits that may or may not have meaning for someone. It is in virtue of such traits, traits of possibility in a complex, that the complex may signify or suggest its prospect. What is possible belongs to a complex as such. What is signified is a further relation between the complex and discoverers or knowers, between the complex and another which is a complex of human expectation. A prefinition is therefore to be distinguished from a sign, which is indeed a trait but a far less comprehensive trait within a complex. A sign is the kind of trait whereby specific limits of the complex may be ascertained by present means. It is through signs that *knowledge* of the complex is extended by awareness of its possibilities, and by the association of known possibilities with their eventual or anticipated actualizations.

But even when the distinction between a sign of possibility and a prefinition is clear, another confusion threatens. Within the standpoint of human expectation, certain kinds of signs may be thought of as directing attention to "what is not yet." To speak of a possibility as "what is not yet" is tacitly to identify "what is" solely with the actual. The possibility prevails; it prevails now; it prevails no less than the complex in which it is a possibility, and no less than an actual circumstance of that complex. Far from being what is not yet, it is only what is not yet actualized. Established, innocent habits of speech notwithstanding, we should avoid speaking of possibilities as getting to be "realized," for the possibility is already "real," already prevalent. A possibility does not get real when it gets to be actualized, any more than an actuality gets real when it acquires new possibilities.

The prefinition is that which is intrinsic to the complex as it prevails, *that* complex, that order of traits. The *order*, with its makeup of traits, is what basically prefines. It is represented by its prefinitions or possibilities. If any complex is thought of as having had traits which it no longer has, it is also readily thought of as having traits which it no longer will have. Likewise, if it has traits which once it did not have, it will presumably have traits which now it does not have. But whatever the scope or character of its traits, and in whatever location they belong to it, its constitutional "chart" takes it beyond any given location. No complex, as we saw, can be said to be "complete" in all respects, because additional traits can be absolutely excluded only in so far as it ceases to prevail. Traits of relatedness to other complexes are imposed upon it. Thus it is always constitutionally framed by—it prefines—limits, no matter what their range or their relative similitude to its previous limits. The constituent traits of its gross prefinition are its possibilities. Possibilities, therefore, it always has, whether they vary in their general pattern or continue intact.

When a possibility is actualized, a natural complex

is modified. But the same possibility may continue to prevail for reactualization. The gross prefinition may be affected only negligibly, the limits prefined being what they were. But when a possibility comes about or expires, a different extension of the complex is prefined; the relevant traits are not the same. A possibility coming about would imply a swelling of the sphere of relevant traits only if all other possibilities in the complex remained constant. The same constancy would be required for the sphere of relevant traits to contract upon the expiration of a possibility. But a possibility never comes about or expires or varies in its relations, it is never alescent, unless the more inclusive complex in which it is located is alescent. Its alescence in this complex reflects a previous alescence of actuality; this actuality reflects a previous alescence of possibility; and so on backwards. (Although a possibility is always coeval with conditions of actuality, and an actuality with conditions of possibility, temporality or succession is inevitable; there are, after all, complexes preceding that with which a given possibility or actuality is coeval.) For a possibility to arise in a company of possibilities that otherwise prevails in all respects may seem "abstractly conceivable." But it is far easier to conceive of a possibility as entailing the alescence of other possibilities (not to mention its own subalterns) *all* of which reflect an alescent actuality. And when the latter is the case, a new possibility may mean not a swelling but a contraction of what is relevant. For example, certain complexes may arise which introduce the possibility of imminent human catastrophe. In the order of ethical action and reflection, this new possibility may entail a contraction in the sphere of relevance. A great variety of previously relevant ethical choices may shrink into the two relevant choices, of surviving or not surviving, each with a correspondingly shrunken number of subaltern options. The new possibility is a spoliative alescence.

When we speak of a possibility as a natural prefinition of relevant traits, we must note carefully what does and does not follow. A possibility is not identical with a limit. Nor can the limits of a complex, the boundaries within which its contour will extend, be said to "depend" upon its possibilities. The limit "depends" upon both possibilities and actualities. Except for colloquial convenience, a limit is not a trait "in" an actuality as such, not a trait "in" a possibility as such. A limit is prefined in a complex. A possibility is a prefinition of the limit—it is the prefined extension—of the complex. We cannot say that a possibility is what "limits" a complex; what limits it is the order of complexes in which it is located. And within this order, both possibilities and actualities are factors in the "limiting." Both are efficacious in the sense that both "count." Neither counts without the other. If we think of limiting as if it had to take the form of a process like physical causation, we are likely to miss the point, namely, that actuality merely as such can no more limit a complex than possibility merely as such, whether the limiting is the limiting of a physical event, a political force, or a religious doctrine.

Taken without qualification, the term "limit" ordinarily suggests restriction. Limits are the natural bases of finitude. If there were no limits, man would be unable to discriminate natural complexes. "Possibility," on the other hand, suggests expansion, at least in popular contexts; and indeed there is no essential connection between possibility and finitude. When a possibility is interpreted as a prefined extension of a complex, and as being therefore the natural definition of a relative limit, this does not imply that all complexes are in all respects finite. An infinite sequential order of numbers has limited and limiting traits, but this does not mean that it must have a final term. The possibilities inherent in the complex known as an infinite series are the natural definition of *its* relative limits, which are such, for example, as to allow any number to be succeeded by another.

viii

Potentialities and powers are those possibilities which are customarily discriminated in complexes having a well-known pattern of traits. It is rarely considered surprising when a complex fails to actualize "all" of its powers or potentialities, but a certain range of regularity if not frequency of actualization is expected. This regularity may define a natural history, or it may measure a natural process; in which cases, it would reflect a type or form. Hurricanes, spiders, and medical graduates are recurrent exemplifications of possibilities that are socially classified. Powers and potentialities are often attributed to complexes in so far as they are unique, perhaps no less often than to complexes in so far as they are typical. A human individual is commonly said to have attained "the height of his powers," that is, as an individual. Somewhat more puzzling is the equally common declaration that an individual has *not* attained the height of his powers. What underlies these ways of speaking is an expectancy based upon the observation of possibilities that have already been actualized and that are deemed continuous with, or similar to, others unactualized, all of them scaled in terms of the greater and the lesser. To speak of what does or does not represent an individual's powers is itself a version of the typical—what is typical of that individual.

Thus powers and potentialities are possibilities that are mainly thought of as prevalent rather than alescent. But even when they are said to be acquired (rather than "innate"), the acquisition itself is assumed to take place within limits that are more or less acknowledged. The general emphasis, in a rather loose way, is upon possibilities that are "essential" and not "accidental."

It is desirable to make a distinction between potentiality and power, partly by way of recognizing certain kinds of ordinal differences, and partly by way of recommending usage. Sometimes a possibility is both a potentiality and a power. The distinction would mean that the possibility has two overlapping traits.[23]

A potentiality prevails as a member of a family or group. In order that there should be a potentiality, there must be potentialities which constitute a body of similars. A potentiality is representative, and it is discriminated as prevailing because of its representative status. A power, on the other hand, though it may have species of its own, is a possibility that is as likely to be discriminated for its unrepresentative status as for its kinship with other possibilities. No power, no possibility of any kind, is isolated or disconnected from others. A man who has the power to sleep and dream at will must certainly have other powers related to this. But in such instances the emphasis on the possibility being a power rather than a potentiality is the emphasis on its idiosyncratic or relatively unique aspect. In the same vein, we should say that an acorn has the potentiality of becoming an oak, but not that it has the potentiality of scarring a toad on which it falls—this would have to be a power belonging to the acorn.

It is plausible to think of certain potentialities as never being actualized. To say of a man that he has the potentiality to produce things that are great and important does not imply that he has done so or will do so. Again it is the representative status of the potentiality that comes into play. The man's potentiality is a promise based on his potentialities. The family vouches for its members. But to say of a man that he has the *power* to produce things that are great and important is a more extravagant claim. A power does imply previous actualization of a possibility—which is then recognized as that power. A potentiality once actualized may be regarded as a power. To say that any complex has the power to effect a result but never has effected it, has proven to be a mischievous way of speaking and suggests a specific claim without warrant. Such claims encourage the gratuitous positing of traits *in vacuo* and the multiplication of powers (including "occult" powers) by groundless speculation. Mankind has the potentiality of destroying all its democratic institutions. It can be said to have the power of so doing only in the sense that it has approximated this degree of power by achieving powers which increasingly resemble the required destructiveness.

Although a power as such is not necessarily representative of a group of possibilities, it may be present in a group of possibilities which are potentialities; and indeed, some power must belong within a family of potentialities. The man who has the potentiality to do important things represents not only other and allied potentialities, but some which have been actualized. Although the human potentiality of destroying all democratic institutions does not amount to the power of doing so, it presupposes various powers among its allied potentialities—powers of destroying *this or that* democratic institution; powers of *destroying,* in one way or another.

A potentiality, then, is a possibility located in a range of conditions that are associated, that prevail all together, in a kind of collective identity. It is a possibility in a family of possibilities. A given potentiality may never be actualized. But one or more of its kin— other possibilities belonging to the family—must have been actualized for the family to prevail. This latter condition, in other words, is that among the potentialities in a family, some must be powers.

A power is a possibility that has been actualized in some degree and can be recognized as [that] generic [power] in the next instance of its actualization.[24] Not every power is a potentiality, and not every potentiality is a power. A given power does not presuppose a family of [similar] possibilities to which it belongs, but it does of course presuppose other possibilities to which it is related.

Powers and potentialities are most often attributed to complexes regarded as agential. (An "agent" is presumably a "patient" too, and vice versa. "Active" and "passive" powers, as traditionally distinguished, alike apply to what is here designated as an agent.) Although every complex is efficacious in the sense that its prevalence makes a difference (see section v above), agents are said to be "causally" efficacious. More specifically, powers and potentialities belong to individuals and associations of individuals. They belong to trees and forests, ants and ant colonies, chemical solutions, governments, books. They seem not to belong to structures, processes, or histories as such, but only to the complexes partly constituted by traits of structure, process, or historicity. Thus, powers do not belong to a catenary, to speech, or to the history of George Washington, but to a bridge with catenarian cables, to organisms endowed with speech, to George Washington throughout his history.

The attribution of powers and potentialities to "agents" has its justification. The problem involved is a problem not so much of correctness as of adequacy. The notion of an agent, like the identification of specific agents, suffers from a good deal of uncertainty. It implies the magnification of one complex above others in a chain, and it reveals the usual cravings of both philosophers and laymen for "solid" subjects which at bottom are no more than products of pre-established interest. Attribution of potentialities and powers to the solid subjects, in priority to less easily namable complexes, underestimates these very subjects as bearers of possibility. There are innumerable possibilities "for" an agent or subject. Since these are more comprehensive than that agent's "own" possibilities (his potentialities), they are in a sense more fundamental. In order to understand complexes like bureaucracy or personality, it is imperative to pass from the smaller sphere of possibility to the larger and more fundamental one.

But even aside from the matter of how large should be the sphere of possibilities defining an "agent," the agent's "own" powers and potentialities must be construed as subaltern complexes correlative with actualities. The powers of George Washington belonged to him *in* his historical being, and *as* a historical being, and not merely throughout his history. Washington as a complex was not temporally encased in a "history." Powers do certainly belong to a bridge. But a bridge-structure as a complex must be understood as an order or relational multiplicity of traits, some of which, namely potentialities and powers, prefine the traits of its continued prevalence. So powers and potentialities must be seen, not merely as representing a unity, but as embedded in a multiplicity.

ix

Possibility is fundamental to the metaphysics of laws and universals. The question whether laws and universals are "real or unreal" is as empty as such a question always is when applied to discriminanda. Even if the criterion of "reality" were value and importance, laws and universals would not be outranked, for in human thought about the world they are incredibly pervasive.

If we think of law as we do when we speak of laws of motion or laws of heredity, the most insistent conviction is that a complex prevails which does not consist [only] in a way of speaking, difficult as the analysis of its traits may be. Obviously the complex does not prevail in the same sense as a body in space does. It should be plain also that traits like "here" and "now" or questions concerning "where" and "when" are inept as well as elliptical. Through all of the repeated convictions, doubts, and perplexities about law, the sense of a prevalence becomes more meaningful rather than weakened. Whether law is held to be in an eternal realm or in the mind, whether it is held to be a form of statement or a form independent of statement, whether it is held to be a "construct" or an "objective reality," a complex and order of traits [indomitably] obtains.

Once the prevalence of a law is conceded without further qualification, the question arises whether we are dealing with an actuality or a possibility. If a law is an actuality, what is the kind of possibility of which it is an actualization? A law is exemplified. But what could it mean for an actuality to be exemplified? Actualities are imitated, and they may even be said to be "manifested," both directly and remotely, by their effects. But only possibilities are exemplified through actualization.

A law is a possibility with continuous or recurrent actualization. It is the possibility that under certain conditions certain relations will obtain; relations, for instance, of dependence or sequence. It is one of the possibility-traits in an order. It prefines and contributes to the gross (or collective) prefinition of relative limits in the order. The social conditions under which laws are initially discriminated (discovered, enunciated) express the human concern with possibilities that are stable and abiding. The specific conditions under which laws are actualized, in contrast to other possibilities, arouse perennial interest because the very notion of law suggests wide scope—pervasiveness or comprehensiveness of a high degree. Such scope makes a dramatic impact upon inquiry, entailing relatedness among complexes that have been independently encountered, complexes as yet unencountered, and complexes not encounterable except in the most indirect ways.

Although the point is evident from what has been said in various contexts, we must distinguish between (a) the conditions under which a possibility prevails as such within an order, and (b) the conditions in the order which actualize this possibility. The distinction accordingly applies to law. There are conditions under which a law as such (as possibility) prevails, and there are conditions which actualize the law. The former conditions are unique to the order, the latter conditions typical or recurrent within the order.

(a) A law of capitalist economy prevails as long as the conditions of capitalist order prevail. Geological laws prevail as long as the earth prevails. Economic and geological laws themselves may be alescent; that is, there may be variation which arises in the regularly actualized possibilities of the capitalist economy and the earth. The economic and terrestrial orders are in turn located in more comprehensive orders, such as the order of socio-economic behavior and the planetary system. These orders have their laws or regularly actualized possibilities. The relation between the more and the less comprehensive orders is an actuality.

(*b*) Alescence in the conditions under which a law is actualized—for example, variations in the frequency with which these conditions are present—does not affect the integrity of the law as possibility, nor the integrity of its actualizations.

The actualizations of a law constitute a class of conspicuously similar complexes. In relation to one another, they are marked by what may be called a thematic or rhythmical trait—thematic where the actualization is continuous (as in laws of motion), rhythmic where it is recurrent (as in laws of heredity). Sometimes, as in the law of non-contradiction (which is not a "stipulated" or a "legislated" law, any more than the laws of motion are), the actualizations or instances seem less strikingly similar because of the very pervasiveness of the law, or better, the pervasiveness of the order within which the possibility resides. And yet upon reflection, the similarity of the instances (as we may call the repeated and continued absence of contrary instances) is the more impressive. For in the case of this law, unlike laws prevalent in other types of order, we cannot describe conditions that would spoliate its integrity or diminish its scope, though we can describe conditions under which it would not be relevant.

Similarities and universals are not the same. But they are first cousins. The vexatious problem of universals derives from puzzlement over the "reference" of universal terms, and the same problem arises with respect to classes, kinds, or forms. To say that universals are "nothing but terms," verbal devices used to manipulate particulars (to identify, classify, compare them), rests on the opinion that these particulars "in reality" have nothing in common and are absolutely particular. Absolute particulars would have to be absolutely unique. Since the notion of absolute uniqueness, as there is small need to repeat, implies disconnectedness and unrelatedness to anything else, each particular would have to inhabit an inaccessible domain of its own. But whether these particulars are "in the mind" and invested with similarity (including common involvement in a relation) to cover their unintelligible nakedness, or in the world and utterly alone "in themselves," the notions of similarity and difference are inevitable and indispensable.

Wherever complexes are comparable or commensurate, they show similarities and differences from each other. A similarity or a difference between two complexes is an actuality. Nor is it a matter of great consequence whether we say that two complexes are "similar" or that they are "the same in a given respect." If we are to avoid the absurdity polar to "absolutely different," namely "absolutely the same," we always require specification of the respect in which a trait prevails, its order and ordinal location. Notoriously, philosophers have been much more willing to regard as an actuality A's being different from B than A's being similar to B. When the actuality of the latter state is accepted, it becomes relevant to ask what it is an actualization of. An actuality presupposes some possibility in a complex. The actuality of traits in so far as they are similar presupposes the possibility known as a universal. And a universal may be defined as the possibility of different complexes having traits that are similar in a given respect.

"But what about universals without instances?" "What would triangularity be if there *were* no triangles?" "And what is perfect honesty when there *are* no perfectly honest people?" Laws and universals are possibilities bearing generic and specific names, although there are innumerable possibilities which have been and always will be socially identified, especially among powers and potentialities. Whether at any time there are triangular shapes or not, whether at any time triangles are thought about or not, and named or not, the possibility of such a shape may prevail. It prevails, of course, in an order consisting of actualities and other possibilities—not in heaven. In an order where bodies and shapes, and the possibility and actuality of relations prevail, [the possibility] triangularity is a subaltern complex. Actual triangles belong to this same order. As for "perfect honesty," if it has enough meaning to be *discerned* as a possibility, it would be located in a social and moral order of complexes about which men are confessedly far less clear. If such a possibility were as yet without any actualized instances, it might be regarded as an "ideal," a possibility the actualization of which is never "completed" but "approached" through indefinitely greater degrees of a specified activity.

The question whether what are said to be universals are to be regarded *as* universals, *as* possibilities, becomes more important than the question whether universals "subsist," whether they have being "apart from particulars" or only "in particulars." When we know what we are talking about in the employment of universal terms, we can usually trace and discover some traits of the order in which the universal is relevant. Tracing and discovering is made difficult when universals and laws are regarded as "essences" in an eternal realm of essence, or as "eternal objects." Such versions of laws and universals mirror that view of possibility according to which "pure possibilities" or "pure potentials" were and are and always will be possibilities, the same possibilities, no matter what prevails and what arises, no matter what actualities there are and what actualizations have taken place. Possibilities, we are to believe, must be both eternal and everlasting: eternal in the sense of being inherently exempt from alescence; everlasting in the sense of being always subject to actualization—or should we say embodiment, perhaps incarnation?

There are kinds of universals and laws, kinds of possibilities, just as there are kinds of actualities. Possibilities, naturally, resemble one another as well as differ from one another. If particular possibilities can exemplify a general or universal possibility, and if a universal is itself a possibility, then there are possibilities of possibilities. In a "realm of essence" the ensuing complications might be troublesome. Among the complexes of nature, it is no less possible for possibilities to arise than it is possible for actualities to arise. But this also is evident on general theoretical grounds in the metaphysics of complexes. For the possibility of any complex is the possibility of all its traits, including possibilities. Only the locution is troublesome before it is expanded and qualified, and before the language of "entities" and "subsistences" is shown to be irrelevant to the theory of complexes. Since every actuality has its possibilities, the possibility that *it* reflects is reflected by these possibilities.

x

In Chapter III and earlier in this chapter, the distinction was made between (*a*) the cloudy idea of "knowing what is possible," and (*b*) rationally establishing that a possibility prevails. When it is said that it is always much easier to know what is possible than to know what is actual, the implication intended is that possible states of affairs can always be "imagined": just think "consistently" of any traits believed relevant and juxtapose them. Since "thought is free," and there is no constraint by "the facts," an unlimited range is open to us. Such a view, it was shown, ignores the ordinal traits under which any genuine knowledge of actuality or of possibility is achieved. To establish that a possibility prevails, and that it is not simply a verbally non-contradictory specification, one unsure even of its own non-contradictoriness, the knowledge of inclusive complexes is prerequisite.

But the objection may be raised that with such restrictions we never can know what is a possibility belonging to a complex. First, we do not know how determinate are the boundaries of any complex within which the possibility is to be sought. And second, even a clarification of the boundaries or limits would not help, for what has not yet been actualized cannot be identified. If the ascertainment of possibilities by non-contradictory supposition or "conceivability-criteria" is excluded, then, far from knowing innumerably more possibilities than actualities, we can know none at all.

In effect, this argument is one of a kind which denies to knowledge of possibility what would not be expected in knowledge of actuality, namely, absolute certitude and perfect awareness of limits. It also conveys the impression that knowledge of actuality is essentially a "long hard look" affair, as if the history of human inquiry, and the natural and social sciences in particular, were not witness enough to the contrary. And the argument suggests, finally, that knowledge of possibility and knowledge of actuality are separable.

Knowledge of possibility and knowledge of actuality would be separable if possibility and actuality were separable. No doubt, a man who has been swindled of his money knows the actuality of his loss without making an analysis of all the possibilities involved. But of possibilities he must think if he thinks at all—what made the theft possible and how it might have been avoided, what possibilities are open in the wake of the theft, what redress is possible, what possible meanings there are in the situation. Identification of a possibility depends upon encounter with similar possibilities previously actualized, or upon encounter with an actuality made understandable in the light of such possibilities. Not that we abstain from imagining or conceiving traits. But the traits imagined must be indicated or aroused by the traits of an order about which the thought is taking place. On the basis of the order as known previously, we generalize about its present possibilities. We guess what "may be" on the basis of other, analogous "may be" guesses. Some of these earlier possibilities were not actualized and others were, and the company of possibilities then present for consideration permitted parallelisms, continuities, and resemblances to be detected.

Practical knowledge and identification of possibilities rests basically upon having expectations, not necessarily about future occurrences, but about the outcome of processes and the efficacy of methods. Everyday expectations reflect knowledge of an order within common experience. Novel expectations reflect more intricate avenues of query. Expectation implies possibilities entertained. More meaningful than to ask how possibilities are identified or known is to ask whether possibilities can ever be humanly ignored. The merest breath a man takes favors one possibility and renders others obsolete. At this end of his scale, with such lowly maneuvers of his organism, he keeps pace with other animals and the plants. All are unwitting producers as well as executors of possibilities. At the other end of his scale, where he is unique in the manner of his kind, he methodically actualizes possibilities that he has produced or apprehended. In so doing, he also keeps actualizing himself. He is not the sole or even the most basic determinant of his own actualization.

His is not the only kind of complex that is continually in process of actualization. His kind alone, however, is able to dwell with the possibilities, and this is crucial for his degradation or salvation.

NOTES TO THE ORIGINAL EDITION

1. Conceptual portrayal is part of the exhibitive function of philosophy, as distinguished from the assertive function. Philosophic method is discussed in each of the three predecessors of the present book (which have been listed in the Preface).

2. G. H. Mead, *The Philosophy of the Present,* edited by A. E. Murphy (Chicago and London, 1932), p. 1.

3. Methodic activity is the purposive ramification of judgment in any of its modes—assertive, active, exhibitive. When methodic activity is informed by the interrogative spirit, by invention and probing, it constitutes *query.* Query is the genus of which inquiry or science is one species—the species concerned with the ramification and validation of assertive judgment. See *The Concept of Method,* passim; *Nature and Judgment,* Chapter II; and *Toward a General Theory of Human Judgment,* passim.

4. Quite apart from the definition of metaphysics, there are champions of the term "existence" who consider it adequate and versatile enough. W. V. Quine, for example, derides "those philosophers who have united in ruining the good old word 'exist.' " See his *From a Logical Point of View* (rev. ed.; Cambridge, Mass., 1961), p. 3.

5. John Locke, *An Essay concerning Human Understanding,* IV, vi, 11.

6. John Dewey, *Experience and Nature* (2d ed.; New York, 1929), p. 85.

7. G. W. Leibniz, *Discourse on Metaphysics,* translated by G. R. Montgomery (Chicago and London, 1931), Proposition VIII.

8. Edmund Husserl, *Cartesian Meditations,* translated by Dorion Cairns (The Hague, 1960), p. 18.

9. J. H. Randall, Jr., *Nature and Historical Experience* (New York, 1958), p. 131.

10. Not only "being" but "existence" and "actuality" have been said to allow of degrees. And degree is sometimes expressed by specific kinds of "more" and "less." Thus: "Intuition not only exists, but is the most intense form of existence." George Santayana, *The Realm of Spirit* (New York, 1940), p. 94. Or to quote a more recent position: "What is actual *is* in a more intensive sense than what is merely possible or potential." Albert Hofstadter, "Truth of Being," *Journal of Philosophy* (1965), p. 171. What it means to *exist* more or less "intensely," or to *be* in a more and a less "intensive sense," does not emerge satisfactorily, if at all, from the context of the statements quoted.

11. According to Whitehead, "a coordinate division of an actual occasion . . . can *be conceived* as an actual occasion with its own actual world . . ." Such conception is described as "hypothetical" and as "potential." Whitehead says that "just as for some purposes, one atomic actuality can be treated *as though* it were many coordinate actualities, in the same way, for other purposes, a nexus of many actualities can be treated *as though* it were one actuality." Otherwise stated: ". . . In addition to the merely potential subdivisions of a satisfaction into coordinate feelings, there is the merely potential aggregation of actual entities into a super-actuality in respect to which the *true actualities* play the part of coordinate divisions" (italics added). See A. N. Whitehead, *Process and Reality* (New York, 1929), p. 439.

12. See A. N. Whitehead, *Process and Reality*, pp. 126, 129; and *Adventures of Ideas* (New York, 1933), p. 262.

13. See Chapter IV, section iii, for a generalized statement of this point, namely, that every natural complex may be said to be efficacious.

14. See the study by Milton K. Munitz, *The Mystery of Existence: An Essay in Philosophical Cosmology* (New York, 1965).

15. This order is the proceptive domain; the relevant com-

plexes in this order are procepts; and it is in this order that the individual is a proceiver. See *Toward a General Theory of Human Judgment* and *Nature and Judgment*.

16. For "perpetually perishing parts of succession," see Locke, *Essay*, II, xiv, 1. For "actions," "each perishing the moment it begins," see II, xxvii, 3. See also II, xv, 12: time as "perishing distance."

17. Perhaps it is unnecessary to say that "arising" here has nothing to do with the notion of "rise" so often used by historians ("the rise of nationalism," "the rise of the West"). Both rise and decline may be manifestations of alescence or "arising."

18. W. V. Quine speaks of an "overpopulated universe," with its "slum of possibles." He deplores "expanding our universe to include so-called *possible entities*." One can hardly deny that there are philosophers whose ontological notions have not been of the most defensible kind. But Quine's own formulation of the issue loads the dice in the opposite direction. His continual use of "entities" as a generic term tends to make even a sober analysis of possibility suspect. He speaks seldom of "possibilities," and repeatedly of "possible things," "possible entities," and "possibles"—preserving the suggestion of actualities misplaced or fabricated. His metaphors, witty as they are, carry their own dubious assumptions. Concerned about gratuitously "expanding our universe," he does not consider whether the universe has been gratuitously contracted, perhaps by sheer philosophic failure. Ockham's razor is an instrument that requires the utmost judiciousness and delicacy of philosophic perception: it is exceptionally dangerous, and exceptionally difficult to use. It has, of course, been wielded with greatest relish by those who, like Quine and in his phrase, "have a taste for desert landscapes." See *From a Logical Point of View*, Chapter I.

19. A locution similar to that of Quine ("entities or experiences that are possible but not actual," "possible entities") is used by Nelson Goodman, who reaches the conclusion: "We have come to think of the actual as one among many possible

worlds. We need to repaint that picture. All possible orders lie within the actual one." But neither of these alternatives is satisfactory, and no satisfactory theory can be achieved without adequate categories and a positive framework. Logical apparatus can expose problems in a given theory of possibility. But by itself it cannot "repaint the picture." See Goodman's *Fact, Fiction, and Forecast* (Cambridge, Mass., 1955), p. 56.

20. See the analysis of the status of logical principles by Ernest Nagel in *Logic without Metaphysics* (Glencoe, Ill., 1956), pp. 55–92.

21. See Henri Bergson, "The Possible and the Real," in *The Creative Mind* (New York, 1946).

22. I too have spoken of a power as "actual," in the sense that "it is different, for example, from the supposition or notion of a power" (*The Concept of Method*, p. 136). The "actuality" thus referred to, however, is clearly the actual *possession* of a power.

23. There seems to be no easy way of deciding whether the less frequently used English term "potency" has the connotative force of "potentiality" or of "power."

24. This definition is a somewhat more precise version of that given in *The Concept of Method*, p. 100.

APPENDIX I

SELECTIONS FROM *THE SOUTHERN JOURNAL OF PHILOSOPHY*, 14:1, 1976

REPLY TO RECK:
THE STRUCTURE OF THE WHOLE,
THE LOCATION OF THE PARTS‡

After discussing in some detail various innovations, features and values of my philosophic structure, and after describing how the leading ideas are related, Reck concludes that the whole setup is arbitrary. It is not clear, however, whether he considers all systematic philosophy arbitrary to some extent, and whether he considers such a conclusion to be an inevitable paradox.

Ordinarily, when we say that a philosophic view is arbitrary, we mean (a) that it has no justification whatever and is supported at best by non-philosophic reasons; or (b) that the reasons given in its behalf are no better than the reasons given in behalf of a contrary view; or (c) that the same reasons given in its behalf could be given in behalf of the contrary. The latter two senses entered into my account, a few years ago, of what I called a *strain* of arbitrariness in Whitehead's system. But to speak of an †

---

‡Originally published in *The Southern Journal of Philosophy* 14:1 (1976), pp. 47-53.

entire philosophy as arbitrary, to ask, as Reck does, whether a categorial scheme is arbitrary, is quite another matter, and one which I find perplexing....

If a philosophy is significant in any way at all, if it provides a mode of interpreting and clarifying major complexities of the world, what sense does it make to call it arbitrary unless we are to despair of philosophy altogether? It makes more sense to think of philosophies as illuminating or sterile, provocative or unimaginative. What would be the antonym of "arbitrary" that would give it meaning when used in this wholesale fashion?

Reck, however, seems to have a specific line of reasoning concerning the alleged arbitrariness of my outlook. Stated largely in his own words, it runs as follows: "Buchler's own philosophy is primarily exhibitive....As exhibitive it would seem to be devoid of cognitive significance." Buchler indeed does say that the exhibitive aspect of philosophy is no less cognitive than the assertive. But he fails to show how "the cognitive significance of a categorial scheme construed as exhibitive judgment may be determined; how, in brief, its truth value may be ascertained....If Buchler's philosophy depends ultimately on exhibitive judgments, on what grounds should it be accepted? Ultimately it can be supported by no arguments, since it is supposed to establish the standards to judge the validity of arguments. Ultimately, therefore, Buchler's philosophy is arbitrary."

I call to Reck's attention the following considerations:

(1) What does it mean to say my philosophy is "primarily exhibitive?" How did Reck arrive at the "primarily?" Is there a way of measuring the relative amounts of assertiveness and exhibitiveness? Strangely enough,

Reck says that my own movement back and forth between the two proves "it is difficult if not impossible to render precise the complex interrelation between exhibitive and assertive judgments in philosophy." Now this point too is seen as an objection to my conception of philosophy. But the two sets of objections don't jibe. And Reck can't have it both ways. If you can't clearly determine the interrelation of the exhibitive and the assertive in my philosophy, you can't say my philosophy is "primarily exhibitive."

(2) Both in what I have just quoted and in what I quoted from the argument about arbitrariness, Reck speaks in the plural of "exhibitive judgments." He speaks of "exhibitive judgments in philosophy" and of my philosophy as "depending on exhibitive judgments." The locution and its context suggests that he tends to think of exhibitive judgment in philosophy as consisting of units, as premises, corresponding to the way assertive judgment typically is thought of as consisting of propositions. But a philosophy judges or discriminates exhibitively not through individual units or compounded units but through its categorial order.

(3) Reck seems to assume that we can stand off, look at a philosophy, and ask: "Should it be accepted, or should it not be accepted?" as if we were interviewing an applicant for a job. He also sees the whole structure as either supported or not supported by arguments. Where these arguments should come from, and on what philosophic basis they should be used to exercise their autocratic function, he does not say. Apparently in evaluating a structure we are to ignore such questions as: how people might be influenced or stimulated by it, what applicable ideas it can give them, what analyses, attitudes, or

distinctions they can profit from, what unsuspected patterns or relations in the world it might enable them to discern, what comprehensive viewpoint it can afford them and what conceptual language it can provide them with. We are to suppose that these considerations have nothing to do with the general question, on what grounds should this philosophy be "accepted" or "not accepted?"

(4) Reck, wondering how I would determine the cognitive significance of the exhibitive categorial scheme, sums up by asking "how, in brief, its truth value may be ascertained." He thus equates "cognitive significance" with "truth value." In traditional terms the equation might be understandable, but in my structure it is confused. For exhibitive judgment is neither true nor false. That kind of determination pertains to assertive judgment. Exhibitive judgment may be knowledge, but it is not true. It does not contend and it makes no claim. Thus my rejection of an exclusively propositional conception of knowledge and my rejection of the truth-value mode of determination as universally applicable makes Reck's crucial question unmeaning in my framework. If he wishes nevertheless to ask how the cognitive value of exhibitive judgment is ascertained, and thereby disregard the types of gain I have mentioned, I offer two brief answers. The first is a counter-question: How is the cognitive value of *assertive* judgment in philosophy ascertained, regardless of whose philosophy we are considering? The second is that I do not know how to *measure* cognitive value in philosophy, but that if I have not conveyed at least an *awareness* of the kind of cognitive value philosophy can achieve through its collaboration of assertive and exhibitive judgment, I have no further explanation to give.

Thus, because Reck's assumptions about arbitrariness do not apply to my philosophy, his conclusion could only be true on grounds other than those he has specified. I turn now to his point, also presumably about arbitrariness, that "Buchler affirms naturalism; but he reveals a humanism which undermines his naturalism." There seem to be three sets of statements in which Reck spells this out . . . . :

(1) "It is not merely that the general ontology is subordinate to the metaphysics of utterance because it is expressed in judgment; it is rather that man, understood by means of the categories of the human process, so permeates judgment and most emphatically exhibitive judgment that he is writ larger than nature."

(2) "The metaphysics of the human process embraces the general ontology as its own portrayal"; "all the categories are products, human judgments."

(3) "Buchler's philosophy is grounded in the human individual."

Now *all* philosophers who employ categories frame or shape these categories. Each category as expressed is the product of one who uses it, and sometimes the product of a tradition. But being a product doesn't mean that what it discriminates and finds is a product. We produce the finding, not what is found. Our theory of finding does not swallow up our theory of the found. The fact that I have given much attention to products and their status as judgments does not imply that the world I judge is subordinated to the theory of judgment. According to my conception of philosophy, every philosopher judges complexes of the world. Are only those views of the world not swallowed up which are unaccompanied by a theory of judgment? And are such views swallowed up and subordinated when a theory of judgment is developed? The moral

seems to be that if it is not your intention to write man
larger than nature, don't write too much about man, and
above all, don't develop a theory of human judgment; and
by the way, arrange the order of your publications so that
you write about nature first and then about the nature of
man.

I get the impression that the chronological priority of
TGT to MNC tacitly influences Reck's view that my
general ontology is a phase of my theory of the human
process. I also get the impression that the greater number
of my books ostensibly dealing with man further influences this conclusion. Is it necessary to say that the
chronological and the logical order of the sub-divisions
are independent of each other? So far as I am concerned,
my entire work may be called a philosophy of natural
complexes. For the human process is not merely one kind
of natural complex; it is delineated in my work only by
heavy reliance upon broader categories of nature. Process
as such is not a major category of my general ontology.
The larger number of books on the philosophy of man is
itself highly deceiving. From the beginning, the general
ontological categories (which of course are later elabo-
rated) enter into the theory of man and guide its structure.
The notion of natural complex and the term "natural
complex" pervade the whole of TGT. "Procept," one of
the main ideas in the theory of experience which constitutes the first chapter, is defined this way: "A procept is
whatever natural complex can be identified or discriminated in the life process of the individual" (TGT 11).
Procepts are repeatedly described as natural complexes
which modify or reinforce the proceptive direction. How
can one fail to see from the beginning that, far from the

philosophy of natural complexes being grounded in the human individual, it is the human individual that is grounded in the philosophy of natural complexes? Nor is it unimportant to note that, like the concept of process, the concept of individual is not a major category of my general ontology. Recurrent warning is given, especially in ML and in MNC, against taking the individual (human or non-human) as the paradigm of whatever is said to prevail.

From the beginning of TGT, the general ontological concepts of relation and relevance join the concept of natural complex in making the theory of experience intelligible. Procepts are described as "natural complexes in a unique relation," or as natural complexes relevant to a proceptive direction. Also present at the beginning is the major concept of ordinality. Perspective, which is defined in ordinal terms, is required for the definition of proceptive domain. "A perspective is a kind of order, that kind of order in which a given set of natural complexes function as procepts for a given proceiver or for a community of proceivers" (TGT 124).*

In NJ the human individual is explicitly located in a limited world within the world at large. The category of possibility is required for the conception of query as entailing a spoliation of possibilities. The use of the category presupposes the approach to possibility later developed in MNC. TGT had explained experience as "nature proceived." NJ says, "No sentiment about the

---

*This is Buchler's quotation as it appeared in SJP. The original in TGT is: "A perspective is a kind of order, that kind of order in which a given set of natural complexes function as procepts for a given proceiver or (distributively) for a community of proceivers."

ultimate eternality or the potential infinitude of the self can conceal its littleness in the natural order" (NJ 117). I could show the same pervasiveness of the general onto-logical framework in CM. Suffice it to say that method is not only discussed but formally defined in terms of possi-bility, natural complex, and ordinality: "A method is a power of manipulating natural complexes, purposively and recognizably, within a reproducible order of utter-ance." ML, in terms of its immediate subject, the concept of poetry, would appear simply to be classified as an application of my metaphysics of utterance. But of course the concept of poetry is shown to require ontological assumptions at the most general level, no less than any other explained manifestation of experience and utter-ance. Thus the principle of ontological parity and the concept of prevalence are made fundamental in explaining the distinctiveness of the poetic stance. This metaphysical level is present not merely in the formal theory of poetry but in the critique of poetic theories which make unarti-culated assumptions about "concreteness" or an "inner world," as well as about possibility and actuality. The ordinal conception of actuality in the last chapter of ML is designed to dispel age-old confusion about the so-called fictional and "imaginary" aspects of poetry.

Accordingly, it is outlandish to say that in my outlook "man is writ larger than nature." Indeed, there are those who would be prepared to say that in no other outlook which seeks to preserve the multifariousness of human existence is the contrary so emphatically the case. And it is an error or misquotation to say, as Reck in one place does, that according to me judgment is a way of "transcending nature." For me this is an unintelligible notion. What I actually said was that through judgment it is possible for a man to transcend his own *self,* since the product can live beyond its producer and yet represent that producer.

I would like to sum up what I have said so far with this statement: My general ontology of natural complexes can be formulated independently of my metaphysics of the human process. My metaphysics of the human process, on the other hand, presupposes my general ontology.

What I have shown should serve also as the response to Reck's contention that "Buchler reveals a humanism which undermines his naturalism." I want nevertheless to add a comment or two. The terms "naturalism" and "humanism" are prepared rubrics which may or may not have the rough function of locating a viewpoint in relation to others. What they certainly cannot do is to clarify an undertaking which finds so much that is unsatisfactory about both traditional and current philosophy. "Naturalism" is not, of course, a term that I decline to be identified with. But it has had such varied and confused meanings that it can only lump together viewpoints which should be severely distinguished. It needs far more clarification than it brings. "Humanism," especially at this period of history, is impossibly vague. It is a name that has been applied at one time or another to writers of virtually every shade of opinion from St. Augustine to John Dewey, and to religious and moral trends some of which actively oppose each other. Reck even says that my conception of man has a "romantic" emphasis. Since this term, like "humanistic," when left unqualified, makes no impact on me, I plead *nolo contendere.*

Addressing himself to the concept of natural complex, which for me permits universal identification of any discriminandum prior to analysis, Reck says it has connotations which jeopardize the principle of ontological parity. The term "natural," he says, implies a judgment of what is "really real;" it involves ontological bias, bias against the non-natural or supernatural as unreal or less real. But the way I use "natural" does not imply that the non-natural or supernatural is a lesser realm or a lesser reality; it implies that these notions are only confused ways of referring to nature. To call any complex non-natural would have to mean—using the formulation in ML (104)—that it is "intrinsically and necessarily discontinuous with any of the possibilities or actualities of the world." How can it be "other than a nature of some kind?"

It is wrong to say with Reck that for me "an example of order is nature." I have opposed the idea that nature is an order; it is the provision of orders. In certain contexts, if we find it necessary to steer our rhetoric to phrases like "the natural order," we must speak of it, I have said, not as including but as permeating all orders. The phrase "the order which permeates all orders" means the *ordinality* which permeates all complexes. It is better yet to say that nature *is* ordinality, so long as this is not all we say. Nature is ordinality and relationality, prevalence and alescence, possibility and actuality. This fortifies the view I first preferred and still like, that nature is "provid-ingness"—the "provision and determination" of traits or complexes....

REPLY TO ANTON:
AGAINST "PROPER" ONTOLOGY‡

For many years I have been telling students that propriety is not a philosophic value, and that those who are

---

‡Originally published in *The Southern Journal of Philosophy* 14:1 (1976), pp. 85-90.

preoccupied with what is proper and improper procedure seriously divert our philosophic energies. Anton wonders whether I *really* have categories, whether I *really* have an ontology. If I do, why haven't I defined ontology? Why haven't I defined metaphysics? Why don't I have a theory about the nature of categories? And where is a survey of category-theory to be found in my writings? With one fell swoop Anton has demonstrated unwittingly that there is hardly any ontology to be found anywhere, and that there are hardly any respectable categories in the history of philosophy. For most philosophers, including the classical philosophers, do not bother to deal with his type of questions at all. Alas, poor Spinoza! Your categories are so limited, and you have failed to prove the legitimacy of your procedure! All you have done is to arouse thought!

Yet I do not wish to evade discussion of categories. . . . As I have just indicated, I am not much concerned with categories as constituting a formal scheme, or with the so-called problem of "justifying" the categories. The work the categories do is their justification. . . . Although relatively few philosophers have made formal lists, all philosophers, in my opinion, do have categories, even those who repudiate metaphysics. Among those who have made lists, some take the categories to be universally applicable in the sense that whatever there is, is considered to exemplify one or another of the categories. Others regard each category as applicable to whatever there is. I for one cannot see fit to tell anyone what a category must be like or what it must do. Even though I am obliged to regard some philosophies as better and richer than others, I see no compelling ground to legislate to philosophers how they should philosophize. Criticism always is necessary, but it cannot anticipate invention. All philosophers

have categories in the sense that in their thinking, whatever its level of generality, some concepts function more
regularly and effectively than others, toward the end of
making distinctions or making observations or framing
principles. Those concepts which are indispensable in
determining the character of a philosophy are its categories.

It is the actual functioning of categories that I would
prefer to stress. . . . I don't believe that worthwhile categorial schemes are "proposed." Categories are framed on
the basis of insight and discriminative power, not on the
basis of prior regulations. There are, to be sure, implicit
policies; but policies are much more dependent upon and
shaped by categorial insights than vice versa. Whitehead's
categories, both principles and concepts, are . . . incredibly
numerous, and sometimes one feels that there are more
principles than there are cases for them to apply to. But
the very length of the lists suggests that, so far as
membership and mention are concerned, one more or one
less, even several more or several less, are not philosophically crucial. The sheer abundance of Whitehead's
concepts may dull our craving for economy, but it is an
inspiring disregard of *a priori* restrictions, and it suggests
the folly of thinking that any categorial scheme can be
complete or final. The same suggestion is implicitly
conveyed by Aristotle, some of whose most important
categories, in the sense in which I am speaking of categories, are not listed, and not included in the Ten. On
what basis can it be stipulated how criteria for categories
should be arrived at? Such decisions themselves can be
based only on philosophic considerations, and whose
philosophic perspective, whose categorial outlook should

be deemed legislatively mandatory? It would have to be categorial principles of a particular kind that would determine categorial principles of any kind—a *reductio ad absurdum* if ever there was one.

Is it strange that I should talk of, say, compulsion and convention as categories? For me a category is a concept of broad scope functioning to interpret and explain on a given level of generality. We can always ask, how broad in scope is a given category? How broad in scope is the complex with which it is concerned? There is a level of generality on which the categories are as broad as we can make them—this is general ontology. And there are levels of lesser generality—areas with a lesser degree of comprehensiveness. The very broadest categories may be applicable on all levels, as I have shown in my own work; but on each level there may be categories commensurate with the subject-matter. In other words, there are less restricted and more restricted types of generalization. This has been recognized in practice for a long time. There has been a metaphysics of morals, a metaphysics of experience, a metaphysics of poetry. . . .

I add only one further point. It is becoming more and more widely recognized that there are unstated, implicit categories that function in philosophic thinking. Some of these are to be found in a particular philosophy, others seem to be present in every philosophy. An example of the latter are the categories of similarity and difference. These would not seem at first to fit the description I gave of categories as those concepts which are indispensable in determining the character of a philosophy. Indispensable they certainly are. They are presupposed by the mere process of attempting to make comparisons, distinctions,

APPENDIX I

identifications, generalizations. And they may even be said to determine a specific philosophic character, not by themselves, but by the way they are utilized or applied in conjunction with the explicit categories....

According to Anton, "Judgment...refers not to... things as they are, but to human products. Hence it is restricted to the world of the human self." He goes on to attribute to me the view that to know natural complexes is to know what our metaphysical judgments produce. Hence, he concludes, in my view the world is not related to us as it is, but as it is represented or created in our products. What Anton is saying is that on my view we cannot judge complexes as they are, but only as they are judged. But how confused it is to infer that because we produce judgments, they must *refer* only to products. The vehicle of discrimination leads us to the complex discriminated, but that complex is still a complex and discriminated as a complex. The world judged is not a product. It is the judging alone that is a product. A judgment about the world is a finding, sometimes in the form of a shaping, but what is found is not the finding. Of course, what is found is found in the way it *is* found. It is known in the *way* it is known. Can it be otherwise in *any* view of knowledge? Can the world be known in the way that it is *not* known? Anton wants to say that the world is in a relation to us as it is, not as it is judged. The world is indeed in a relation to us, both when it is judged and when it is not judged; and in both cases it is related as it is, even though the two relations are not precisely the same. When we judge the world, the world is no less the world as it is. The world preceded all judging, and will remain after all judging has ceased. The judgments of query, far from being restricted to the world of the human self, are the way the self transcends itself.

Anton says, "I take it that his theory of proception is the key to his philosophy." There are keys but not *the* key. Each major concept provides access to the others. But even if we were to accept the colloquialism, the theory of proception could be at best a key to my philosophy of man, not to my philosophy as a whole. Anton further says, "upon analysis it can be shown that for Buchler the world is what it becomes for human proception." And finally: "The consequence seems to be that there can be only one natural complex which is also theoretically defensible and all-encompassing: the human self." We need clues to explain these extraordinary readings. Anton's phrasing "becomes for human proception" suggests that "proception" is used analogously to "perception" or "thinking." Of course there is no analogy at all. This blunder would also make "procept" analogous to "percept" or "idea," so that the essential meaning of proception would be lost. In contradistinction to "ideas in the mind" or "sense-data in experience," procepts are natural complexes of the world which happen to modify or maintain human individuals. The original rationale of the concept of proception was to demolish once and for all the insidious notion of experience as a chamber in which a self is confined—to demolish it not by resolution but by conceptual reorientation. The proceptive order is one among innumerable orders of the world. Natural complexes may be related to the proceptive order as to any other order. There is no foreground or background, no privileged location, only more and less inclusive orders. I said earlier that my MNC is a self-sufficient work which would constitute a general ontology all by itself. In that book the word "proception" does not occur. In a four-line footnote at the end of the book, the words "procept" and "proceiver" are used to help illustrate the general ontological category of relevance.... †

The final correction I am forced to make has to do with the meaning of the concept of natural definition. Anton says: "It should be made clear that by 'natural definition' Buchler means definition 'understood as a human product'." My meaning is the exact opposite of this. Natural definition need have nothing whatever to do with human judgment or human beings. It would pervade the world whether there were life or not. It is the kind of definition in which any natural complex sets limits to another, inherently demarcates the boundaries between it and another. This conception, as I have pointed out in MNC, is rooted in established usage, as when we say that a cat's whiskers define its relation to close spaces, or that weather conditions define the prospect of a harvest, or that a river valley defines a territory, or that the ice age defined the topography of a continent. Far from leading us back to experience, natural definition leads us to infinite ramifications of the actual and the possible. In this conception, every natural complex defines its contour. That kind of natural definition which I call prefinition, wherein a complex defines the *extension* or *continuation* of its contour, is what we mean by a possibility. Since I consider this concept to be as important as any I have introduced, I am troubled by grooved approaches to its meaning.

REPLY TO GREENLEE:
PHILOSOPHY AND EXHIBITIVE JUDGMENT‡

I shall take up one by one the questions which Greenlee poses at the end of his paper, although needless to say it is to the discussion behind the questions that my answers will be directed.

(1) "Is philosophy to be identified with metaphysics?" For me, no. Metaphysics is not the whole of philosophy. When I say this I do not mean that metaphysics is one subordinate subject-matter within the subject-matter that is philosophy. The term "metaphysics" is not analogous to the terms "aesthetics," "epistemology," "ethics," etc. It is not a subject-matter area in the same sense. It is one of the functions of philosophy. As Greenlee reminds us, we can speak of a metaphysics of art, a metaphysics of knowledge, a metaphysics of conduct, law, history, society. The metaphysical function is to frame "the most fundamental and general concepts of a given subject-matter," as Greenlee puts it. It is not the breadth of the subject-matter that distinguishes metaphysics, but the breadth of the complexes discriminated in a particular subject-matter. I think I should hesitate to say "any subject-matter." Philosophy does not ordinarily pursue metaphysical query into microbiology, physical education, crystallography, ceramics, or electrical engineering. The reason is not that it is impossible, but that part of the metaphysical motivation is to link concepts pertinent to one area with those pertinent to another, and the transition from a

---

‡Originally published in *The Southern Journal of Philosophy* 14:1 (1976), pp. 139-143.

special area to, say science generally, is subtle and difficult. By the same token, a metaphysics of weaving or baseball is more precarious than a metaphysics of poetry, visual art, or music. We tend to generalize first in art or the broader arts, then in arts of smaller scope; first in science, or theoretical physics, then in sciences of smaller scope. Yet the philosopher needs to keep an eye on the desirability, at times, of moving in the opposite direction.

I said that metaphysical query is one form of philosophic query. Other philosophic functions cannot be reduced to the metaphysical, e.g. the articulation of important concepts, principles, and symbols; the comparison of disciplines and methods; the weighing of philosophic evidence; the criticism and organization of arguments; the strategy of formulation; the refinement of philosophic observation (including forms of aesthetic, phenomenological, and historical observation); the practice of the history of philosophy; and the reflexive concern with the philosophy of philosophy. Such functions embody and apply kinds of philosophic discernment which are not necessarily connected with the quest for increasingly comprehensive relations and structures. The building of a philosophic system, which we at once associate with metaphysics, cannot dispense with most of the other functions I have mentioned. If, furthermore, we acknowledge that philosophy is a form of active judgment, in its practical, moral, and educational aspects, we cannot equate it with metaphysical query alone.

What I do feel strongly is that most of the non-metaphysical functions of philosophy profit from being *accompanied* by metaphysical awareness, by a capacity and readiness to discern broader aspects of any complex dealt with. My own concern with the metaphysical factor for systematic philosophy explains in part why I have often spoken indifferently of the philosophical and the metaphysical. Part of the explanation also is the type of context in which the linkage has made sense and done no harm.

(2) "Can the generality Buchler ascribes to metaphysical categories be restricted so as to avoid reflexive paradoxes?" This question, I am afraid, presupposes too much. The logical paradoxes, including the so-called reflexive paradoxes, involve problems of linguistic formulation. They never have and never can inhibit substantive theory. But the Grelling paradox does not even apply to the categories I am using. It is applicable only to certain kinds of words or expressions,and it has little to do with the matter of unrestricted generality as such. The word "natural complex" is itself a natural complex, and there is no meaning in my system to its not being (or to saying it is not) a natural complex. The word "prevalence" itself prevails, and there is no meaningful alternative. It does not follow, however, that we need to tolerate usages like "prevalence prevails." Like the usage "Being is," I regard it not as tautological but as nonsensical. Nor do I consider such nonsense phrases inevitable. In every case the transition in reasoning that seems to culminate in them can be satisfactorily modified or clarified.

(3) "Is a philosophy a conceptual perspective?" Yes, in the sense that it is an order of concepts, and in the further sense that it is an order of *philosophic* concepts. There are orders of scientific concepts and of theological concepts. And these orders belong to the sciences and to theology, not to philosophy, though of course they are philo-

sophically examinable. To say that a conceptual perspective is a scientific one does not in itself mean that it has to "shade off" into a philosophic perspective. The concept of "concept" is philosophic, but not concepts merely as such. For the record, I should comment on Greenlee's statement, "Whether being a conceptual perspective distinguishes philosophy from every other enterprise. . .is not, so far as I can see, decided in Buchler's work." If I have not explicitly used a phrase like "conceptual perspective" with respect to science, it is either because I took its applicability for granted or because I simply had no occasion for that phrase in particular. I have, however, in discussing the kinds of perspective in science, gone so far as to say: "Another type of perspective in physics is an 'external' one—external to the actual subject matter but intrinsic to the method—namely, the selection of central and organizational concepts in the process of systematizing, or the selection of experimental techniques" (TGT 119).

(4) "Is it not wrong to speak of philosophical works as products of inquiry?" At bottom, Greenlee is justified in observing that if philosophy combines art and inquiry we should hesitate to speak of "philosophic inquiry." His point that "philosophy is integrally a mode of query that is uniquely what it is" could not more accurately reflect my position. But for this very reason, it should be clear that in my occasional use of the phrase "philosophic inquiry" I cannot possibly be referring to philosophy *solely as* inquiry, but to philosophy *in so far* as it is inquiry. In the same way, the expression "the art of philosophy" would not imply that philosophy is solely an art, but would refer only to the artistic aspect of

philosophy. And again, to speak of "the assertions that philosophy makes" could not imply that philosophy makes only assertions. I might comment also on the statement in TGT that "Philosophy, resembling both science and art, is both assertive and exhibitive." I am suggesting in this statement that the scientific aspect of philosophy is broadly representative of its assertive dimension, and that the artistic aspect of philosophy is broadly representative of its exhibitive dimension. I am not saying that every philosophic assertion is a scientific assertion in the sense that it could belong to one of the sciences; or that every exhibitive aspect of philosophy is identifiable in terms of the conventionally classified arts. As Greenlee makes clear, the concept of assertive judgment is more generic than the concept of scientific assertion, and the concept of exhibitive judgment is more generic than the concept of exhibitive judgment in art.

We may say now, more fully: Philosophic query sometimes takes the form of inquiry. But even in this form, there are limits. Thus, philosophic assertion resembles scientific assertion in its appeal to evidence and weight of evidence. It does not resemble scientific assertion in its process of validation. For even on the assertive level, the *kind* of evidence is not the same. In its fullest sense, then, the phrase "philosophic inquiry" must be taken to mean: philosophy in so far as it uses scientific criteria, but not necessarily scientific criteria alone, even on the assertive level. And we could not speak of philosophic works as "products of inquiry" but only as "products partly of inquiry."

(5) "Is the appeal to a sense of satisfaction concerning an order of traits *as* an order or arrangement somehow

intrinsic to the function of an exhibitive judgment?" In the context of his question, Greenlee is thinking of exhibitive judgment on the level of query. In strictest terms, an exhibitive structure of query *need* not appeal to a sense of satisfaction, so that the terms in which the question is couched—"intrinsic," "necessarily"—are too strong. But we can always ask whether or not the structure compels assent. The producer of such a structure does seek to compel assent, and in so doing appeals to a sense of satisfaction. Sometimes the firmness and the recurrence of a sense of satisfaction constitute the core of assent, and in so doing provide a basis for eventual articulation. I would venture to say that this applies to the exhibitive aspect of mathematical demonstration as much as it does to that of philosophy and the arts. Mathematicians often speak of a proof as elegant, beautiful, or perfect; and this seems to refer not merely to an incidental delight, but to a model that enriches the art of demonstration. What I think philosopher, artist, and mathematician are *not* appealing to is the mere quality of an impact that their product may make. A sense of satisfaction, like many other forms of sensing, is rather to be thought of as a viable acceptance which may transcend the more special fact of liking or disliking. The worth of an exhibitive judgment lies in its being worthy of articulation.

(6) "In the kind of judgment which is a contrivance, is what is exhibited that contrivance itself or is it whatever part of the world (if any) that contrivance represents?" Here I must take issue with the way in which the question is formulated and with some of the assumptions Greenlee makes. He says that the two kinds of showing-functions which the question poses are quite unlike, that this no

doubt explains why I nowhere bring them together, and that in fact I never distinguish them. To which I answer: I never distinguish them as unlike, because they are not at all unlike. And I never bring them together, because they are already together, by virtue of the nature of judgment.

The question Greenlee is raising was raised in CM, where I pointed out that exhibiting a contrivance and exhibiting complexes found in the world are both realized in the same process. They come together in a single function, which I described as "providing the means . . . to look and find."

> It is misleading to ask whether what is exhibited (in philosophy) is a structure of "ideas" or a structure of "existence." All judgment, whether it takes the form of action, contrivance, or assertion, manipulates by ordering natural complexes and endowing them with a recognizable identity. . . . The philosopher perforce exhibits a structure of concepts. . . . He perforce manipulates one or another part of the world (CM 166).

Thus in philosophy the conceptual scheme is the discriminative finding; the complex discriminated is what is found. What is exhibited may be called either a scheme revealing a complex or a complex revealed by a scheme. The conceptual structure is a conceptual portrayal, and there is no portrayal without something portrayed. We know from age-old criticism in art that a portrayal is a discrimination of some kind. To think of a philosophic "order of concepts" as exhibitable independently of "the world which a philosophy is about" is to regard the order not as a conceptual order at all but as a body of marks, and the world not as the world but as that which is "out there" and apart. In this connection, I would like to comment on the use of the term "represents" in Greenlee's question. For the theory of judgment, this term is not necessary and often undesirable. We need no longer say that a work of music or architecture does not represent the world and a work of philosophy does. Music, architecture, and philosophy all exhibitively discriminate natural complexes; they all are involved with the world: the world of time, sound, and emotion; of space, mass, and habitation; of possibilities and actualities.

(7) "Can not the exhibitive function of disclosing a represented part of the world be served by the assertive, as well as by the constructive, side of philosophy?" I would agree. A philosophic structure, after all, is a structure not only of concepts but of principles. Each of these principles we deem to be true in an exhibitive order. Ideally speaking, if not always in practice, the assertive and exhibitive functions of philosophy articulate each other. Each can subserve, and even extend, the other's role. Assertive judgment ties the exhibitive structure to our craving for belief, and distinguishes it from other exhibitive structures which are non-philosophic. And the structure, in turn, firms each assertion by defining exhibitively a society of assertions.

JUSTUS BUCHLER

APPENDIX II

NOTES ON THE CONTOUR OF A NATURAL COMPLEX‡

I HAVE described a contour as the continuity and totality of a complex's ordinal locations, and as the interrelation or gross integrity of the integrities determined by these locations. I should like to comment on what is and what is not implied by this formulation.

The concept of contour is required for an adequate account of the concept of natural complex. Since a complex (whether temporal or not) may have a different integrity in each of the orders wherein it is located, and since we wish to be able to regard it as the same complex despite its different roles and aspects, its variations, we must provide a means of dealing with the way in which such ideas as identity, integrity, and continuity stand to one another. Identity, for example, is a vexed notion if ever there was one; but it is not exactly easy to dispose of. I define it as a relation of a certain kind. But what kind? Between what and what else? Here is where the notion of contour enters. It not only helps us to define identity; it accounts for why the different integrities of a complex do not dissolve the complex into a chaos. A contour is the

---

‡Written in 1977. Heretofore unpublished.

constellation or direction of a complex. The constellation or direction may alter. This continuity of a complex, its contour, in no way excludes discontinuities. The most basic form of discontinuity is the unrelatedness of sub-complexes within a given complex, along with the relatedness of other sub-complexes.

When I said that I define identity as a relation of a certain kind, I was referring to the following formulation: "The identity of a complex is the continuous relation that obtains between the contour of a complex and *any* of its integrities" (MNC 22, italics added). We cannot regard identity as the continuity among the different integrities. We would still be subject to the old question, how can that which consists of many differences be continuous, or identical with itself? We cannot equate identity with sameness, for that would beg the question how sameness can admit of difference. The concept of contour permits us to reconcile sameness with difference. The answer to the old paradox is that the sameness of a complex lies in its contour, while the differences of a complex lie in its constituent integrities.

A contour should not be thought of as a kind of closed vessel containing antecedently all the traits of a complex, possible and actual, past, present, and future. I have stated in MNC that "the integrity of a complex does not lie in the totality of its traits" (MNC 106). As itself an integrity, a contour thus cannot be "all-inclusive"; it does not include all of a complex's traits. As a changeable totality of the subaltern integrities, it has no fixed value, implying only that all of these integrities are relevant to the complex's identity, even if not all need to be known for an identification. The "totality" in this sense is not a numerical notion; it is indissociable from continuity and interrelated-ness. A merely numerical totality does not imply related-ness of its elements. A contour is made up not of indifferent elements but of constituents which affect its value—of integrities which shape the complex cumula-tively. Adding or totaling as such is not relevant. It ignores the complex as an order. If *a* is a complex and *r* is a complex, it does not follow that there is another complex *ar*; for *a* and *r* may be wholly unrelated, and located in different and unrelated orders. "A contour" means: a complex in so far as it is manifested by many integrities, a complex which in and through its multiplicity retains an identity.

"Contour" does not signify the primacy of a complex's "unity" and the secondariness of its multiplicity. I have pointed out at various times that the notion of a unity "first and foremost" is without meaning. "It makes sense only to say that given complexes are unities of such-and-such a kind, in such-and-such a respect. The integrity of a complex belongs to it not in spite of but because of its multiplicity and relatedness" (MNC 24). A contour does not shape the constituent integrities of the complex; it is the integrities that shape the contour. *Each* integrity does. We cannot speak of an integrity that does not belong to the contour of a complex. This would be to say that it is not an integrity of *that* complex. I have stated that every integrity is "conditional," in the sense that it is determined by some ordinal location of the complex. The contour or gross integrity of the complex always admits of continuation or extension. This, as it turns out, is basic to the concept of possibility. Possibility requires that a contour be indefi-nitely extended or continued. Yet a contour cannot be other than the contour of a given complex. For, being the direction, the variable gross integrity of the complex, it continuingly defines that complex's limits or boundaries. In this sense it is the most comprehensive aspect of the complex.

Any complex, any order, may be presumed to have generic traits of its own. Its contour or gross integrity, by definition, is more comprehensive than a constituent integrity. But by the principle of ontological parity, a gross integrity is no more of an integrity than a constituent integrity, and vice versa. When we understand the core consideration to be that every complex has an integrity, and abstract from the distinctions of level and scope, there cannot be an issue about the use of the term "gross integrity." The basic distinction is then seen to be between integrity and subaltern integrity, whether or not we add on the word "gross" to the former term. The force of the word "gross" is to preserve the distinction between a complex and any of *its* constituents. Any integrity, any subaltern integrity, is a contour or gross integrity of its constituent integrities. Every order and sub-order has its relative breadth, its relative comprehensiveness and pervasiveness. Every integrity unifies other integrities. Thus a denial of gross integrity would be a denial of integrity— of any kind of determinateness in a complex. It would also be a denial of generic traits in any complex.

At this point, by way of applying the concept of contour, I turn to the concept of proception. Consider the statement in TGT, "Proception is the process in which a man's whole self is summed up or represented" (TGT 5). Is it meaningful to ask "whether a man's whole self *can* be summed up"? I have pointed out that a contour cannot be a mere summing up or totaling of elements as such. The "summing-up" here referred to is not a summing up by any person or machine. It is the proceptive *process itself*. It is a representing, a reckoning that is always going on. The summing up is ever cumulative. Theoretically, it can be determined in narrower perspective as the impact of the process at any given moment or in any extended present; as the bearing of the whole self on the self regarded in cross-section; or more precisely, as the process represented in the imminent proceptive domain or in the floating proceptive domain. Failure to see that the proceptive process of summing up is not terminal would be a special case of the failure to see that the contour of a complex is not synonymous with "all the traits" of the complex, is not an arithmetical notion, and is modifiable by the complex's further ordinal locations. Proception entails, interdependently, both a proceptive direction and a plurality of procepts, including of course constituent processes.

Some philosophers fear that in speaking of *an* individual human process we threaten to erase plurality and diversity. "Unity," we are told, cannot be assumed or taken for granted; it may have to be achieved—presumably by an individual who is not yet an individual. This type of concern reflects chronic historical blurring of ontological and moral considerations with regard to "unity." Ontologically, in any case, I have suggested at various times that unity does not imply simplicity and therefore cannot exclude plurality. Thus:

> Every unity is constitutionally and relationally plural. And each plurality, as an order of constituents, is that order, that plurality. The important consideration here is not unity as

such, plurality as such, but the *respect*[s] in which any
complex is unitary and the *respect*[s] in which it is plural.
(SJP 107)   †

We may continue along the line of practical application.
The complex known as Napoleon Bonaparte was located
in many orders, and thus had many integrities. The
identity of Napoleon was a continuous relation between
any of these integrities, such as his role of soldier, and his
ongoing cumulative direction or constellation as a man,
the contour of his life—the contour being not the *sole*
"direction" but rather that emergent direction on the basis
of which certain high-level generalizations can be made
about him. This, the proceptive direction, comprising
both a typical human process and a circumstantial
individual history, was variable. It was shaped by all the
Napoleonic procepts—the complexes relevant to him as
an individual. The patterns of these procepts formed the
orders in which Napoleon was located, some more inclusive and some less—the bourgeois revolution, the emotional order, the order of persons encountered, the order of
war. The possibilities of variation in his life required for
their prevalence that its proceptive direction or contour be
indefinitely continued. This contour was a cumulative
reckoning, its values representable both in broad terms
and in terms of moments or situations. Like any other
contour, it defined the limits of the complex "Napoleon"
and continues to define them. Any of its constituent
integrities, Napoleon as husband, as emperor, as prisoner,
could and can be seen as a constellation of subaltern
integrities.

Are the integrities of a complex all related to one
another? This question can be understood in either of two

ways. (1) Are all the integrities of a complex *inter*-related, in the sense that all belong to a constellation which is the contour or gross integrity of the complex? This question we have already answered in the affirmative. (2) Is each integrity of a complex related to *every* other integrity of that complex? This question is hard to decide. If we were speaking merely of *traits,* generally, we could say that not all traits of a complex are related each to every other. In the case of the complex's *integrities* we must remember that each integrity *is* the complex, the complex in a given order. To say that these integrities are not necessarily related each to every other is to say that a complex as defined by its functioning in one order may not be related to itself as functioning in certain others. It is to say, for example, that a tree as having a cellular structure may not be related to itself as having interest to photographers. If, in general, a complex may be related to itself in respect of some integrities and not related to itself in respect of others, we need to be much more critical about the idea of "reflexiveness."

Question two being thus expanded, it is difficult to ascertain whether, let us say, each integrity of a complex affects the scope of a complex's *possibilities* with respect to all its other integrities. If this were always so, then each integrity would relate to every other by limiting or augmenting certain possibilities for it. But *is* this so? In any case, an affirmative answer to question two is not required either by the concept of contour or the concept of identity. A continuity of the ordinal locations of a complex does not mean that each must be, as it were, contiguous with all the others. And the identity of a complex depends upon a relation of each integrity to the contour, not upon a relation of each integrity to every other.

I pointed out in MNC that when certain traits of a complex are not related to certain others, all remain nevertheless constituents of that complex. I called the unrelated traits "commensurate," in the sense that "'between' them there are traits of access, mediating routes" (MNC 95). We may say the same of a complex's integrities. The ordinal locations which provide these integrities are accessible to one another via the contour of the complex. Thus the biographer of a person would write the latter's history by moving from one integrity to another, in various combinations and directions.

Many years ago (in a discussion of Bertrand Russell's ethics) I introduced the idea of a guiding moral tone. It is a principle of continuity in moral choice (more generally and accurately, in what I have since called active judgment, which may have nothing to do with language). In TGT I said that both the individual and society "are characterized by a guiding moral tone, that of the individual reflecting the proceptive direction, that of society reflecting the accumulated structure of its institutions" (TGT 40). Guiding moral tone corresponds to the more comprehensive notion of proceptive direction, as the latter corresponds to the very much more comprehensive notion of contour. I quote the following in order to yield another illustration or application of the latter notion:

> Every moral choice is the expression of a guiding moral tone. This guiding tone is the fundamental directed sensibility of an individual with respect to moral situations. Choice that is spontaneous is not genuine approval, even though it be the result of a deliberation. As a man does not

believe simply by asserting that he does, so he does not value simply by feeling assent. The guiding tone underlying all valuation is not a fixed property, innate or acquired. Though it involves a propensity to feel in particular ways, it is not itself a particular feeling or a mere flavor of consciousness. The tone that emerges in the complex of native endowment, experience, compulsion, and imagination is variable and plastic. It is not to be confused with "character," a more general term that fails by itself to convey the presence of a developed and directed sensibility. The intellectual value of the two concepts is, however, the same. Both render intelligible specific acts and specific choices, and both help to distinguish between mere behavior and moral conduct. The guiding tone of an individual is what accounts for his *contingent* as well as his *characteristic* choices. "Intuition," "direct sense of value," "appreciation," even Hume's "sentiment," inadequately represent the general factor in choice. These labels and the views they represent have served to obscure the presence of prior inclination. If goodness comes home to the individual in positive satisfaction, this cannot consist in merely a direct instance of feeling; it must consist in a modification or ratification of some underlying temper. The guiding tone and the guiding principles embedded in an individual's conduct are closely related. Both may be more or less explicit in the individual's awareness. In his capacity as moral agent his guiding principles—the policies according to which he acts—are reflected in his moral tone. The concept of tone represents no hypostasis of individual intuitions but rather the continuous basis of any choice. Ultimate approval does culminate in feeling. But guiding tone explains why a given feeling is likely to be that feeling and not another. ("Russell and the Principles of Ethics" in *The Philosophy of Bertrand Russell*, Edited by Paul Arthur Schilpp. Library of Living Philosophers. Evanston and Chicago: Northwestern University, 1944, pp. 530-531.)

JUSTUS BUCHLER

APPENDIX III

ON THE CONCEPT OF "THE WORLD"‡

i

Considering the vast extent of its use, the idea involved in the terms "the world" and "the universe" has received less than adequate philosophic attention. Common speech, religion, literary art, theoretical physics, and philosophy all seem to require and apply the terms frequently. Yet it is safe to say (for any of these areas) that no one is very confident about their meaning and that no appreciable *range* of meaning has developed cumulatively. In their most rudimentary and most insistent sense, the terms suggest "everything," "all there is," and perhaps we must in some way cling to this sense, whatever else we emerge with. Some people like to speak of an all-embracing totality, but they are uncertain about what is implied. Beyond this, and more precariously, "the world" (or universe) is often tied to the notion of a whole or wholeness, regarded not only as inclusive, but as an overarching unity which encompasses whatever pluralities there are, and as an overarching continuity which encompasses whatever discontinuities there are. These ideas are notoriously full of difficulties, although it may be ques-

‡*The Review of Metaphysics*, 31:4, June 1978, pp. 555-579.

tioned, as it will be here, whether the most serious underlying difficulties have been identified or metaphysically formulated in a satisfactory way.

The general problem of defining "the world" is initially complicated by the use of expressions which qualify "world," such as "the academic world," "the world of the self," "the physical universe," or "the universe of discourse." This introduces the notion of "worlds." The word "the" will be seen to imply either uniqueness or manyness-within-a-kind. Both these uses of "the" seem always to be translatable in terms of "a." Thus *the* academic world is *a* world distinguishable from others, but induplicable; *the* physical universe is *a* universe distinguishable from a universe otherwise described, but induplicable. On the other hand, *the* universe of discourse is *a* universe distinguishable from others, but duplicable; *the* world of the self is *a* world distinguishable from others, but duplicable. In the framework of established intent, it doesn't make sense to speak of another academic world or another physical universe, but it makes perfectly good sense to speak of another universe of discourse or another world of the self.

A further preliminary complication arises from a usage of "world" which is historically widespread, that wherein "world" is indeed *the* World (henceforth capitalized) and emphatically not *a* world, yet qualified, nevertheless. In this usage, we speak of God and the World. If the notion of world may be said always to suggest inclusiveness, then *a* world would be all-inclusive in a specific respect, while *the* World would be all-inclusive in *all* respects, except for that which is trans-worldly or non-worldly. This exception to the all-inclusive World introduces a contrast, and it is the contrast which yields exhaustiveness, God *and* the World. A tacit principle of exhaustiveness underlies most metaphysical outlooks. It also underlies common thinking and common usage. The rhetorical intent of phrases like "the whole World," "in all the World," "nowhere in the World" is to express unqualified exhaustiveness as opposed to the qualified exhaustiveness of "my world" or "the animal world." The contrast God and the World represents, of course, only one type. In various outlooks, Self and World, Inner and Outer World, Knower and World are the factors of exhaustiveness. In effect, such outlooks make "the World" a restricted notion. Others express exhaustiveness by the word Reality or (in a quite different spirit) by the pair Reality and Appearance; by the word Being or (again in a quite different spirit) by the pair Being and non-Being; by the word Nature or by such pairs (sometimes designed to contrast, sometimes not) as Nature and God, Nature and Mind, Nature and Man, Nature and Art.

The concept of the World is indispensable to most metaphysical approaches, regardless of whether they are directly concerned with a principle of exhaustiveness. For this concept makes possible a primitive but sobering type of contrast, between what is dealt with by man as specific and chartable and what is always to be acknowledged as indefinitely greater in scope. The World provides conceptually what is greater in scope, incomparably greater, than anything "in" or "of" it. But this contrast imposes itself even where the emphasis, plurally, is on worlds. A distinguishable or circumscribed world is yet indefinitely greater in scope than any discriminandum of that world. The academic world, the underworld, the world of letters, are called worlds because their character and extent are indefinite by comparison with given events, relations, or individuals. We cannot call an aggregate or a mere structure a world. A business firm, a literary organization, an athletic club is not a world. Each of these is progressively traversable, and accessible in terms of the conditions (such as rules and actions) that made it. A world, by contrast, is "indefinitely greater" not in statistical terms but in the sense of being, as it were, dark wherever it is light and remote in its very presence. Yet it is not uncommon to say of this or that world, as of any particular structure therein, that it has disappeared or has been destroyed. If this way of speaking is otherwise justifiable, then it is easier to understand why for human experience the sense of what is indefinitely greater in scope may arise and perish in specific respects.

Both philosophically and colloquially, phrases like "being in the World" and "having a place in the World" are taken for granted and are assumed to make sense. In many contexts, we are prepared to look upon "in" as having other than spatial import: "a woman in labor," "a person in trouble," "keeping a date in mind," "in many contexts." But "in the World" has always had strong spatial suggestiveness. This suggestiveness is by no means rhetorical only. It carries a rationale which might be put this way: Isn't the inclusiveness we wish to convey by the idea of the World a spatial inclusiveness whatever *else* it may be? The main influence on this way of thinking is the astronomical orientation. The expression "the universe" is assumed by physicists and astronomers to be the system delineated and explained by physical formulae. Only rarely is it qualified by them as "the physical (or astronomical) universe." On this assumption the most pervasive of all traits are space and time. The next most pervasive traits, whatever they may be, are assumed to *pertain* to the spatio-temporal. Space and time lend themselves most readily (some would say "intuitively") to the notion of encompassing, embracing, comprehending, or containing. This seems to fit the requirements of the concept of the World as we cannot help thinking of it: everything is *in* the World (the all-inclusive universe), even that which is *also*, more specially, in trouble or in the right. This tendency to think of "in" as, most authentically, physical containment is reinforced by the tradition which emphasizes the primacy (the "basic reality") of space-time individuals and their sufficiency for the account of what human experience discloses.

Now such complexes as mathematical validity, conscience, and aesthetic possibility, unlike stars and mice, seem not datable or not spatially placeable. They are assuredly *in* the World in the sense of being related to other trait-complexes, which in turn are related, and so on. They, like all complexes, are (as we shall put it when we adopt the language of a metaphysics of complexes) *ordinally* located. Since space and time as such have been interpreted in quite other ways than as being containers, the astronomical conception of the World, if it is to be metaphysically useful and to be regarded less crudely than as the model of an Enduring Box, must itself be seen as dependent upon a more fundamental "in," one that signifies "being related to" ("in this or that relation," "in relation to"). Otherwise, we cannot help asking: If the Box is the World, is space in the Box or is the Box itself in space? Is time in the Box or the Box in time? If space and time are in the Box (or are "part" of it), what is outside of it? If "outside" is meaningless, then presumably so is "inside." Not physics, but metaphysics suffers from such perplexities. Physics need only substitute or tacitly accept "physical world" for "World" in order to avoid the morass, thenceforth continuing its exploration and production of problems. We do say that physics explores the physical world, biology the vital world, anthropology the cultural world...and we may say that metaphysics can profit from the increased knowledge of worlds. But knowledge of worlds cannot clarify the concept of the World. Instead, it teaches the need for wariness when framing analogies and models. The approach of philosophers like Hume, Kant, and James, in the exposure of perplexities concerning the World, helps to preserve this wariness. It does not help in the constructive development of a more adequate conception of the World.

ii

Hobbes says that by "the world" or "the universe" is meant "the whole mass of all things that are." This seems at first to come as close as possible philosophically to dignifying the common man's notion of the World as "everything." But there are uncertainties that crop up when we contemplate this plain-sounding description, and in particular the phrase "all things." For, as we know, Hobbes goes on to say that the World and every part of it is "body": "that which is not body is no part of the universe; and, because the universe is all, that which is no part of it is 'nothing'."[1] But it is evident in Hobbes (though not

---

1. Hobbes, *Leviathan*, chap. 46.

made clear by him) that God and the Laws of Nature or
Reason are not body and yet are. They are therefore no
part of the "universe"; but their thus being "nothing"
must mean that they are "no *thing*." The universe is "all
things." It is not literally all-inclusive but inclusive only
of all that lends itself to inclusion. The Hobbesian
conception of the World would thus be restrictive despite
the initial sound of its formula. We cannot prove that this
way of reasoning reflects Hobbes's deliberate intention.
But whether it does or not, we should observe (or for once
take seriously the observation) that the term "things" is
ambiguous, as it is in most philosophers. It serves two
functions. It is the term for bodies, and it is also the term of
generic identification, the term for anything, for whatever
we are talking about, whether a goat or a natural law. In
this generalized vein, Hobbes speaks, for example, of
"those things which concern the common peace and
safety."[2]

Historically, the problem of inclusiveness and exhaustiveness has bred recurrent confusion, and this century is
no exception. For example, in Wittgenstein's general
ontology the World is declared to be a totality. But it is
"the totality of facts, not of things," the totality of
"everything that is the case." "What is the case, the fact" is
equated with "the existence of states of affairs." (States of
affairs are combinations of "simples," that is, of "objects,"
"things," "entities.") Is the World, then, all-inclusive?
Answers found in Wittgenstein oppose one another in
several ways. (1) It can be argued that the World is all-
inclusive. For the World is also called "the sum-total of
reality," and to say that it is a totality of facts, not of

---

2. Hobbes, *Leviathan,* chap. 17.

things, cannot (it would seem) mean that things or simples are excluded, but that the World cannot consist of things alone, of simples uncompounded.

But (2) it can be argued that the World is not all-inclusive. (a) The World "divides into facts" any one of which "can either be the case or not be the case." It is not clear how the World, which is everything that is the case, can divide into facts some of which are not the case ("do not exist"). For even if there are "negative facts," they are not part of the World as it is defined. (b) Things are said to make up "the substance of the World," and "substance is what exists [or "subsists"] independently of what is the case." Things, then, are independent of "what is the case." If they are independent of *whatever* is the case, they are both the substance of the World and independent of the World. (c) The World is also described as consisting of "the facts in logical space." Logical space consists of the possibilities—possibilities of being the case or of not being the case. Possibilities, then, or at least some possibilities, are not encompassed by the World; it would seem, rather, that the World is encompassed by the possibilities, by logical space.

Wittgenstein asserts the following three dubiously compatible propositions: (1) "The totality of existing states of affairs is the World" (2.04). (2) "The existence and non-existence of states of affairs is the reality" (2.06). (3) "The sum-total of reality is the World" (2.063).[3]

---

3. Ludwig Wittgenstein, *Tractatus Logico-Philosophicus*, trans. C.K. Ogden (London: Routledge and Kegan Paul, 1949); also trans. D.F. Pears and B.F. McGuinness (New Jersey: Humanities Press, 1974). Translated passages are mostly from Pears-McGuinness, but in one or two cases from Ogden. I have taken the liberty of using "World" for "world." The citations in these last three paragraphs are from propositions between numbers 1 and 2.063.

Contributing to this massive unclarity and contributing in general to much indistinctness in metaphysical thought, has been the lack of a satisfactory concept by means of which universal identification can be achieved. We should be able to speak universally about "whatever" without being stultified because we think it impossible to name what is "common to everything." We should not have to make a specific reference when specification is unnecessary, distracting, or irrelevant. Nor should we have to persuade ourselves that abstraction at this level is futile or useless. We should not have to say countless times "We're talking about sticks or planets or civilization or buttons or no-matter-what—get the point?" On the other hand, universal identification cannot be achieved by adopting a purely mechanical device, avoiding "thing" and using "any x at all." For a mere variable sign admitting of any value has no meaningful connection with principles that must use it repeatedly and in many contexts. The concept required should have the resonance to affect other leading metaphysical concepts. To hold, for example, that "not every x in the World is related to every other" is a safe but inane means of generalizing. The x is even less satisfactory if not less empty than "thing."

In the history of philosophy, "thing" is seldom used critically. It functions, as we have said, with two ranges of application, which are not likely to be distinguished from one another: (1) as the term for universal reference, and (2) as the term designating individuals (not necessarily "bodies"). Hence, not surprisingly, the persistent assumption that whatever there is must "ultimately" prove to be an individual. Function (1) is exemplified by a phrase like "all the things we discussed"; function (2) by a statement like "Things, not abstractions, are real." The motto "Back to the things themselves" seems to be in the province of the latter function, though it is actually not always oriented toward individuals.

The commingling of both these functions without concern for their difference may be illustrated in the use of "thing" (*res*) by Spinoza. He says that an *idea* and a *thing* express, respectively, the attributes of thought and extension. But he also speaks of "a thinking *thing*" and "an extended *thing*." Beyond this, he says that a circle existing and the idea of a circle existing are one and the same *thing* displayed through different attributes. All this means that "thing" is used to designate: (a) a mode of extension (via function 2); (b) a mode of extension *or* a mode of thought (via function 1); and (c) Substance (also via function 1). Thus, chaotically, yet in completely admissible terms, we could say: An idea is not a thing. An idea is the kind of thing that is a thought, while a thing is the kind of thing that is extended. But a thing existing and the idea of a thing existing are one and the same thing.[4]

iii

The concept which I have introduced as a primary access to the framing of metaphysical principles is that of "natural complex." The term is held to be applicable to whatever there is, whatever we can talk about. In one direction of emphasis it means "any complex of nature," which in turn means any among the indefinitely many complexes. In another direction, the idea means a "complex of traits," which emphasizes the manyness within

---

4. See Spinoza's discussion of Proposition 7 in Part 2 of his *Ethics*.

any one. "Natural complex" thus has both a distributional and a constitutional sense, and these will be found to merge. For brevity's sake we shall speak most often of a complex or of complexes. Contrary to a tendency in certain philosophical and rhetorical traditions, there is no implication that we must or can correlatively dignify "non-natural" complexes or natural "simples." Dwelling briefly on the denial of such an implication, exposing the ontological repugnancies inhering in it, will facilitate explanation of some fundamentals in the theory of complexes. And this in turn will permit us to reflect anew on the concept of the World.

Since "non-natural complex" is not accepted as meaningful, "natural complex" in all strictness is redundant: a complex cannot be other than "natural." But the redundance is retained strategically. First, it serves to remind us that whatever complex is held to be "non-natural" ("anti-natural," "supernatural") would have to be intrinsically unrelatable to and necessarily discontinuous with any of the actualities and possibilities of the World.[5] Second, it serves to remind us that nature admits of complexes infinitely more pervasive and comprehensive than those which are framed or devised by man, or than the complexes man and men. The first of these considerations reinforces the universal applicability of "natural complex" by metaphysical precaution against a destructive or unintelligible assumption. The second guards against the equally destructive possibility of conceiving "nature" in terms of man (and a fortiori in terms of cognitive powers or structures) rather than the other way around.

---

5. A formulation that I gave in *The Main of Light: On the Concept of Poetry* (New York: Oxford University Press, 1974), p. 104.

Like "natural," "complex" has no applicable contrary: "natural simple" is not ontologically meaningful. This may be shown by expanding the idea that every complex is a complex of traits. A trait is a constituent of a complex. (Both "part" and "component" are more limited terms and could not replace "constituent.") There cannot be traitless complexes, complexes unconstituted. But in the same way, each constituting trait is itself constituted by other traits. (Again, "affected," "conditioned," "determined" are here deemed less general and less precise than "constituted.") "Trait" and "complex" are clarified by means of each other. Each trait is itself a complex, constituting and constituted by (at least) conditions, relations, and patterns. For example, a color trait, the trait of being yellow, is constituted by the traits known as conditions of light, spatial extensiveness, relation to eyes, contrast with environing traits. The trait of being loud is constituted by the traits or complexes known as duration, relation to ears, location in a perceptually discriminable environment. To call a trait simple is either to deny that it is constituted or to affirm that it is constituted by a single trait that is indivisible. Supposedly indivisible traits are also commonly called indescribable and unanalyzable; they release us from the responsibility of scrutinizing and defining, and they tolerate (in effect, they mandate) without good reason the termination of an instance of query. The answer to the claim of indivisibility is that a trait is undivided as a trait, but not indivisible. All traits, of whatever kind, in so far as they are the traits or complexes they are, are undivided. But every trait is related to other traits, and these relations are traits. They are constituents of their relata. A "simple" trait, a trait unrelated, is (pace Hobbes) "nothing," "nowhere." A trait that is relationless, conditionless, unlocated, inaccessible to and by other traits, is no trait at all.

An ostensible path of escape from the principle of complexity lies in the traditional distinction between "internal" and "external" relations. It may be contended that simples have no relations internal to their being and that the relations otherwise alleged to be constituents of their being should not be called traits. This view would exclude from the category of trait all the universally acknowledged traits which involve potentialities and a span of time and the manifestations of which cannot be either compresent or joined in a timeless cluster. Such, for example, are the traits of honesty, solubility, reliability, and tensile strength: patently relational, but in fact no more relational than any other. Ontologically, there is no difference between "internal" and "external" relations. All relations are "internal" to the complexes of which they are traits, in the sense that all contribute to the aggregate of our judgments about their relata, what is assertible about them, what is "true" of them, not to mention what is do-able to them and make-able with them, forms of judgment as yet scarcely recognized by philosophers. Many distinctions, of course, can be drawn among relations. None in any way proves that relations are not constitutive, do not make a difference. They prove only that there are contrasts in the *way* relations constitute and in the practical appraisal of certain modes of constituting, e.g., "essential" and "extrinsic" relations. The traits commonly called "internal" are those deemed "essential" in a given respect.

Complexes, then, are *of* complexes. The traits of any complex are its subaltern complexes, its constituents. All complexes are traits which constitute other complexes. Stated otherwise, every complex has its sub-complexes and is itself a sub-complex. From this we can infer that whatever there is bears multiplicity within its identifiable unity as a complex. From this, in turn, we can infer that whatever is, is explorable or analyzable, if it is humanly accessible.

Each complex has an integrity, a trait-constitution whereby it is differentiable from any other. No complex is a mere collection of traits. It is an order of traits. Conversely, any order must (by definition) be a natural complex. We may speak of oceans, symphonies, histories, concepts, physical laws, illusions, meteors, as complexes or orders, and we may (we do in common practice) compare complexes in regard to their scope, their relative pervasiveness or comprehensiveness. Whether order A embraces or encompasses order B, whether B is included in A, reflects questions of common interest, and not least when we speak of worlds in relation to one another. In so far as a complex is a sub-complex of some other (located in that order of traits), it is of lesser scope than the other.

When a complex is said to be located in an(other) order, reference is being made to its relational "position," to one way in which it makes a difference *for* other complexes, and hence to one way in which it is different *from* other complexes. Every complex, being thus ordinally located, has its own efficacy, its own sphere(s) of efficacy. We have to get rid of the prejudice that only space-time individuals make a difference. Any complex is efficacious; it makes a difference, whether it be a possibility or an actuality. Without an ordinal location a complex could not have an integrity. It has an integrity defined by each of its ordinal locations; so that, strictly, it has a network of integrities, which is modifiable by integrities that may arise.

Ordinarily, we would say that a career is of greater scope than a deed done in the course of that career. But in another respect, a deed of (say) symbolical import may be more pervasive in significance than the career within which it occurred. The different "respect" means a wider order (say, the public historical order) within which the two complexes (the deed and the career) are differently related. The possible intricacy and diversity of ordinal and sub-ordinal relations may of course make comparisons difficult and unbearably qualified. But then, we have nowhere made the assumption that nature must be depicted in elegantly compact and "simply intelligible" terms. The aesthetic character of a metaphysics is not a necessary condition of that metaphysics but its contingent outcome. Complexes intersect and overlap in endless ways. Human discrimination and isolation of complexes, the determination of what shall be extricated as the complex relevant to a given purpose, reflects the ontological condition facing methodic judgment.

A teacher located in the order of scholarship is also a scholar located in the order of teaching, and in any number of intersecting orders, such as marriage, employment, and politics; peaceful marriage, gainful employment, radical politics; peaceful interracial marriage, burdensome gainful employment, clandestine radical politics. The teacher as an individual sub-complex would typically be a complex of lesser scope than the encompassing professional orders. In another respect, individual scholarship of a certain kind may be a more pervasive complex of enlightenment than the social complex of scholarship by which it is generated and encompassed. The comparison, once again, presupposes another order in which the two complexes are located. Comparison may be continually re-determined by invoking many orders in which both are located.

Complex and order, complexity and ordinality, are coextensive but not wholly the same in meaning. Each requires the other for its definitional coherence, and the difference is one of emphasis. An order is a complex in so far as it comprises a *multiplicity* of traits. A complex is an order in so far as it *delimits* traits and serves as a *location* of traits. The phrase "an order" here carries the sense of a sphere or a domain rather than the sense of an arrangement or a structure. Arrangement or structure, we may say, is pertinent to a complex and (what is the same) embodied in an order.

The chains of relatedness inherent in any complex are unlimited, non-terminal. This follows from the principle that every complex has subaltern complexes and is subaltern to other complexes. The latter notion, which we said is required for the complex to have an integrity, may not seem obvious and may need an additional argument For we are being asked why, if every (order or) complex encompasses, must every complex be encompassed; why must that which has sub-complexes itself be a sub-complex. The reply can only be that a complex which would not be a sub-complex would not be located. If it were not located in any order, it could not be related to any complex other than itself or its constituents. This means either that it is not a complex (whatever that could mean) or that it includes all complexes. If it includes all complexes, it does not delimit, and this means that it is not an order. But if it is not an order of traits, it is not a complex either. A complex has its own traits. If all complexes are its traits, no complexes are.

The traits of any complex may be, we said, more comprehensive or less. One way of distinguishing traits on the most comprehensive level is to classify them as possibilities and actualities. We may convey this more accurately by saying that in every complex (in every order) there are traits of possibility and traits of actuality. The important point is that we cannot speak of possibilities or of actualities *except* as traits of a complex (as complexes in some order). A "pure" possibility independent of all complexes would be a complex unrelated and unlocated —an absurdity. Possibilities alleged to be of this kind have also been called "abstract" or "logical" possibilities or "conceivabilities." Abstraction is imperative and inescapable. But it is necessarily abstraction from a complex of some kind, abstraction relevant to that complex. Thus to speak of possibilities as complexes is itself an abstraction from the fuller consideration that every complex is also a sub-complex; so that a possibility is a sub-complex, and no complexes lack the kind of sub-complexes called possibilities. This is recognized in the common observation that so-and-so "has its possibilities," the presence of possibilities in any complex being taken for granted, and the emphasis being on the distinctive possibilities of the complex at hand. In the same sense, there are no pure or absolute actualities. "Are none" means that it is contradictory to suppose an actuality not pertinent to (or not located in) an order. Any actuality is the actualization of one possibility and the condition of some other. It is the actuality of some complex, not a "mere" actuality. Every complex is an order of actuality-and-possibility.

Now, just as the conception of possibility in terms of a trait belonging to a natural complex curbs the idea that "anything conceivable is possible" and therefore makes possibilities *less* readily discoverable than commonly supposed, so the parallel ordinal conception of actuality whereby there is not a realm of actuality as opposed to a realm of "fiction," "illusion," or "fabrication," but rather actualities in any order whatever (along with that order's possibilities), makes actualities much *more* readily discoverable than commonly supposed. Thus, first, actualities no longer can be thought of merely on the model of bricks, feet, and houses, but must equally be thought of as revolutions, obligations, and pleasures, none of which can serve as exemplars of individuals. Second, actualities are exemplified also by human products and exemplified *in* these products (these products as orders) no less than by and in their producers. Thus Cézanne, Mme. Cézanne, and Mme. Cézanne-portrayed are three distinguishable actualities. In the case of the third of these, we have a complex produced, with its own traits of actuality and of possibility. Some of its traits of actuality were intended by its producer, others were not. Mme. Cézanne-portrayed is a complex in the order of visual art, and she is not "less authentically actual" than the Mme. Cézanne who changes in the order of public space and historical time. Further, Mme. Cézanne, Mme. Cézanne-portrayed, and Balzac are none of them more or less actual than Balzac's product Cousin Bette, located in an order of literary art and in a sub-order of social life within that order, just as Balzac, a product of his parents, is not less actual than they. To understand the order which determines the integrity of

Cousin Bette, as to understand any other, we need to
search and interpret; we need to ascertain traits of actuality
and possibility. The best evidence is that both scheming
and truth-telling are recurrent possibilities in her constitution. Gentleness and candor are not among its actualities,
while embitterment and turbulence of spirit are. Should
we deny the actual duplicity of Balzac's Cousin Bette and
accept the actual slenderness of Michelangelo's David?

We are ready to get back to the World.

iv

We suggested at the outset that to speak of the World as
"everything" is unassailable but unilluminating. One
might think that the same is true of more consciously
devised equivalents like "the totality of all totalities" or
"the all-inclusive whole." But these are scarcely less vague
and much more shaky. The slightest move toward elaboration causes trouble. Thus if the World is called the
Totality of all totalities, and we ask why it could not just
as well be called the Totality of all that composes these
totalities, we get into what may be termed Wittgenstein's
Difficulty. Or if the World is called the All-inclusive
Whole, and we ask whether this whole includes all
possibilities and all actualities, we get snarled in the
question whether there are "possible Worlds" which are
not included. (Innocently spread out among these unclari-
fied positions is the grammatically unavoidable habit of
referring to the World as "it.") Prospective analysis does
not promise much for either of the above phrases, one
relying on "totality," the other on "whole." For, generally
speaking, the dictated angle of approach is not promising.
It falls back on still other ideas which invite vulnerable

assumptions. Bergson, for example, wishes to think of the World not simply as the Whole but as "the real whole," which he further characterizes (though not without some hesitation) as an "indivisible continuity."

The problem at this point is to speak of the World in such a way that, if we cannot yet define it with some degree of explicitness, we can avoid referring to it in precarious terms. The problem is not with the conception of *worlds,* it is with the conception of the World as satisfying a principle of exhaustiveness. The other type of problem earlier alluded to, that raised by the contrast God and the World, cannot be ignored. But one way in which it can be moved toward resolution, in the sense of achieving at least a coherent philosophic outlook, is by developing a sufficiently radical conception of the World as encompassing God. The objective would be to contrast God and the World in the way that we can contrast Man and Nature, Art and Nature, Mind and Nature, the first concept of each pair being ontologically and even dramatically definable in terms of the second. The opposition within each pair can remain genuinely oppositional, reflecting a perennial philosophic vacillation between making a more comprehensive and making a less comprehensive idea serve as the key to understanding.

When we speak of worlds, we are speaking of orders with the kind of scope that affords them distinctive recognition. Recognition of this type is not debatable or nominal, but compulsive. The order, a world, is what inculcates the recognition in us. The complexes of the order elicit from us a characteristic sub-order of judgment: of assertion, action, or contrivance on our part. It is not any order that can compel in comparable kind. Our location within a world carries with it a continuing sense of that world, though not necessarily a sense of vastness. The sense is rather that of indefinitely comprehensive scope. A world is an order of which relatively little is appropriated in the typical situations of that order. This does not mean that every world is mysterious, any more than that it is always felt to be vast. It might be more accurate to say that every world is elusive, in some degree remote, but again not as being frustrating or recalcitrant at all times (people say "I am at home in *this* world"), but as imposing the indefiniteness of its extent. No one can be aware of all the orders he inhabits. Nor can anyone even be aware of all the worlds he inhabits. Despite the unmistakable sense of the "indefinitely greater" that distinguishes some orders as worlds, we do not, after all, formally represent to ourselves the most deep-seated responses. Besides, we can never adequately articulate our whereabouts. It is no wonder, because a world, like any other order, is itself located in other orders. Considering that each order is a sub-order with sub-orders of its own, where should we say we are?

If each world is an order of complexes, are we on the way to concluding that the World is the Order of all orders? Since there has been less philosophic concern with worlds than with the World, there has been correspondingly less readiness to categorize them on the basis of analogy. We hear it asked whether the World is a Process or an Individual or whatever, but to ask whether a world ought to be so named is apparently much less interesting or not discriminated as an issue. Metaphysicians of today, even in the face of their own impatience with metaphysics, still feel driven to ask,

"What is the ultimate nature of the World?" Among those who do not, some (fortunately) wonder what the difference is between a "nature" and an "ultimate nature," and whether the question itself is a compound of confusions. But many who feel in no way obliged to deal with such a question will speak, nevertheless, as philosophers so often have, of "the World order," "the natural order," "the order of nature." "Order," here, *cosmos*, is used, for the most part, in the narrower and traditional sense earlier mentioned, pattern, structure, arrangement. The issue dealt with concerns the kind of pattern that the World has. (Within this more restricted sense, there is a jumble of "order" and "orderliness." Opposed to "order" is "chaos" or "non-being," treated as if they could be the alternatives. Opposed to "orderliness" is disharmony.) In this way of thinking, the concept of orders, ordinal scope and ordinal location, does not enter at all. The question we are raising and are not quite prepared to answer at this point is whether, in *terms* of the concept of order and natural complex, "all" orders, including worlds, should be regarded as subaltern to an Order called the World.

The so-called World-Order of traditional philosophic usage has been described sometimes in adjectival and sometimes in substantival terms. Thus when it is said adjectivally that the World-Order is (an) intelligible (order), we are being told something about its knowability. Often both its relative knowability and its inherent structure are referred to; for instance, calling it rational or causal or mathematical is designed to explain why it is knowable. Certain adjectival approaches lend themselves to substantival versions. The World-Order is described in a more reductive way by calling it a mathematical or causal *system*. The adjectival approach is less reductive in so far as it can emphasize the primacy of a trait without emphasizing its exclusiveness; it can allow for the "mathematical" World being more than mathematical.

The question whether the World should be said to be a Complex of all complexes must be preceded by the question whether the World should be said to be this or that kind of complex. The core traditional issue is whether the World as a Whole is describable as an A-kind of being, a G-kind of being, an R-kind, each of these analogically based.

First of all, is the World a Whole? In terms of the conception customarily accepted, a whole has parts. Presumably the World would be an undelimited whole with an indefinite number of parts. The notion of a part, however, also customarily requires a distinction between what is essential and what is inessential. Thus we say that the flatness of the top surface of a table is essential to it, while the roundness of the table is not. The former is a "proper" part, the latter a contingent part. In the putative whole called the World, this distinction is inapplicable. Of course, it could be shown that the distinction in the case of any complex is applicable only with respect to an assumed order. The table's proper parts will vary according as the table is located in an order of writing and eating, or in an aesthetic order, or in an order of curiosities. For the World, however, there is no way of ascertaining what is required in *any respect*. Everything is equally a part and therefore required. On the other hand, nothing in particular is required. For if anything is changed, the World is neither more nor less the World. It could not be the World as a Whole that would be described differently; it could only be a *part*. In fact, qua Whole, the World could be "described" only in the most questionable sense.

Would it be better to circumvent the inelastic notion of whole and part by asking instead whether the World is an Individual? To this day it remains difficult to say convincingly what is meant by "an individual." If an individual is held to be that which, among all kinds of "being," alone satisfies the requirement of "not being dependent upon anything besides itself," then the consequence would seem to be that the World is the only individual. If, on the other hand, it is insisted that there are indeed many individuals, and that each is "in itself," each would be "a world unto itself," yet not a world in any sense that would be credible to anyone. Moreover, absolutely independent individuals would not belong to the World, for as absolutely independent they need not belong to anything. Similar absurd consequences follow from thinking of individuals as simples or as the perfect manifestations of "unity."

Most philosophers think of individuals on the basis of their own recurrent encounters with what are *called* individuals. Implicitly, they find in these complexes what amounts to a certain *kind* of unity, a certain *kind* of homogeneity, certain limits for diversity and multiplicity. When we ask whether the World should be regarded as an Individual, we are asking both whether analogy is our best resource and whether the best analogy is that of the individual. Regardless of the relative clarity with which we can approach the concept of individual analytically, we harbor certain assumptions which collectively establish for it a meaning: Individuals are related to other individuals, are distinguishable from them in some respects and similar to them in some respects, are involved in activities or processes, are subject to grouping and class-membership, and are environed by conditions of one kind or another.

Now if the World were an Individual, it might perhaps be said to be distinguishable from other individuals. But this amounts to a distinction between whole and part, for there cannot be individuals aside from or outside the World. Whether there is a commensurateness that would permit comparison between an inclusive Individual and any individuals included is doubtful. But in any case, the World cannot be environed; it cannot be a member of any class; and it cannot be involved in an activity or process more pervasive than itself. Nor is the thesis of Individuality supported by claiming that the World is a very special kind of individual. This begs the question. We have no prior grounds that would allow us to take it for granted. How great a degree of speciality can the attribution of individuality tolerate? The paradox is evident. We want to characterize the World in terms of a complex which is encompassed by it; yet we also want to deviate from the very complex chosen as its model. The exception, the deviation, is not of the type wherein one individual is said to depart from the ways of another. It is from the model's most fundamental traits. If the analogy has not broken down utterly, it is seriously inadequate.

The assignment of individuality to the World has taken even more specific forms. Thus the World has been interpreted as an organism. Although no theological implication necessarily follows, this bears out the charge of Hume's Demea that, in "narrow partiality, we make ourselves the model of the whole universe." The partiality, however, is somewhat more far-reaching; it is to the *kind* of analogy chosen. It would be no less present if the World were regarded as an individual machine. Neither analogy is tenable. An organism is no organism if it lacks a habitat, lacks an individual history, and is unrelated to comparable organisms. A machine is no machine if it accomplishes every result and yields every product. There is a great difference between saying that among the complexes of the World we can discriminate organic and mechanical processes even where least expected and saying that the World as such is an organism or a machine.

Although difficulties arise whenever we think of the World as a singular subject to which traits are attributed, there are deceptive types of formulation. When it is said that the World is a Process or an Interrelation, the emphasis on singularity seems to vanish. But the concept of an integrity certainly does not. An interrelation and a process are complexes which have an integrity, even as an individual has. Some formulations have subtle loopholes and uncertain consequences. They represent weaknesses which can be found in philosophical cosmologies, especially theories of evolution like those of Peirce, Bergson, and Whitehead. If these theories are not open to simple definite indictment, it is only because their framers are sensitive, in principle, to the pitfalls of cosmology. Peirce and Whitehead seem aware of the trouble that may develop in treating the World as if it were one among many. Yet, being themselves much attracted to the kinds of analogies that generate dilemmas, they are impatient of self-imposed warnings, and it is a fair question whether the metaphysics of cosmic chance and love, and the metaphysics of creativity and creative advance do not further obscure the concept of the World.

We may now deal directly with the question whether the World should be regarded as the Order of all orders, the Complex of all complexes. We are about to integrate and to restate in a more generalized and precise way objections previously made under the handicap of limited formulation in limited contexts.

There cannot be a World Order, a Complex of all complexes. Every natural complex, itself an order, is located in an order. In other words, every complex is also a sub-complex, every order a sub-order. The World cannot be a complex, because it cannot be a sub-complex; it cannot be an order, because it cannot be a sub-order. Every complex is related to a complex other than itself and its subaltern complexes. The World cannot be a complex, because there could not be anything besides the World to which it could be related. The World cannot be located, for it would have to be located in an order which would be more inclusive. The World cannot be included, for it would then be not the World but one more order, one more sub-complex. The World cannot be environed, as every order can and must be, for that which environs would be a complex distinctly additional to the World— an absurdity. "An all-encompassing order" could not be the World. It could not be anything but an expression, a verbal complex, and not a very useful one, except through its indirect instructiveness. Though it speaks of an order, it contradicts the concept of an order.

Since the World cannot be ordinally located, it cannot have an integrity. But why, it may be asked again, this time on the more general level, must *every* complex be a sub-complex and sub-order? May there not be a Final

complex, an Extraordinary order? The answer is that the exception proposed would destroy metaphysical principles which are useful and defensible on other grounds.†
To insist upon ordinal location as a necessary condition of an integrity is merely to reiterate that an order defines a complex in a given respect. Each ordinal location delimits, delineates, bounds, demarcates a complex. An unlocated complex, one without an integrity, would be one without traits—another absurdity. If we admitted it as theoretically tolerable, an unlocated, unrelated complex might then have no sub-complexes, since these by the same token would not need to be located. The World, or what would be left of it, would be without events, relations, or possibilities. Again we see the doubly unsatisfactory outcome of employing an analogy for the World (this time a generic category, that of complex) and basically evading the analogy. The analogy cannot be carried through, and neither can the evasion.

V

By "the World" we must mean: Innumerable natural complexes (each located, each locating) which distributively include any given complex and which have no collective integrity. For "complexes" we may of course read "orders of complexes." "Innumerable" is intended both in the sense of being indefinitely numerous and in the sense of being not in all respects numerable. The two senses combine to yield "indefinitely numerous where numerable." The present formulation is in non-singular terms and embodies a principle of exhaustiveness, an "everything" principle. It avoids the notion of a universal container, and it avoids the possible re-emergence of an absolute Order by avoiding the idea of a set, a collection, a class, a totality, a grouping, a whole, for any of these implies a complex. The formulation will not allay the habitual philosophic craving for some familiar assurance of overall unity, a craving which has no rational force and which reflects no conceptual imperative. On the other hand, the concept of natural complex expresses the very basis of the interdependence of unity and plurality. There is no final Unity, but there are and can be unities of overwhelming pervasiveness. There is no final Order; yet whatever is, is an order.

In speaking now of the World we shall abbreviate its defining conception and speak equivalently of Innumerable Complexes. A concern which directly follows definition of a term as difficult as "the World" is the extent to which established locutions remain viable. Several such locutions revolve about the word "in." First of all, if we wish to speak of given complexes as "in the World," we must beware of drawing the conclusion that they are *located* in the World. It is not the World as such that determines for them an integrity. It is not Innumerable Complexes, not complexes at large, so to speak, that locate a given complex ordinally. No assumption has here been made that "all" complexes are related to all complexes in all respects. Such an assumption, we have argued elsewhere, destroys the concept of relation. No assumption has been made that, because any given complex is never unrelated, it is therefore related to all others. The idea of total interrelatedness might be held to justify "locating" a complex in a single universal scheme. But positing such a scheme and providing a map of it are two different matters. Complexes are not related to, not located in, the

World as World. There is no location for them beyond
their ordinal locations. There is no "ultimate" location.
"In," as we first pointed out near the end of section one,
may be construed generically as an ellipsis of "in relation
to." More precisely, it means "belonging to an order or
complex (of which it is a constituent or sub-complex)."[6]

With this precaution, the phrase "in the World" can be
useful in certain types of contexts. "Man is in the World"
is sometimes a disavowal of the view that man is bottled
up in his consciousness. "Anything in the World" suggests
"any complex we can think of." To say of some complex
that "it has its place in the World" is a bit more tricky; the
statement should be the signal for specification and
definition. Every complex does have its "place"—its
places—in various orders of the World. Rhetorical emen-
dation would turn "its place in the World" into "its place
somewhere in the World," the "somewhere" understood,
perhaps, as an order not yet known or found.

Not all usages are innocuously or meaningfully translatable. Philosophically formulated questions like "What
if there were no World?" or "Why is there a World instead
of nothing at all?" grammatically resemble questions like
"What if conditions on earth had not permitted am-
phibians to evolve?" or "Why are there mountains in this
area instead of plains?" They refer to the World as if it
were a complex. It is fair to ask whether they should be
called "questions." The phrases "no World" and "nothing
at all" do not identify a subject-matter for consideration.
The negation of World is not an alternative identification.

---

6. This conception satisfies, for example, all eight senses of "in"
distinguished in Aristotle's *Physics* 4.3.

The phrases seem to communicate only because they approximate, or reduce to, something like "totally unknowable World" or "absolutely empty World" or "wholly other kind of World." But these are of equally doubtful coherence.

What bearing has the notion of "possible worlds" on the concept of the World? The phrase assumes certain possibilities the actualizations of which would mean that the World is a world. Presumably, there could be either (A) possibilities of a World other than the World, or (B) possibilities of the World undergoing the kind of change which transforms its character as the World. (A) implies alternative Worlds, (B) alternative transformations of the World. In view (A), the World is the present actuality and other Worlds are possibilities: they may be or might have been actualized. From our defined standpoint, (A) is meaningless. One can speak of the possibility of worlds "within" the World, that is, the possibility of certain kinds of orders among Innumerable Complexes. But one cannot speak meaningfully of the World as belonging to a class (of "Worlds" that are possible). For again we have a brand of speculation which refers to the World as if it were a given complex. (B), however, is not an intelligible view either. It implies much more than that there may be unprecedented transformations. It implies a conclusion similar to (A), namely, that the World has a character as a whole, and that it is possible for this whole character to be replaced by another, in effect, for the World to be replaced by "another." But Innumerable Complexes have no collective integrity, are not a collection. There is not a whole character of Innumerable Complexes. Any kind or degree of transformation is a given complex.

The remarks on possibility previously made (toward the end of section three) must have indicated already why most versions of "possible worlds" rest on an unsound approach to the concept of possibility. It is an approach which assumes that although some possibilities are dependent on actualities, dependent on (ordinal) conditions, there are also "pure possibilities" which are wholly independent. Not all who hold this view believe that there is a "realm" of possibility. But the view does appear to assume a realm of pure intellection or conception. Pure possibilities are held to be discoverable by pure calculation, to be ascertained by ascertaining what is free from contradiction.

In accordance with such an approach, we often hear something like this: "Insects don't talk, because that is biologically, empirically, impossible; but it is logically or abstractly possible that they could, for there is no contradiction involved." But a contradiction certainly is involved, a contradiction of the concept of "insect," an area of knowledge, and the conditions of linguistic meaning. That is, the so-called logical or pure possibility turns out not to be about insects at all. The alleged pure possibility free from all ordinal limitations *is* in fact determined in and by an order of complexes, but an order covertly introduced—in this case, an order of envisioned images. It is this order that serves as the guarantor of "non-contradiction." For behold, we envision "insects talking." And indeed there are creatures plainly doing so in this visual order. But they are not insects. Insects, of course, may belong also to an order of reverie. But the integrity determined by this order must be reconcilable with the integrities determined by their other ordinal locations, otherwise we are thinking only of animals arbitrarily given the same name. Thus claims of this kind not only rely on an order for their content and meaning, but unconsciously introduce such an order, one in which the alleged possibility is deemed to be actualized. There are no exceptions to the principle of ordinally determined possibilities. The so-called formal possibilities are not "pure" in the sense of being certified as possibilities *apart* from an order. Their order is an abstract system with complexes of notational signs, rules of combination, and rules of inferential procedure. Like all orders, this one has its possibilities and its actualities.

Possibilities of any kind, then, are to be found among the Innumerable Complexes as traits of orders. There cannot be possibilities of the World "as a whole," because the World is not an order. Nor can there be possibilities "for" the World, if this implies the absurd idea of a complex apart from the World and of which the World would be a trait. If God were a complex of great scope and significance, that complex would be among the Innumerable Complexes. We can therefore say that various worlds are possible in the World or that among the Innumerable Complexes there are actualizations which have the distinctive character of worlds.

The phrase "actual World" is as confusing and unnecessary as "possible World." The World is not "an actuality." It is not an actualization. For these are traits of an order. But in a good many philosophic works "the *actual* World" appears to be contrasted with "what anyone may *think* the World is" rather than with "a possible World." The so-called actual World is then equated with "what the World *is*." Plausible as this may sound at first, the comparison involved comes close to presupposing an integrity for the World, the question at issue apparently being whether we know what this integrity is or merely think we know. The comparison is made as if it were analogous to one between "what we may think the moon is" and "what the moon *is*."

Since the Innumerable Complexes do not constitute an Order, and since in consequence no order has an "ultimate" location, it follows that no order has absolute priority over any other. The dynamical order in which railroad tracks actually never converge has no intrinsic priority over the visual order in which they actually sometimes converge. Priorities of all kinds there surely are—causal, logical, explanatory, ethical, literary—but all are conditional. Being conditional means being ordinally determined, and this is what is meant by priority being always priority in some respect. No complex is prior "in nature." On the other hand, a complex prior in any given respect is indeed prior in that respect. Thus a complex which is prior in a given order of human evaluation definitely is prior in that order, and the same complex, if it is not prior in another order of human evaluation, definitely is not prior in that other order. Among Innumerable Complexes there are innumerable differences and innumerable similarities, but there is no final hierarchy of complexes. The World has no form, no boundaries, no constitution. It is not mappable. There are complexes which have a beginning and complexes which have an ending. Innumerable Complexes, the World, has no beginning and no ending.

The discrediting of non-ordinal priorities, priorities in the World at large, has further consequences for metaphysical theory. For example, it undermines the view that actuality is "ultimately prior" to possibility. Holding a view of this kind is like holding the view that one trait is more of a trait than another, one trait-type more of a trait-type than another. The elimination of absolute priorities also removes one of the supposed grounds for the view that certain complexes may be more "real" than others, the ground being their relative position in an Ultimate Hierarchy of Being. But regardless of whether we commit ourselves to accepting ultimate or functional hierarchies, and indeed whether or not we speak of hierarchies, no basis can be established for an ontological distinction between more and less "real" complexes. For, once again, no complex is more of a complex than any other. Equally meaningless and more obviously pointless is the metaphysical question *whether* a complex is "real," which is like asking whether it is a complex.

In the well-known everyday sense, "real" expresses conformity to or attainment of a given standard; "not real," failure to meet the standard. Sometimes "real" is a term of emphasis ("That is what I really mean"). Sometimes it reflects appraisal in comparative terms ("He is a real man," "That is the real issue," "She has lost sight of the real world"). These seemingly uncomplicated usages can be more than troublesome. Human individuals occupy different orders at any given time and successively within the comprehensive order or perspective that is their life history. ("Perspectives" are humanly occupied orders.) To describe anyone as having "no sense of reality" must be translated to mean that such an individual chronically confounds one perspectival location with another or has lost the power to differentiate in this regard, say, between an order of sensory imagination and an order of public association. To describe an individual as living in "an unreal world" reflects also a predetermination with respect to importance. For that individual, the world in question could equally well be described as "all too real." The case with the two worlds is not that one of them is the "real" one, but that it is difficult to live simultaneously in both. Yet even to say that both are "real" adds nothing meaningful to what has already been acknowledged, that each is a world. The notion of "reality" has never been helpful to theoretical understanding and has often impaired it. At times it has played no positive role but has only served as a separate hindrance to clarification. Thus in the classical refrain of metaphysics, "What is the real nature of the World?" the word "real" only adds to a confusion that (as we can now see) is present in the question to begin with.[7]

JUSTUS BUCHLER

---

7. In dealing with the concept of the World, the meaning we have provided is conveyed in terms of Innumerable Complexes (as qualified and amplified above). If we were dealing with the concept of Nature, the meaning provided would be conveyed in terms of Complexity and Ordinality (though incompletely). There is an inevitable difference of focus, and the two approaches are complementary. See my *Metaphysics of Natural Complexes* and *Southern Journal of Philosophy* 14 (Spring 1976) p. 52.

APPENDIX IV

PROBING THE IDEA OF NATURE‡

i

Both in colloquial and in methodic discourse the idea of
nature has functioned in a large number of ways, and the
variety of these ways makes it seem impossible to find
significant relatedness among them. Nature has been
distinguished from man, from art, from mind, from
chance, from purpose, from history, from eternity, from
irregularity, from society, from civilization, from God,
from evil, from good—to name some of the best known
historical contrasts. Yet with respect to every one of these
same ideas, nature also has been made inclusive of it or
synonymous with it or continuous with it. I have no
intention of trying to explain how all this has come about.
But it will not be irrelevant to remark that the very fact of
the concept "nature" lending itself to so many and conflicting uses can be seen as a cue, a hint to metaphysical
thinking rather than as a ground for despair. My subject
will take the form of considering two broad philosophic
tendencies which have determined specific conceptions of

‡*Process Studies* 8:3 Fall 1978, pp. 157-168. This paper was also
presented to the Metaphysical Society of America prior to its publication in March 1979. (*Process Studies* 8:3 was actually published in late
1979 or 1980.)

nature. One of the tendencies is to regard nature as limited, and the other is to regard nature as unlimited. After asking what the difference comes to, and after persuading you to think exactly as I do, I shall propose a possible way of defining nature. But first, some observations that are more or less historical.

According to Collingwood's book *The Idea of Nature*, the two most frequently used broad senses that have been given to the word "nature" are: first, the collective sense of a "sum total or aggregate," and second, the sense of a "principle" or *arché*, a source which defines or informs whatever is called "natural" and which justifies our speaking also in the plural, of "natures" or "essences." This second sense is held to be the original and so-called proper sense of *physis*. I think it would be better to identify these two ways of conceiving nature as "orientations" rather than senses or direct meanings. The first of them I would call the domain-orientation; the second, the trait-orientation. Thus reframed, each can be seen in a way that permits certain distinctions to emerge. For example, with regard to the first orientation, nature conceived as a domain may be, but *need* not be, conceived as a collection or sum or aggregate; instead, it may be conceived as a certain *kind* of domain. And with regard to the second orientation, nature as the principle or source of traits that are called "natural" can be thought of as just that—a principle of traits—and not a principle only of those traits that are called "essential." Thus it is at least possible to omit the notion of inherent essences without violating this second orientation. We may observe, in general, that it is a trait orientation which has given rise to concern about the natural vs. the *un*natural, or the natural vs. the artificial, and that it is a domain-orientation which has given rise to concern about the natural vs. the *super*-natural. In the present discussion such concerns are reduced to the general issue of the natural vs. the nonnatural, which is one way of rendering our question of nature unlimited vs. nature limited.

It is within what we are calling the domain-orientation that Collingwood believes the difference is to be found between nature conceived as unlimited and nature conceived as a limited or restricted domain. A restricted domain in Collingwood's version is one that is not independent but dependent on some other. He believes that in the basic tradition of European thought the dominant view by far is this view of nature as limited: it implies that nature has "a derivative or dependent status in the general scheme of things," that "the world of nature forms only one part or aspect of all being." It is dependent "on something prior to itself." Historically, the reasons underlying the restricted view, the one called dominant, are extremely diverse. But the view as such is held or presupposed by scientists as well as philosophers, and it goes back to the time when the entire general issue of the scope of nature was debated in early Greek thought.

It is very hard to assess a contention about what is the dominant view. My interest here is mainly theoretical rather than historical. But even historically, we cannot gauge the issue solely by trying to figure out a numerical majority of opinions. For among them there are implicit emphases which have been as influential as those which are visible on the surface. We could also cite powerful counter-examples like Erigena, Aquinas, and Spinoza, who in their different ways conceive of a divine nature and in effect make nature the inclusive, or an equivalent of the inclusive, category. Probably many others were likewise convinced that, since whatever is has a nature, the notion of a nonnature is absurd. Collingwood, as we might suspect, pays small attention to that particular medieval tendency which dwells on *natura naturans* and *natura naturata*. When, however, he alters his angle and calls the dominant view the "modern" view, he is on securer ground. Then we recognize the so-called world of nature as the spatiotemporal world, and we begin to understand why science, for so long called "natural philosophy," still wishes to be called "natural" science.

I still have a bone to pick on the historical level. It is surprising for a historical account (especially a serious account like Collingwood's) to interpret a restrictive conception of nature as one in which nature has "a derivative or dependent status." In the modern restrictive tendency what is called the world of nature, far from being considered necessarily dependent, is as often assigned the reverse status, namely that upon which any other "world" is "dependent" (e.g., the "world of number" or the "moral world") or that of which any other world is an appearance or that which is "more real" than any other world.

ii

The notion of "the world of nature" usually involves the cognate notion of "the order of nature" or "the natural order." It is interesting to reflect that philosophers like Peirce and Whitehead, esteemed for their intensive concern with science as well as for their independent spirit, tend to think of nature in the limiting or restrictive way. They deal at considerable length with "the order of nature," a phrase the components of which seem to receive from them a certain type of explicit consideration, but which as a phrase remains dim in both of them. I suppose that the order-of-nature habit of thought is an oblique commitment to the idea of "laws of nature," which would be a much more difficult idea to defend if the domain-orientation were of the unlimited kind. Whitehead says in *The Concept of Nature*, "Nature is that which we observe in perception through the senses." In *Process and Reality* he says that when "we speak of the 'order of nature'" we mean "the order reigning in that limited portion of the universe...which has come under our observation." And as late as *Modes of Thought* he says, "Nature, in these chapters, means the world as interpreted by reliance on clear and distinct sensory experiences, visual, auditory, and tactile." Whether these statements of the same theme are perfectly harmonious in themselves or with one another, I am not sure. But they surely accentuate the restrictive position. In *The Concept of Nature* Whitehead had said also, "Natural science is the science of nature." And again, "[N]ature can be thought of as a closed system whose mutual relations do not require the expression of the fact that they are thought about." In *Process and Reality* the term "nature" serves the purpose of defining subject-matter basic to science. Treating philosophically of nature thus apparently boils down to focusing the more general metaphysical categories on such concepts as space and time. In contrast to what is sought by science, there is said by Whitehead to be "an essence to the universe" which is sought by metaphysics or speculative philosophy. Metaphysics, he believes, seeks to understand "the system of the universe." I refrain from comment for the time being, except to note that Whitehead also occasionally uses phrases like "the womb of nature" and "the divine nature," which may or may not suggest a tacit alternative usage of nature in a wider sense.

Let us return to the idea of "the order of nature," which often seems to function less as an idea than as a name or slogan conventionally identifying a roughly associated group of problems. In contexts where it is presumably under discussion, specifically those of Peirce and White-head, it is hard to find out whether the phrase presupposes order *in* nature or nature as *an* order. If there is any difficulty in taking "the order of nature" to mean "that order which is called nature," then the difficulty should attach also to the expression "the world of nature," which has the same type of import. But leaving aside the question of what sense we should accept, the distinction between order as belonging to nature and the order called nature is of utmost importance. It reflects the difference between "order" as a definite familiar kind of trait and "an order" as a complex of traits, a location of traits, regardless of what kind. Order in the former sense is contrasted with "disorder," whereas *an* order, construed as a complex of traits, can be contrasted only with other orders: as we will find, there is no meaning to a nonorder. "Order" contrasted with "disorder" is not a distinction at the most general ontological level. But "an order" in the sense I am suggesting has little to do with order in the sense of arrangement or pattern, such as a pattern of regularity or of chance. It is to be understood as a complex with an integrity. In other words, the concept of an order or complex is universally applicable.

We pursue this now in more detail. Let us suspend

temporarily the entire issue of the scope of nature, of whether we can maintain a distinction between natural and nonnatural. And in our metaphysical stance, let us think of anything at all, whether it be classified as an individual, a sensation, an event, a relation, a structure, a grouping, a change, a process, an eternal form, a hallucination, or whatnot. It has traits. It is a complex of traits. It is a plurality of traits. The plurality will follow if only from each trait's being itself ramified, from each trait's standing in relations; from each trait's, in other words, being itself a complex. No trait is at some point cut off relationally from *every* other. If there is such a point of absolute disconnectedness, we have yet to identify it or certify it in the history of man. The traits of a given complex will differ in some respect from those constituting any other and will resemble them in some respect. This is another way of saying that each complex limits and relates its traits in the way that it does. By "the way that it does" or "the respect in which it does" we imply an order. We have already posed the reciprocal idea of an order as a complex of traits. And we have just now been speaking in ordinal terms.

To improve the cohesiveness of this truncated account, we must lay fuller emphasis on two concepts which are interwoven with the others in the reciprocal way just employed. These are the concepts of integrity and ordinal location. Insofar as each complex both differs from and resembles others, it has a trait makeup. Yet if our description went no farther than this, we could not say that a complex has an integrity but only certain constituents thereof, including plurality. The other and indispensable factor is the location of the complex in an order, that is, in an order other than itself, a more inclusive order. By its location the complex is delimited and hence distinguished in a given way from other complexes. As ordinally located it may be thought of as playing a role in a setting—a spatial setting or a moral setting or an occupational setting or any environing complex—even if the role at bottom is that of excluding other traits and being in a specific relation. But a complex may be located in many orders and may therefore have many integrities. If not located in a given order, it does not have an integrity relevant to that order. It is not defined or delimited in that respect. But ordinally located it must be. To omit this consideration is to inject contradiction into the concept of a complex. It follows directly that every complex of traits is not only located or included in various orders, but locates and includes other complexes, subcomplexes, and is an indispensable determinant of *their* integrity. Orders, being complexes of traits, thus derive their integrities from their status in more inclusive orders, and no order is an order if it is not inclusive and included, locative and located. But the "no order if" phrase is, of course, a merely rhetorical addition, for on the approach I am describing, what is not an order *is* not.

Returning to the problem of nature and the natural: the issue as formally stated was put in terms of the domain-orientation, i.e., is nature a limited or an all-inclusive domain? But the issue also can be put (as we have implied) in terms of the trait-orientation, i.e., is nature a source or principle of traits limited to the so-called essential traits of any being, or is it a principle universally applicable to any trait whatever? We stated a miniature argument for the unrestricted conception, attaching it to the outlook of such as Erigena, Aquinas, and Spinoza. It went: since whatever is has a nature, we cannot give meaning to the notion of a nonnature. To this it might be objected, first, that the use of the expression "a nature" to apply to whatever is, decides the issue by definition and settles it in advance; and second, that the use of the expression "a nature" confounds the domain-orientation with the trait-orientation, for we are talking about the scope of nature and not about this or that nature.

But in fact, as we now can see, we do not need the expression "a nature" at all. We are able to say that whatever is has an integrity; it is the integrity of a complex. We are able to say that a complex, necessarily being located in *some* order, cannot have a nonintegrity. And in general we are now able to see that a trait-orientation and a domain-orientation are merely two sides of one and the same effort of interpretation. For a domain is an order, and there is no order without traits, just as there are no traits, no complexes, unlocated in any order.

The view of nature as restricted amounts to the view that there is a widespread order of complexes called nature, which is either located in another or other orders or includes other orders but not every other. In the now popular but actually more customary language of "worlds," nature restricted is a world that is seen as somehow related to other worlds. Of course, once we see each of these worlds as an order, the pressure to specify the order and to clarify its relatedness, to get rid of the "somehow," becomes greater.

As for the unrestricted view, it too now can be stated without interference by old associations of the term "nature." We seem required to say that nature unrestricted must include all worlds, indeed all orders whether they are to be called worlds or not. But a careful statement of the unrestricted view cannot be achieved all at once. There are problems that have to be solved.

iii

I introduced the common term "domain" to help clarify a historical distinction and to help launch the present discussion. At this point we are in a position to see that although we can speak of a domain as an order, and perhaps vice versa, we cannot speak of a domain or order of nature in the unrestricted sense. The reason is emphatically not the Kantian view that nature or the world as a whole cannot be "given in experience," cannot be "objects of possible experience." To begin with, on the basis of such a reason we could argue that *nothing* as a whole can be an object of possible experience or be given, since we must take into account the indefinite spread of its relations and its potentialities. Actually we are aiming at an affirmative metaphysical conception instead of a conception based on a supposedly necessary structure of knowing and experiencing. Yet even if we approach the matter in epistemological terms, we certainly need not accept Kant's sense-appearance paradigm of the content of "experience," or what is meant by "given in experience" or "object of experience." And we certainly need not accept Kant's view of nature as "an aggregate of appearances." We shall have to say, instead, that though nothing at all is present as a "whole" in experience, yet nature is present in every instance of experience and every process of experiencing.

The reason that nature unlimited is not a domain may be put in the following way. A domain is an order, an order of traits. There is no order without delimitation, trait-delimitation. If nature were an order, it would be an order of all orders. But if it is unlimited, not delimited, it cannot be an order at all. For it would have to include every order without being included in any. It would have to locate every order without being located. If it is not ordinally located, it has no integrity. If it has no integrity, it cannot itself be the location of any other order and determine *that* order's integrity. An order cannot be defined by another which has no constitution of its own traits. And an order which does not locate and is not located does not constitute and is not constituted. The conclusion, then, must be that if nature is an order it is limited in scope and that if it is unlimited it is not an order. In familiar terms we would say that nature is not analogous to *a* nature. But of course it is the metaphysical explanation for the unsoundness of the analogy that is important.

A consequence of all this is that a conception merely of nature unrestricted is not enough. It needs to be augmented and clarified. If, as we have seen, it is so formulated that it can both utilize and abandon the concepts of a complex and an order, the idea of unrestrictedness is jeopardized. The way Kant, for instance, identifies the meaning of the terms "world" and "nature" jeopardizes the idea, by our standard. "World," he says, "signifies the mathematical sum-total of all appearances and the totality of their synthesis"; and "[t]his same world is entitled nature when it is viewed as a dynamical whole." Actually Kant cannot be speaking of nature in an unrestricted sense as that is here understood, if only because he associates nature intrinsically with a principle of causality, which is itself a restrictive condition. But what is relevant to our problem is the kind of formulation that we find in Kant. "Syntheses" and "wholes" are complexes of traits. They are integrities determined by ordinal location. Thus World and nature as identified by Kant would have to be ordinally located. But their location would mean inclusion in another order. And this contradicts the requirement in terms of which they are identified, namely, being inclusive and not being included.

The position that nature unlimited cannot be an order of all orders will remain puzzling to those for whom the latter idea has an emotional no less than an analytical aspect. They are inclined to think that nature unembraced is nevertheless all-embracing in *some* sense. The sentiment as such is not only understandable but acceptable—when we say *what* sense and say it more satisfactorily. But if it entails bald commitment to a superorder, then the burden falls on its exponents to develop another conception of what an order is or to discriminate two conceptions, one of which is uniquely applicable to nature. Pending that development, there is no good reason to exempt the idea of nature from the criteria of the ordinal conception we have found basic. After all, we are not faced with an impasse or a hopeless paradox. I shall define nature-unlimited otherwise than as an order, even if the result is not conveyed in the form of a conventional package. I think that behind the insistence on an order that is to be uniquely distinguished from all others there are no doubt various convictions mirroring conscious or unconscious models. But whatever models are adopted, the issue of integrity and demarcation must be explained or explained away. An order differentiated only by the all-inclusiveness ascribed to it, and itself without a principle of integrity, is as self-contradictory as an infinitely extended enclosure, a territory without boundaries, a habitation without environment, a definition without limits.

From the viewpoint at which we have arrived thus far, two general observations are pertinent. The first is that there is no longer any need to speak nor any meaning in speaking of "the unity of nature." This idea, which is another of the venerated metaphysical slogans, seems most at home in a restricted view of nature and in particular the historical view defending the universal applicability of scientific law and explanation to all that is measurable in the world. Another and even older version of the unity of nature is the idea of the inherent purpose or purposes of nature, "what nature intended." It too is familiar, morally and metaphysically—and remarkably obscure in meaning.

The second general observation is that no reason can be assigned for speaking of what Whitehead (among many others) calls "the system of the universe." "The universe" appears to be Whitehead's term for the most comprehensive order, and "nature," as we saw, is called by him a "portion" of the universe. We will recall also that intimately related to this assumption of a system is his view of "an essence to the universe," an essence allegedly sought by metaphysics. But, once again, the universe, deemed all-inclusive, cannot be itself an order and, therefore, cannot be called a system. A system is differentiable not only from its own subaltern systems but from alternative systems. If it is inclusive of all others, it is left without an integrity and is therefore not a system at all. Hence there is also no meaning in saying that it has an essence.

On the basis of the unrestricted view as stated thus far, science would be said to be concerned not with nature in an unqualified sense but with a given world or worlds— the physical world, the social world, the psychological world. These worlds are pervasive orders of nature, for we no longer can make sense of "the" order of nature. The diverse problems of science emerge in suborders or levels and, when resolved, provide integrities expressed in formulae. Included among the complexes of these orders are the methods and processes of scientific activity itself. And just as we no longer need struggle to make intelligible "the" order of nature, we no longer need to dignify the so-called rationality of nature. Aside from the meta-physical ineptitude of this particular attribution, the notion as such was framed to fit applied mathematical thinking. A tenable conception of nature recognizes many orders occupied by man among the innumerable orders not occupied by man and many orders devised by man. Among the latter are the orders of query, of which science or inquiry is one and art or contrivance is another, both, of course, indefinitely subdivisible. It is orders of query which yield different possible forms and manifestations of rationality.

We are obliged now to translate the foregoing considera-tions into terms which convey an idea of nature more directly. If nature is undelimited and therefore to be identified as coextensive with whatever is, we can say that by nature we mean "orders, of whatever variety and number." This is safe from the difficulties mentioned, if

not altogether congenial psychologically. Nothing is
implied about a totality or whole or collectivity, no
embarrassing commitment made to an ultimate integra-
tion which lacks an integrity. But needless to say, it is a
somewhat clumsy way of expressing an equivalent meaning. In calling it clumsy I do not want to be saying that
every adequate metaphysical conception must be rendered
in a grammatically facile way. If I had the time, I would
argue that philosophic and in particular metaphysical
judgment is not always best articulated or even best
understood in the form of assertions. Not less fundamental
is the force of mutually enhancing ideas which recur in
different contexts. These form a conceptual array. The
array is what communicates metaphysical query in the
firmest sense and preserves a structure over and above
specific weaknesses. A structure of metaphysical query has
an assertive dimension, but it also is one type of exhibitive
judgment. In the exhibitive mode of metaphysical judgment we discriminate traits that are not only comprehensive (at the level chosen) but meant to be satisfying in
virtue of that comprehensiveness as *portrayed*. The degree
of satisfactoriness (and I do not mean acceptance) will
reflect itself in continuing query compelled by the original
portrayal, by the conceptual array. But let us resume the
effort to define nature.

Now the term "the World" is what we may well think of
as the most highly generalized notion that can serve to
express the human sense of encompassment. In a parallel
and correlative way, the term "nature" may be thought of
as the most highly generalized notion that can serve to
express the human sense of characterization and traithood.
Elsewhere I have defined the term "the World" partly

through the following statements: "By 'the World' we must mean: Innumerable natural complexes (each located, each locating) which distributively include any given complex and which have no collective integrity.... 'Innumerable' is intended both in the sense of being indefinitely numerous and in the sense of being not in all respects numerable." In accord with this, and complementary to it, "nature" may be defined as the ordinality of any complex—any of the innumerable complexes. We define more fully by adding that nature is the complexity of any order—any of the innumerable orders. And more fully yet by adding that nature is indeed the complexity of any complex, the ordinality of any order; it is the ordinality that limits each complex, the complexity that pluralizes each order.

I can imagine someone questioning whether ordinality is not itself an order, whether complexity is not itself a complex, and whether therefore we do not lapse back into the idea of nature as the superorder. But I have already said that nature can be defined as "orders, of whatever variety and number" and that we are introducing only a more fluent, equivalent version. This leaves no implication of a superorder. In speaking of nature as the ordinality of any order we are affirming distributively that complexes named at random (say, a political community or the order of traits known as an apple) are first and last ordinal, whatever their specific traits may be. But it is not ordinality that includes and locates, it is one or another order. It is not ordinality as such that will provide an integrity. It is not nature that locates but an order of nature. It is not the World that locates but one or more of the innumerable complexes. The integrity of a complex is determined at a given level. A carpenter is defined by the order of activity to which he belongs. The integrity of a hereditary trait is determined by the genetic order in which it is located.

When nature is defined baldly as "orders, of whatever variety and number," too little is suggested of a difference in emphasis between the concepts of nature and the World. The focus is on *natura naturata:* we are given the crop, but not the seeding, not the productive principle. The definition in terms of ordinality corrects this. Some years ago I defined nature as providingness, the provision of traits. The intent was to abstract from the partly eulogistic common suggestion of purposive or planned accumulation, as well as of agency, and to amplify the suggestion of sheer putting forth or bringing forth, sheer geniture, for better and for worse. The conceptions of nature as providingness and as ordinality are continuous with one another and with the conception of nature as "orders." This continuity can be conveyed by utilizing both members of the twin *natura naturans* and *natura naturata*. Nature as ordinality is *natura naturans;* it is the providing, the engendering condition. Nature as "orders" is *natura naturata;* it is the provided, the ordinal manifestation, the World's complexes.

The foregoing conception of nature means that no complex can be regarded as, so to speak, transcendently free-floating, as nonordinal, as superseding all orders. It means, for example, that what are labelled as fictions, illusions, and contradictions also have an ordinal environment and an integrity or integrities, whether these be verbal or logical or emotional. It means that nothing is "contrary to nature," nothing distinctively "in accordance with nature." But one important way to see what the proposed conception implies is to understand its impact on the concepts of possibility and actuality. In denying "free-floating" status to any natural complex, we are, first, identifying any possibility as a complex and hence a subcomplex; and second, denying that any is a so-called pure possibility, one undetermined, unaffected by conditions both of actuality and related possibility. If ordinality is ubiquitous, then possibilities must be ordinally located. What is possible is possible only under given conditions. The conditions may be broad or narrow, constant and perpetual, or fleeting. They may be temporal or nontemporal, contingent or mathematical. When allegedly pure possibilities are thought of, they are in fact thought of ordinally, but the relevant conditions which are latently implied are unwittingly suppressed or overlooked. If a possibility were wholly independent of all other complexes, we surely could not conceive or envisage it, nor could we describe or formulate it. For whatever we could be talking about would relate to some complex that we bring to bear. It would relate to what we know or envision or can think of. We certainly can think of new possibilities, but not in complete discontinuity and isolation from all else. The complexes which we choose to talk and think about are partly but necessarily determining factors of the way we talk about them. A nonlocated possibility could not be identified. An integrity could not be framed for it. By contrast, to acknowledge that possibilities are traits and have subaltern traits is to acknowledge that each is bounded, limited. Perforce we ask: possibility of what, possibility in what respect, what direction?

The case is precisely the same with actuality. Every

actuality is native to an order or orders. A complex is determined ordinally to have the actuality and kind of actuality it has. Some philosophers who would not wish to speak of pure actuality in the way they speak of pure possibility nevertheless think that way and presuppose a notion of what is inherently and distinctively actual. Their model is the spatiotemporal, publicly measurable world, and even then, most often only the individuals of that world. Shakespeare they would consider actual—actual at one time, at least—but not the man Hamlet. If they became aware of the ordinal levels and locations that are relevant to the validation of all our judgments and modes of judgment, they might come to say (with the appropriate qualifications) that Shakespeare no longer is actual and that Hamlet still is or that since Shakespeare is indeed actual in an order of history his present efficacy is the efficacy of all the persons and relations he has actualized. It is not unusual to hear that art poses possibilities. It is less readily perceived that art produces actualities and that such actualities can be and have been more influential in the life of man than many actualities of the familiar public historical world. A genuinely ordinal conception of nature recognizes products of art to be orders in the same sense as other products, like technological orders and legal orders. Orders may, of course, interpenetrate one another. Having identified the relevant order, the order we are interested in, we accept what we find. We accept the actualities and possibilities of that order. Gertrude actually is the mother of Hamlet. Ophelia cannot possibly be that. Hamlet actually sees the ghost of his father. Those who would deny that Shakespeare's persons actually have eyes would hesitate to deny that Donatello's angels actually have wings. It must be that a bias toward certain kinds of art goes along with a bias toward certain kinds of actuality.

But we do not have to depart from everyday situations to grasp the ordinality that is nature. The first note of ordinal metaphysics was struck in 1951, when I suggested that a house may fluctuate in its actual size, just as it may fluctuate in its monetary worth. Many philosophers who would agree that when we stand before a house it is the house that we see, not an image or sense-datum or appearance of the house, would balk at the ordinal consequences. As we move away from the house, it becomes smaller. I am not saying, in the manner of certain epistemologies earlier in this century, that the house appears smaller, each appearance being just as much a reality as the house itself. I am saying that if what is called the "house itself" appears smaller, it is because it *gets* smaller. It is in the order of vision that it gets smaller. That is one of its ordinal locations, as much an ordinal location as its geometrical or financial location. As we move away from the house, it actually occupies a progressively smaller space in the visual order. This can be predicted and measured. The house is the same house, but in a different order. The different order yields a different integrity, another integrity of the same complex. What we should call the "nature" of the house is its network of integrities, its contour of ordinal locations.

There is, finally, a broad danger of ambiguity and confusion that needs to be guarded against. A persistent view of actuality is that it *is* an order, the order called "the world of actuality" or "the actual world." And there is a corresponding description of possibility as well, often associated with the idea of pure possibility, namely, that there is indeed an order called the realm of possibility.

Now, we know that it has been chronically difficult to give a plausible account of how a realm of possibility and a realm of actuality are related or get related. But my main concern here is that this pseudo-ordinal stance not be confounded with an ordinal conception of nature. For all actualities to be massed together in one realm and all possibilities in another is to remove them all from the various orders in which they belong or in which they arise. It is to remove them from their spheres of relevance and thereby to reject if not to destroy the conception of ordinality. Orders may not only prevail but eventuate or cease to prevail. The reason that a special realm of possibility or of actuality must be denied is that *every order* is a realm of possibility and of actuality. *Every* order or complex of traits has its traits of possibility and its traits of actuality. Even what we might abstractly call an order of possibilities arising in reflection or confronting social action has its aspects of actuality; for example, there is an actual succession of one possibility by another in the course of thinking or in the course of social occurrences.

In these remarks I have said nothing at all about how possibility may be defined or how actuality may be defined. I have tried only to argue the status of possibilities and actualities as natural complexes. The further explicit definition of these concepts adds support to the ordinal approach in general. But it requires further theoretical apparatus that cannot be adequately introduced here. The same must be said of other concepts I have scarcely mentioned, specifically those which I name prevalence and alescence. These are required for the fullest conception of nature along the lines indicated. They are designed, as a team, to do work which other philosophers may prefer to assign to the concept of Being.

Yet, notwithstanding these omissions, should it be hard to see that every natural complex has its mode of actuality and has possibilities that represent its limits? Or that whatever we produce, whatever we discriminate, whether a technological trend or a unicorn, a teapot or the bush that was not consumed, cannot be dismissed, ruled out, or declared null, but calls for ordinal definition? Should it be hard to see that an order of poetry, like an order of poets, is an order of nature?

JUSTUS BUCHLER

EDITORS' NOTES TO THE
SECOND EDITION

P. 1, Line 2: Buchler's method could be described as one of cumulative definition. No single statement suffices as *the* definition of a concept. Rather, his works are best read with, as he says in his Preface to MNC, a "willingness to accept a highly sequential exposition in which the earlier and later parts are mutually clarifying." There are a few places where he addresses this issue. We cite one here. (We also refer the reader to our Editors' Note to page 165, line 20.):

Singer's paper gives me the opportunity to suggest, not by way of remonstrance but as a general observation, that conceptual precision cannot always be thought of in terms of a concern to guard language from pitfalls. Sometimes it takes the form of holding together carefully the various constituents of an insight, and actualizing them linguistically when a particular stress is required. To think of these actualizations as competitors in an attempt to produce the one precise definition is to miss their role as contributors to definition. Looking at any formulation in the "competitive" way increases suspicion of ambiguity. Looking at it in the "contributive" way enables us to put two and two together. I think that my own tendency toward extreme economy of abstract formulation, seeking to trim away as much inessential matter as possible, has been partly responsible for the assumption that in my work there is one definitive version of each major concept. ("Reply to Singer: Alleged Ambiguities in the Metaphysics of Natural Complexes," SJP 68.)

P. 3, Line 7: Buchler comments on the meaning of providingness in his "Reply to Reck":

I have opposed the idea that nature is an order; it is the provision of orders. In certain contexts, if we find it necessary to steer our rhetoric to phrases like "the natural order," we must speak of it, I have said, not as including but as permeating all orders. The phrase "the order which permeates all orders" means the *ordinality* which permeates all complexes. It is better yet to say that nature *is* ordinality, so long as this is not all we say. Nature is ordinality and relationality, prevalence and alescence, possibility and actuality. This fortifies the view I first preferred and still like, that nature is "providingness"—the "provision and determination" of traits or complexes. ("Reply to Reck: The Structure of the Whole, The Location of the Parts," SJP 52, here 200.)

P. 3, Line 15: "Conceptual portrayal is part of the exhibitive function of philosophy..." begins Buchler's own note to this passage. We refer the reader to his passage on the same topic in Appendix IV, "Probing the Idea of Nature," p. 274. Also see Appendix I, "Reply to Greenlee: Philosophy and Exhibitive Judgment," pp. 207-214; and CM 166-169.

P. 22, Line 22: Buchler provides further clarification and amplification of the concept of contour. The first quotation is directed to the question of the relation between scope and contour. The issues of totality, continuity and unity of a complex are addressed in both quotations.

[N]ow, what about the relation between scope and contour? Since I distinguish the integrity of a complex from its scope, and since the contour of a complex is itself an integrity, how can I say that the scope of a complex is a factor in its contour? Here I am concerned not to correct but to avoid a misunderstanding. One of the reasons for distinguishing between the integrity and the scope of a complex is that a change in its comprehensiveness or pervasiveness—i.e. in its scope—may not affect its integrity. Thus, to take an example I have given, the arrival or departure of one resident in New York City's population of eight million should not be said to affect the integrity of the complex known as New York, even though technically the scope of this complex has altered. But there is all the difference in the world between saying that the integrity of a complex may not be affected by a *change* in its scope, and saying that the integrity of a complex may not be affected by its scope. In my structure of concepts the former is true, the latter false. The scope of a complex, its whole scope and not this or that change in scope, is a constituent of its integrity. Thus the city of New York derives its integrity partly from the kind of scope it has, its immense pervasiveness, even though particular changes in scope may be of no consequence for its integrity. The general conclusion is that the contour of a complex embraces the scope of that complex in so far as the scope severally enters into the constitution of the subaltern integrities. I say "in so far" because this or that trait of scope may be irrelevant, as may be many other traits of a complex. An integrity is not the sum of all the traits of a complex. Correspondingly, a contour is not a numerical aggregate of traits.

As to the question why the contour of a complex, being an integrity, should yet be thought of as the continuity and totality of the complex's locations, the answer is not difficult. First, though it is true that the notion of integrity is not identical with the notion of ordinal location, the integrity of every complex is dependent upon its ordinal location. Second, though I have called the contour the gross integrity, I have never regarded this phrase as either primary or self-sufficient. In my sense, a gross integrity *implies* continuity and relation. As an integrity of integrities, it is *eo ipso* a continuity of their ordinal locations. ("Reply to Singer: Alleged Ambiguities in the Metaphysics of Natural Complexes," SJP 67-68.)

[F]or the metaphysics of natural complexes there are no simple unities at all. Every unity is constitutionally and relationally plural. And each plurality, as an order of constituents, is that order, that plurality. The important consideration here is not unity as such, plurality as such, but the *respect* in which any complex is unitary and the *respect* in which it is plural. The first two sentences of TGT state the issue plainly enough: "To ask whether the human individual is best understood as a multiplicity or as a unity is unprofitable, not because the answer is impossible but because the answer is obvious. The humanity of the individual implies a plurality of functions, and the individuality of the man implies a focus of movement and of utterance."

On the more general level, we may say of the contour of any complex in relation to its constituent integrities what we have said of the proceptive domain in relation to its plurality of procepts. The notion of a contour is merely the recognition that the many integrities and suborders are yet the integrities of a complex, a more inclusive order. The more inclusive order is precisely the continuity and interrelatedness of these subaltern orders. It is the continuity and relatedness prevailing, no matter what discontinuities and aspects of unrelatedness also prevail. In this sense alone is it a gross integrity. The contour is not closed and absolute. It is not prior to its constituent integrities. It is itself a subaltern integrity in some other, more inclusive order. The notion of a contour is the recognition of sameness along with difference—the sameness of a complex within the differences of its integrities. The sameness is a unity and continuity of a certain kind; the differences are a plurality of a certain kind. The sameness does not annihilate the differences. Conversely, the contour is shaped by the integrities in relation to one another, and is affected by any integrity that may newly arise. The concepts of relative sameness and relative difference are required for intelligibility and for sanity.

Should it bother us to think of a contour as a "totality" of integrities? There are totalities, whatever we may think. There is a totality of the seats in each room, of the roles an individual has played, of the odd numbers. There are finite and infinite totalities, totalities possible in a given respect, totalities actual in a given respect. A contour, as the name suggests, is the kind of totality that consists in a continuing or inclusive interrelation of elements. The totality does not abolish the distinguishability or the analyzability of the elements. ("Reply to Ross: Aspects of the Theory of Judgment," SJP 107-108.)

P. 31, Line 1: Buchler examines in some detail the roles of a principle of ontological priority in Whitehead's thought in his article, "On a Strain of Arbitrariness in Whitehead's System," *The Journal of Philosophy*, 66: 19 (October 1969) pp. 589-601. (Reprinted with small emendations in *Explorations in Whitehead's Philosophy,* eds. Lewis S. Ford and George L. Kline, New York: Fordham University Press, 1983, pp. 280-294.) Hereafter, references to this article will be made by title and page number of its publication in *The Journal of Philosophy*.

P. 55, Line 28: There is an extended analysis of the concepts of prevalence and time in Buchler's "Reply to Singer: Alleged Ambiguities in the Metaphysics of Natural Complexes" where he specifically refers to this passage. We quote the entire analysis:

What we may call the conditions of a prevalence constitute its ordinal status and determine its traits. Among the more important conditions, out of an indefinite number, are those which we call temporal. Three pairs of conditions—seriality and irreversibility, continuation and availability, prospectiveness and imminent actuality—very roughly identify orders of a past, a present, and a future. The concept of prevalence is not designed and not required to explain what time is, or at best, no more required to do so than to explain, say, what matter or space is. Time, space, and matter are orders of prevalence. But there are infinitely numerous orders of prevalence. Every complex, in so far as it prevails, prevails both in an order and as an order. Every order is a complex that prevails. Every order is a prevalence, every prevalence is ordinal. The word "prevail" admits of tense-qualification. We can speak, in my metaphysical use no less than in common use, of what prevails, what prevailed, what will prevail. But "prevail" also admits of spatial and physical qualification. Dinosaurs, we should say, prevailed for a certain period, and prevailed as large living masses in certain regions or places.

There is no doubt that in my efforts to communicate the concept of prevalence I have made a number of statements which need further explanation.... On the one hand I say, "A complex may cease to be prevalent in all respects" (MNC 55). On the other hand I say, "Being now, or having been, nothing can erase or undo *that*. The mark is made. The complex prevails" (ML 130). These two statements seem to be opposed. Actually they are not only consistent but complementary. The first is saying that certain complexes which once prevailed may no longer be located in any present order. The second is saying that a complex which once prevailed cannot be reversed and its original prevalence annulled. I ended this second statement in the present tense for dramatic emphasis, but that only made for puzzlement. Let us pursue the points of both statements a bit further, in order to clarify them and see how they come together.

May a complex cease to prevail in all respects? Does a complex that once prevailed forever prevail? Does it prevail timelessly? The answers require ordinal specification. There is certainly *a* sense in which some complexes cease to prevail without qualification. Living dinosaurs do not presently prevail as living dinosaurs in any respect. Nor do *any* Mesozoic reptiles, nor does the Mesozoic era prevail as actually Mesozoic. When appropriate ordinal conditions are specified, we move into the complementary emphasis. Thus: dinosaurs prevail in the present as fossilized dinosaurs, or as objects of study. They also prevail as completed and extinct natural histories in the temporal order that constitutes the history of the earth. They do not cease to be located in the order of the past. Having once been actual, they cannot be de-actualized. Aristotle's quotation from Agathon (*Nic. Ethics* 1139b, 11) is pertinent:

> God himself lacks this power alone
> To make what has been done undone. (Welldon)

In my terms, a complex may cease to be prevalent. But it cannot cease *to have been* prevalent. When I said in ML "Being now, or having been, nothing can erase or undo *that*," I might have added, What now is, or what once was, what now prevails or what once prevailed, must be regarded as sovereign and ineradicable in its order. When, instead, I added "The mark is made. The complex prevails," I did not at all mean to imply that temporality, or any other qualifying trait, was irrelevant. For as I have stated, temporality is one of an infinite number of conditions which may enter into and constitute a prevalence.

Singer says: "If prevalence is more generic than being-in-time, then prevalence must be non-temporal." The statement would be more accurate if "may" were substituted for "must." Then the point would be that some prevalences involve a condition of temporality, others do not. Winter alternating with summer is a temporal prevalence; a logical entailment-relation is a non-temporal prevalence.

According to Singer, "Buchler says that temporal orders

differ from other orders but does not define the way in which the two types of order differ." On this statement I make two comments. The first has to do with the facts of the matter. (1) Although I do not formally define the difference between temporal and non-temporal, my use of major categories in relation to that difference cannot be regarded as having no bearing on it. Alescence and prevalence can be illustrated in both non-temporal and temporal terms. Singer herself has cited my distinction between temporal and non-temporal possibility, and has alluded to the concept of prefinition, which helps to explain why possibility can be of either kind. So that, in the absence of a formal account, the difference between temporal and non-temporal is not exactly ignored by me. (2) My second comment elaborates on an earlier one in which I said that the concept of prevalence does not depend upon and is not required to account for time or timelessness, which are to be regarded as two among the innumerable conditions constituting prevalences. No one would deny that time is one of the most pervasive of the conditions of natural complexes. But this does not require it to be made a category of my metaphysics. There are many pervasive complexes reflected in notions used by all philosophers—for example, similarity and difference, junction and separation, mathematical properties, validity and invalidity, degree and kind. Such notions are as it were the connective tissue between a system's metaphysical concepts and the bulk of discourse. They may be effectively used without being analyzed or formally defined, and ordinarily they are not construed as systematic categories if they do not directly contribute to the distinctive character of a philosophic outlook. (SJP 65-67)

P. 56, Line 7: Buchler addresses the issue of the novel use of words in a 1976 article:

Reck (and others) think my work is replete with neologisms. Actually there are few, perhaps three or four, of which "alescence" and "proception" are the most conspicuous. I cannot sum up what I have written on the subject of terminology and of philosophic language. I merely suggest that what some people find to be unfamiliar in my philosophic style rests not on verbal choices and uses alone but on a certain kind of relation between words and ideas. At times I have employed terms of older vintage, at other times older uses of current terms. But for the most part my words and phrases exploit analogically traits that are embodied in common speech. There are many who do not like this practice, including non-readers. ("Reply to Reck: The Structure of the Whole, The Location of the Parts," SJP 53.)

There are several places where Buchler addresses issues of language and its cognitive and philosophic functions. These include: TGT 81-89 (which is reprinted from his October 1939 article in *Mind*, "On the Class of 'Basic' Sentences"); the Introduction to the second, revised edition of TGT (Dover, 1979) which, as an extended discussion of the concept of experience, is also indicative of why Buchler abandons the term "experience" for the neologism "proception" (TGT xiii-xl); TGT 3-5 on proception. We also refer the reader to Buchler's own comments on the subtleties of linguistic usage in the Appendix to TGT (1979) where he elucidates the intended meaning of certain phrases and words he uses. In NJ, see 9-20; 49-55 on "judgment"; 41-49 on language. *The Main of Light* is on the concept of poetry and is rich in commentary on language.

P. 59, Line 17: From here to the top of page 62 is a discussion of whether prevalence is "prior" to alescence. Buchler further discusses this issue in at least two places:

Finding prevalence and alescence not to be parallel in all

respects, Reck concludes that "in a fundamental sense, perhaps in spite of ontological parity, prevalence is prior to alescence." Thus, he says, Buchler readily maintains that in the midst of an alescence there is always a prevalence, but he does not hold that in the midst of every prevalence there is always an alescence. But why must there be this kind of rhythm or rhyme? I am introducing two categories that develop traits not reducible to traits traditionally identified. I am defining an opposition between these categories considered as different dimensions of any natural complex. Must this opposition be scaled or leveled to some other type of opposition? And how does any of this concern the principle of ontological parity? That principle doesn't deny different kinds of being or various kinds of priority. It doesn't deny differences of scope or forms of incommensurateness. What it denies is degrees of being or degrees of reality. It does not deny degrees where degrees belong or differences where differences belong. On the contrary, as I have contended, the principle is the preserver of differences and degrees, for it cautions against dismissing as "less real" the odd complex or the complex of lower degree in any respect. ("Reply to Reck: The Structure of the Whole, The Location of the Parts," SJP 52-53.)

And again Buchler tackles prevalence and alescence in his "Reply to Singer":

Although I cannot agree with Singer that there is a stronger and a weaker sense of "prevalence," she has convinced me that certain clarifications are required. In MNC I start the chapter on prevalence and alescence by saying that all complexes may be said to prevail; that all complexes "obtain." I refer to this as the "minimal" sense of "prevalence," which is not one of two *different* senses, but *part* of the sense we must grasp before giving the full account. I then go on, not to state another sense, but to elaborate. It would not have been wise, even if it had been possible, to try to say everything at once—a disease by which I have been infected often enough. There is only one sense of "prevalence," but it has various aspects, and it is enforced by all of these aspects.

Singer argues that a complex prevalent in what she calls the weaker or minimal sense, as merely excluding, excludes traits, merely as such; whereas a complex prevalent in a stronger sense, as *dominant*, excludes *alescent* traits. But I see this distinction as naming two different aspects of one and the same point. Clearly, for a complex to exclude *any* trait is to exclude what would be alescent or variant *for that complex*. Dominance, then, is not a second sense but an aspect of *all* exclusiveness or restrictiveness.

Singer's proposed distinction between obtenance, the weaker sense of prevalence, and dominance, the stronger sense, is actually designed to save me from inconsistency. For aren't prevalence and alescence opposite and exhaustive dimensions of any complex; and yet, does not an alescence, merely as a complex, prevail; and therefore, must it not prevail in the weak sense of simply obtaining, since it cannot be dominant and alescent at the same time? Now, had I been able to add at the outset of my chapter that nothing can be said simply to "obtain" but only to obtain with the qualification "in so far as"—which was added a couple of pages later—some problems in the exposition might have been avoided. Whatever defects in clarity there may be, I think there is no equivocation. The following brief account is designed to show that an alescent complex, in the order in which it does prevail, *is* dominant in that order, and that in no sense can it prevail or obtain merely *as* an alescent complex.

A complex prevails in so far as it excludes traits. By contrast, a complex is alescent in so far as traits are introduced into it—in so far as it admits traits. Every complex, as that complex and not another, is exclusive, and therefore prevalent. Hence alescent complexes, as the complexes they are, must exclude, must be prevalent; for although an alescent complex admits traits, it excludes traits it is not admitting. How, then, are we to understand the following positions I have set forth: (a) A complex cannot be both prevalent and alescent in the same order. (b) An alescence, or alescent complex, must be prevalent in *some* order. Let us take a pair of examples.

The ocean tides constitute a prevalence, the kind of prevalence that consists in a process of recurrence. High tide alternates with low, the water rises and recedes. Suppose that within this process there occurs a uniquely tall spray at the crest of a wave. That spray, as deviating from the dominant pattern of alternation, is an addition to the process, an alescence. It is alescent in relation to the order prevailing. But it is also located in another order, an order of non-recurring movements of water. In this order it is dominant, excluding *inter alia* recurrently alternating movements of water. Thus the complex known as the spray is both alescent and prevalent, but in different orders. In the one order it introduces a variance, in the other order it excludes a variance.

Consider a field of daisies which is an acre square. In one corner there is a rose bush. The field of daisies is a prevalence in relation to which the rose bush is an alescence. But in a more inclusive ten-acre area there are rose bushes situated at regular intervals, including the one among the daisies. In this order the rose bush prevails as exclusive. Thus it is located in two overlapping orders. In the one, as alescent, it introduces roses among non-roses. In the other, as dominant, it excludes non-roses.

These examples, of course, are simplified for visualization. Even if the rose bush were the *only* one in the larger area, it would be located in some order—that is, defined by traits—in virtue of which it would exclude non-roses and prevail or obtain as the complex that it is.

In general terms, we may say: (1) A given complex may be prevalent in one respect, alescent in another respect. (2) An alescent trait, a trait introduced into a prevalent complex, cannot obtain as introduced; it can obtain only as excluding.

(3) An order within which a trait is introduced necessarily overlaps with an order in which that trait excludes; but the two orders are not the same. (4) It is not true to say, as Singer does, that "in every order in which it is located a complex obtains or prevails in the weak sense." It turns out that in this weak sense "obtains" means "is" or "has being." But according to the conceptual scheme whose possible permutations I have just been surveying, these words do not add anything. The notion of an alescence "prevailing" or "obtaining" *as* an alescence, regardless of order, subverts the concept of ordinal determination. It covertly restores the idea of absolute or pure "being" which the prevalence-alescence approach is designed to improve upon and supplant.

Thus I reaffirm the statement in MNC which italicizes the words "in so far." "*In so far* as (a complex) is alescent, it is not prevalent; *in so far* as it is prevalent, it is not alescent."

It may be useful, finally, to quote a summary statement which I entombed in a footnote of ML.

> It is not metaphysically accurate to say that any natural complex merely as such and under any conditions—in all respects—prevails. It prevails in so far as its integrity does exclude traits which would modify that integrity. To the extent that the complex *admits* or *allows* such traits, it cannot be said to prevail: to this extent and in this respect, it is not a prevalence but an *alescence*.

("Reply to Singer: Alleged Ambiguities in the Metaphysics of Natural Complexes," SJP 63-65.)

Buchler's final quotation is from the notes to ML, Chapter Six, "Ontological Parity and the Sense of Prevalence." The original note concludes with a sentence which Buchler omits here, "Prevalence and alescence are the exhaustive natural dimensions." (ML 179)

P. 92, Line 21: Buchler provides a succinct statement of

some of his views on knowledge and cognitive gain in his "Reply to Ross: Aspects of the Theory of Judgment." (SJP 103-104) The passages Buchler refers to in his reply are NJ 33 ff. and ML 148-152. There are several other extended passages in NJ where Buchler deals with the concept of knowledge. We also refer the reader to CM 116-117 where Buchler discusses the relation between knowledge and method. From the "Reply to Ross":

Ross thinks that according to me every judgment is cognitive. Aside from the fact that I nowhere say this and specifically deny it, the position is antithetical to my outlook. The quotation on which Ross seems to rely is misread because the burden of the section in which it appears is ignored. In that section I am pursuing a hypothetical dialogue with those who hold a limited view of both judgment and knowledge, and I ask the question "What does it mean to attribute 'cognitive' significance to a judgment?" The answer is that the judgment is a vehicle, a means, whereby knowledge is acquired or transmitted. Knowledge, then, may not be acquired in the process of judging, and need not be. Where cognitive significance may be attributed to judgment, it may be to any of the three modes: acting and making are a means no less than stating. Clearly, no judgment merely as judgment is knowledge. It can only be the condition for knowledge to be acquired, if it is acquired at all.

Ross never doubts that for me judgment and knowledge are either the same or inseparable. . . . What he calls "Buchler's most explicit definition of knowledge" is "the capacity to produce or to experience in different, unprecedented ways." The *full* formulation is as follows: *"knowing is that process by which an organism gains from its own continuous living or from the world available to it* the capacity to produce or to experience in different, unprecedented ways." The whole conception of cognitive gain is missed by Ross.

He is also unaware that, even as adequately quoted, this passage is *not* my most explicit definition of knowledge. That is to be found in ML...and...considerably amplifies my conception of knowledge. But since Ross quotes from NJ, how could he have overlooked the following lines?

> To regard judgment as exclusively an approximation to knowledge, and therefore as a concept in the theory of knowledge, is to err in the understanding not only of judgment but, as we have seen, of knowledge itself. Philosophically, the theory of judgment or utterance is more comprehensive than the theory of knowledge; for in the account of knowledge the notion of judgment is inevitable and indispensable, whereas in the account of judgment the notion of knowledge is not (NJ 52-3).

P. 165, Line 20: This passage and the one following exemplify Buchler's method of cumulative definition. He comments specifically on these passages:

> My conception of possibility is a body of conclusions emerging from various problem-contexts, and no one formula provides all that I would like to think of as essential to the conception. Of course, we normally tend to pick out individual sentences as concise versions of a definition. But if we do so in my case, and do so because we wish to feature the idea of prefinition, we are not limited to one which says that a possibility is a prefinition of the contour of a complex. We might equally well pick one which says that a possibility prefines the extension or continuation of the traits of a complex. Or we might pick one which says that a possibility is a prefinition of the limits or boundaries of a complex. The two latter types of statement permit us to recognize as embraced in the prefinition both the contour and the scope of a complex, whatever may be the relation of contour and scope. From this point of view, it would not be necessary in any case to amend the definition, for it is conveyed by a

number of formulations taken collectively. ("Reply to Singer: Alleged Ambiguities in the Metaphysics of Natural Complexes," SJP 67.)

P. 191, Line 16: This refers to Buchler's 1969 article, "On a Strain of Arbitrariness in Whitehead's System."

P. 206, Line 4: See MNC 123 and 188, note 15.

P. 220, Line 3: Quoted here, MNC 2nd edition, p. 286.

P. 251, Line 3: The concept of 'the World' as a World Order, a Complex of all complexes, is rejected by Buchler because such a concept would be an exception to the metaphysical principles which he has articulated. To be such an exception is to be an arbitrary element. Systematic principles entail consequences which one would have to be willing to accept if one is committed to the theoretical merit of the principles. The alternative of simultaneously maintaining a position which would violate the articulated and acceded to principles would introduce "a strain of arbitrariness" into the systematic structure. (See Buchler's analysis of Whitehead's system for just this fault: "On a Strain of Arbitrariness in Whitehead's System." Buchler argues that there are two systematic trends in Whitehead's thought, each of which tends to impede the development of the other. In "Trend 1" Whitehead formulates concepts with which "to distinguish 'types of entities' [types of 'existence'] and to explain their interrelation," while in Trend 2 he "is concerned not to delineate with increasing refinement the traits of the various types of entities, whether in specific detail or in large patterns, but to determine how 'real' the various entities are" [p. 590].) With the concept of arbitrariness, the issue Buchler is identifying concerns the question of systematicity, and not just logical consistency. Arbitrariness of systematicity is undesirable because it impedes query in the sense of the development of the categorial structure. Finally, the arbitrariness Buchler criticizes in Whitehead and seeks to eliminate in his own view is also exhibitively undesirable to the extent to which it disrupts the elegance and coherence of the system.

INDEX

209, 229, 238, 244, 259, 264, 272, 279, 290

Method, 2, 23, 28, 127, 149, 184, 187, 198, 210, 273, 296

Michelangelo, 242

Mind, 87, 88, 176, 179, 205, 226, 243, 260

Miracle, 9

Mme. Cézanne, 241

Modification, 41, 42, 83, 107, 126, 223

Montgomery, G.R., 187

Multiplicity, 17, 29, 47, 94, 175, 217, 237, 239, 247, 286

Munitz, M.K., 188

Murphy, A.E., 187

Mystery, 10, 97-99

Nagel, Ernest, 190

Name, 28

Napoleon, 220

Nascence, 56, 80

Natural definition, 46, 162, 163, 165, 206

Natural history, 62, 125, 170

Natural order, 99 ff., 198, 200, 245, 263, 284

Natura naturans and natura naturata, 100, 263, 276

Nature, 2-3, 9, 10, 99-101, 196, 197-198, 200, 226, 233, 234, 238, 243, 245, 257, 259, Appendix IV

Necessary, 160, 161

Non-being, 4, 31, 76, 226, 245

Non-contradiction, principle of, 60, 61, 139, 178, 255

Non-natural, 6, 29, 99, 155, 200, 234

Nothing, 4, 229-230, 235, 253, 269

Novelty, 80, 101

Numbers, 151

Object, 5, 26, 230

Observation, 26

Obtenance, 53, 293

Occurrence, 54, 60, 66, 69, 129, 147; see also Event, Fact

Ockham's razor, 189

Ontological parity, 31-51, 53, 198, 200, 218, 292

Ontological priority, xxiii, xxiv, xxv, 30-51, 117, 160, 287

Order, 7, 13, 16, 47, 49, 72, 76, 84, 85, Chap. III passim, 131, 141, 152, 156, 167, 177 ff., 197, 198, 200, 205, 209, 213, 215, 217, 218, 219, 220, 221, 237, 239, 240-241, 243-246, 250, 251-252, 253, 255, 256, 257, 258, Appendix IV passim, 286, 288, 290, 293, 294-295, 298

Ordinality, xvii-xxix, 85, Chap. III, 131, 160, 179, 182, 200, 239, 259, 275-276, 279, 280

Organism, 88, 123, 184, 248-249, 296

Origination, 56, 81, 127

Painting, 154

Parity, see Ontological parity

Parmenides, 31

Part, 16, 20, 24, 34 ff., 44, 45, 229, 235, 246-248

Particular, 39, 64, 106, 179, 181

Pattern, 93, 94, 235, 245, 265, 294

Peirce, C.S., 249, 263, 265

Perception, 14, 26, 27, 205

Permanence, 72-76, 81

Persistence, 73

Perspective, 7, 25, 197, 209-210, 258

Pervasiveness, 25, 36-39, 104, 105, 177, 218, 237, 285; see also Scope

Philosophers, 14, 15, 30, 40, 81, 130, 148, 153, 154, 174, 189, 195, 201,

DATE DUE